The Courage to Love Again

Also by Sheila Ellison

The Courage to Be a Single Mother
365 Afterschool Activities
365 Days of Baby Love
365 Days of Creative Play
365 Foods Kids Love to Eat
365 Ways to Raise Great Kids

The Courage to

LOVE AGAIN

Creating Happy, Healthy Relationships After Divorce

Sheila Ellison

HarperSanFrancisco
A Division of HarperCollins*Publishers*

HarperCollins books may be purchased for educational, business, or sales promo-
tional use. For information please write: Special Markets Department, Harper-
Collins Publishers, Inc., 10 East 53rd Street, New York, NY 10022.

HarperCollins Web site: http://www.harpercollins.com

HarperCollins®, 📖 ®, and HarperSanFrancisco™ are trademarks of Harper-
Collins Publishers, Inc.

FIRST EDITION

Library of Congress Cataloging-in-Publication Data
Ellison, Sheila.
    The courage to love again : creating happy, healthy
relationships after divorce / Sheila Ellison. — 1st ed.
        p. cm.
    ISBN 0-06-251750-3 (cloth: alk. paper)
    ISBN 0-06-251751-1 (pbk.)
        1. Divorced women—Psychology. 2. Self-esteem in women.
3. Self-acceptance. 4. Dating (Social customs). 5. Remarriage.
I. Title.

HQ814.E455   2002
305.48'9653—dc21   2002190211

02 03 04 05 06 ❖ RRD(H) 10 9 8 7 6 5 4 3 2 1

To my husband, Al,
for having the courage to love me

Contents

Introduction

When I was a young girl, I loved the story of Cinderella. In the annual television special of that fairy tale, the prince rode up on a real horse, and you could see the sparkle of love in Cinderella's human eyes. After my divorce, I realized that I had entered my first marriage looking for someone to care for me—someone to manage my family's financial obligations so that I could be a mother. I expected a prince, a dream relationship that matched the fantasy I had created in my mind. In many ways, the beginning of my marriage looked like that fairy tale. I planted my hopes and dreams in my marriage. As time went on, I set what I wanted aside for the sake of the relationship. I stopped asking myself who I was. I took the seed of what I wanted my life to grow into, and I planted it in my husband. I knowingly chose to do this because I held in my mind a vision of the life I wanted to create for my children and a vision of what love was supposed to look and feel like.

When the relationship ended in divorce, I had to accept the fact that I was on my own and nobody was going to ride up to rescue me. I sank into the depths of despair, sure that I had failed my children and myself. I was stripped of all the roles I recognized—no longer a wife, no longer a mother in the way I had been a mother, no longer the person I wanted to be. I sat in this place for many months, unable to heal my wounds. Like most women who are faced with the end of a marriage, I felt the burning desire to get over this loss, to put everything aside, to let it all go, and somehow to find the strength to rebuild my life. I wanted to feel love again, to find and hold on to some positive emotion that might help me to move on. My mind whirled with confusion about what marriage was supposed to be, what it had been for me in the past, and if I would ever find the courage to reach out and love a man again. At times the sinking pain pulled me under to such great depths that I wasn't sure if I actually wanted to surface.

But even in this chaotic, painful place, something within me demanded order and explanation. I wanted to know when my life would get back to normal, how long I would grieve the many losses, and how I might find the will and the energy to visualize a new life. I worked to uncover the pieces of my life and understand them. Through these discoveries, a powerful woman with powerful feelings and needs came to light. I became visible to myself— and the more I saw, the more sure I was that I could rebuild my life. I wanted to bring the powerful, self-assured woman into a healthy love relationship. I just wasn't sure how.

Then I reached a point in this grief cycle when I realized that in order to survive I would have to take complete responsibility for my life. I remembered the last words my attorney said as I left her office on my first visit: "The women who recover fastest from the end of their marriages are the ones who don't sit around and complain about how their ex-spouse is supposed to take care of them. They start taking responsibility for their lives right from the start." My competitive nature came to the fore, and I decided that I didn't want to be one of those women who dwelled on misfortune. I began to work to support my family. I started to set goals for the future. I painted a clear picture in my mind of what my life was going to look like. The picture had room in it for my career, my family, and my personal life. In the end I learned that the journey toward loving again was not about finding the right partner; it was about finding myself.

I decided to jump into the dating scene, hoping the new focus would give me strength. But it didn't take long to realize that a woman with four children and little income wasn't exactly a dream date. Few men write "existing children" on their list of most-wanted girlfriend features! Now that I was a mother with children at home, dating was a completely different game, with more confusing rules than dating had been fifteen years before when I was a single woman. I knew I had to be stronger and more self-confident. I had to know what I wanted and to believe in my chosen direction. For me, there was simply no choice. I discovered that if I brought my weakness into a new relationship with the expectation that my partner would fill any void, the partnership immediately felt off balance and I would again become willing to plant my hopes and dreams in my new partner. I even found myself expecting the relationship to make me whole again. I wanted new love, sex, and intimacy to fill the painful hole that was left in my heart after the divorce.

I did find love, and with it I believed that my life would magically fall back into place. Unfortunately, even a new love relationship did not make the pain go away, and it did not free me from the personal growth work that I needed to do. I made quite a few mistakes coming from that hole-in-the-heart place: one was falling in love right away. Without a doubt, the relationship was an incredibly healing step. After years in a bad marriage, nothing builds self-esteem quite as effectively as a man who wants to make love with you, who doesn't have any history with your faults, and with whom you don't have to co-parent. That first relationship lasted a while. He had no children but definitely wanted some. I had all the children I could handle but was considering having more so that we could stay together. I was scared to fail again, and I found myself putting my own needs lower than his on my priority list, just as I had done within my marriage! I set aside my desires and went along with his ideas about communication, sex, and relationship. He was like a teacher, which was great for me, because at that time, after failing in my marriage, I didn't know myself well enough to know what I wanted or how to get it. But during this relationship I made little progress toward being the kind of powerful, self-sufficient woman I'd set out to find within myself, who could be a partner and not lose herself.

While I was still involved in this first relationship, I met my future husband, Al. It was in the beginning of our relationship that I decided to experiment with the ideas I've written about in this book. By then I was stronger in many ways. It had been two years since the divorce, and I was growing comfortable with my independence. I had a job and felt my career was going rather well. I had successfully found a way to support my kids without the support of a man in my life. After years of healing, self-reflection, and time spent defining the relationship I wanted, I was willing to risk putting all my cards (and myself) on the table. I experimented with letting Al know what I needed, and I showed him who I actually was instead of projecting a person I thought he might want. I never pretended that he would come first—how could he when I had four kids under the age of twelve? In my heart I was sure that he would run from me once he knew all the facts, but he didn't. My honesty allowed him to be honest, and together we were able to grapple with that loaded issue that causes the death of many relationships: expectations.

One day a neighbor remarked that I was lucky to find someone who actually wanted a woman with four kids. With a smile on my face I said, "He isn't sleeping with the kids!" She gave a nervous laugh before walking away. Somehow when our society pictures a single mother, it sees a downtrodden woman, left with a bunch of kids, without enough money to support them; she's gained a few extra pounds during the divorce process and is too busy looking for a way to support her family to take care of herself. The description may be true of some divorced women, but it doesn't have to be your picture. You have the ability—and life offers the possibility—to create whatever you want, once you've decided what direction to go.

This book does not begin with what might seem to be the obvious first step in forming a new love relationship—meeting a man. Instead, we begin with the goal of increasing our knowledge of ourselves: how we feel, how we see ourselves, and what we want. As a society we've often thought of relationship as a coming together of two people into one life or being. Most of us tried that definition in our first marriages without much success! This book challenges and teaches a woman how to stay separate and move independently within her own life before sharing that life with another. The new goal is to enter a relationship able to share what you already have within you instead of expecting the relationship to fill a part of your life that feels empty.

It is possible to enter a new relationship as an independent, whole, and complete woman who is ready to transform old patterns into new ideas and to make fully conscious choices. This book will show you how to find the courage to look at your mistakes, to accept your past choices, to forgive yourself, and to go on to a place of self-acceptance and love. You will discover how important it is to understand past relationship patterns so that you can break the bad habits, learn new skills, and avoid dating the same type of man over and over again. You will create a picture in your mind of what you want your life to look like, complete with new characters, a new setting, and a creative plot.

This book will give you a new set of love skills that, once learned and practiced, allow two people to create a relationship that works. One important ingredient in fulfilling relationships is a sense of equality, so you will also learn how to build an equal partnership. You will learn to balance the life you want to create as a woman with the life you may already have as a loving mother. After reading this book, you will be able to define the emotional and sexual relationship you're looking for and to determine what you need and want from a new partner. In hearing other women's stories, you will gain the confidence, understanding, and support you will need to embark on this new journey of partnership, a journey that doesn't require giving any part of yourself away.

Part 1 of this book explores the inward journey—how we learn to love and to accept who we are, how we choose to fill ourselves with the creative action of forming new lives, and how we have the courage to get rid of the old patterns and behaviors that don't work in order to make room for new ideas and dreams. The first step in changing my old patterns was to believe in my ability to stand independently. I had to learn to love all that I was, to forgive the bad decisions, and to focus on the talents and abilities that could carry me into a new life, full of new relationships and new possibilities. In that process I learned that I could choose the person I wanted to grow into and that I could choose to create a new relationship that worked for me.

So often in playing our roles as wife and mother, we forget that inside our body is a woman's spirit that belongs to us, a girl-child who laughs with glee as she steals out her bedroom window and strolls around the neighborhood with friends late on a Friday night. An excited teen kissing her parents good-bye as she's left alone for the first time in her college dormitory room. A scared mother groaning during labor, wondering how long the pain will continue before her baby will be placed in her arms. We created our lives by the choices we made; we even created our marriages. Maybe we were not conscious that our choices were leading us down the path that we were on. Perhaps we didn't have the tools to make the right choices then, but after reading this book, the choices we make will become conscious, positive affirmations of the women we have grown into.

Part 2 of this book is about the outward journey toward a healthy new relationship. We look at how to present the real you, set realistic dating expectations, learn new couple skills, have great sex, and successfully blend your life with a new partner. This is the fun part, where you have the chance to try out everything you've been working toward in part 1. You get to open yourself up to intimacy in a completely new way, with selective vulnerability and the underlying knowledge that you are strong enough to risk loving. The moment I understood that I was in love with Al was a defining moment in my life. For the first time, I wasn't afraid of what would happen to me if he didn't love me back. I loved me—and I wanted to enjoy the swirling, excited emotions I felt with the solid knowledge that I was finally whole. I loved him and wanted him, but I could create the life I wanted even without him. The ability each of us had to stand independently made the decision to be together much easier. Neither one of us felt the burden of carrying the other's emotional baggage.

When we decided to get married, my friends thought I was crazy. Everyone asked the same question: "Why would you get married when you already have all the kids you want?" Living with someone outside marriage no longer holds the societal judgment it once did, so why be legally or financially bound? To me, my marriage symbolized the completion of a circular path. I lost my dream and fell down into the depth of grief. I lived with the death of my spirit, and that death created space for new dreams. In so many ways, I've risen from the ashes of my old life. I've learned how to love myself. With healing self-reflection and hard work, I was able to enter my new marriage as an independent, self-supporting, confident, competent, and talented woman who expects an equal partnership. That sentence in itself took years of preparation! I may have been devastated by the divorce and heartbroken over the loss of love, but I am still alive and willing to try loving again. I decided that divorce would not be the end, but rather a wonderful opportunity for a new beginning. The following pages contain the story that I worked to create. A new partnership was born. We all deserve that same chance to write another story!

Part One

The Inward
Journey

1

Picture Your life

Suzanne walked down the fruit aisle for the second time. Pausing at the nectarines to squeeze, holding on to her cart, she twisted to look over her shoulder at the man standing by the salad dressing. God, his butt looked great in jeans. She had spotted him first looking through the wine, followed him to the soup, then to the cereal aisle, and now to the fruit. Looking down all the time at her cart full of whatever she grabbed to look inconspicuous.

Batteries, that was what she came in the store for, Brian's remote control car. She hadn't gotten the batteries, couldn't forget those. The kids were gone for the weekend, but she'd promised to fix that car while they were gone.

Rough looking, torn jeans, tanned skin, ruffled hair, and a warm smile.

He did smile back by the soup, she thought. *Could be married, though; he's too cute to be alone.*

She watched him grab a loaf of sourdough and head for the checkout. Still squeezing the nectarines, Suzanne felt her head spin. She began to panic. Should she leave her cart behind and position herself at the magazine rack? Could she let him leave the store without getting a number?

This is ridiculous. What am I thinking? Why would he be interested in me? I have two kids, haven't dated since my divorce, I'm thirty-seven years old, and can't bring myself to talk to this man that I've been stalking for the past twenty minutes. I am acting like a teenager, she said to the stack of magazines as he headed for the door. She dropped the magazine and followed him.

"Excuse me, I don't generally approach strange men in grocery stores, but, in case you aren't married, I'd like to give you my phone number."

"I noticed you in the store. I'm Will—and you are?"

"Suzanne, nice to meet you. Do you live around here?"

"I do, I'm on my way to a friend's party," he said, holding the wine and grocery bag up for her to see. "Would you like to come with me, or should I use this number later?"

We can all remember that feeling of looking at a man and feeling an immediate attraction, wishing he were single, wondering what his touch might feel like. We want to look into eyes full of desire for us and experience a life shared with someone who fully knows who we are. Even if the last experience of romance ended in divorce, we still want to date, to be intimate, and to find the courage to love again. The loss experienced in divorce is a sinking process in which most women feel they have sunk to the lowest place they could imagine. In order to move from that deep sense of failure, anger, and sadness, we need to be able to change direction. How do we redefine our direction? We imagine something new—a life we can look forward to. We use all our mind's power to create a new picture of our life.

It is difficult to imagine something beautiful and fulfilling when our marriage has either crashed and burned or just slowly sputtered out. We have spent years building an understanding of who we are in that one primary relationship. Then love ends, and we have a choice: either we can blame divorce for our difficult life circumstances, or we can create a new picture of the life we want and then allow that picture to inspire us on the journey. The picture we create needs to be specific. It needs to have enough fantasy to tickle us with courage and enough reality to allow us to believe it is possible. If we can see our lives as a journey toward a destination of our own choosing, then it is much easier to live each day, to do what we have to do in order to support ourselves and our children as we keep taking steps in the direction we want to move.

Suzanne had a picture of her life, and that picture included dating, so she made a decision to go for what she wanted and face her fears. She could have let Will leave the grocery store without approaching him, telling herself there would be another opportunity to meet a man she was attracted to, but instead she seized the moment.

Each of us has the same choice. We can let our dreams motivate our actions, or we can let our fears and inadequacies lead the way. We are all afraid to move forward, but we can't let fear sit in the driver's seat or we will lose the power to create meaningful lives full of love.

What are the dreams you have for your life, and how do you begin to dream again when your last dreams didn't come true? These may seem like simple questions, but at this point in your life you know nothing is simple. You have to consider your children, your financial obligations, whether you have to or want to establish a career. Before you were married, you had the freedom to choose where you wanted to live, what you wanted to do, and with whom you would spend your life. Now those choices seem to have narrowed or disappeared, replaced with adult responsibilities. Much of the sadness I felt following my own divorce centered on this feeling of being stuck in a life that seemed to hold no hope. So much of my time was spent figuring out how to survive—like how to pay for food—that dreams for the future seemed a waste of energy. In fact, when I did let my mind wander, I would start to feel a dull pain as the spiral of guilt rose to the surface, followed by sadness. I really missed the life I could have had if my marriage would have worked.

One Sunday I decided to attend a local church, and the sermon seemed written just for me. It was about the magi who journeyed to see Jesus when he was born. The preacher focused on what the journey cost them in terms of time, hardship, even the relationships they had to leave for the weeks they were gone. The magi undertook it, he said, because they had a clear vision of where they were going and why the journey was important. The preacher talked on, but I couldn't hear the rest of his words because my mind had already spun off on a new train of thought about my life and the journey I was on. I could clearly see a dirt road winding through some hills covered with grass and wildflowers. I tried to visualize what I was walking toward and realized that I didn't really know where I was going. The picture I held of my life had been broken by my failed relationship; inner healing needed to happen before I could define my journey. I was walking toward something, getting up each day and making an extraordinary effort to improve my life, but I hadn't created a picture in my mind of what I wanted my life to look like. Exactly where *was* I going?

That day I began to understand that unless I was willing to do the inner healing work, unless I knew where I was going and unless I could create a picture in my mind of the life I wanted, I would have no idea what choices to make or what direction to go. I began that day to create a vision of the life, the relationship, and the career that I wanted. Even though you may be feeling like I was, alternatively wishful and hopeless, energized and scared, overwhelmed and defeated, you can still find the courage to dream about having healthy, happy, fulfilling relationships in your life. You will have to do some inner work and make some outer changes for those dreams to become part of your reality, but it can be done a step at a time. The first step begins with vision.

In this chapter you will have a chance to create a new picture of your life. We will begin by examining personal limitations, assets, and abilities. Then we'll let our minds play for a while with fantasy and dreams for the future. From there we will learn how to bring some of our fantasy thoughts into reality. Once you've established the picture of the life you want and have identified dreams for the future, it is important to look at ways you can hold on to those dreams as you enter into a new relationship. Remember, if you can imagine it and hold the idea in front of you as a source of inspiration when life is difficult, then your dream can become possible.

Limitations, Assets, and Abilities

I came home from church inspired and ready to elaborate on the picture that came to me. I was ready to decide what I wanted and to get it on paper in the form of goals. I spent that evening jotting down ideas. I was inspired.

But the very next morning, my outlook changed. I woke up feeling defeated—and for good reason. My four kids and I had been living in a studio apartment for a year. It was the first day of Christmas vacation. I hadn't bought any gifts and knew I didn't have any extra cash to create the Christmas I wished we could have. Presents would be paid for by credit cards again this year, and then there would be months of stress as I tried to figure out how to pay the bills. That apartment didn't have even a closet big enough to cry in, so I got out of bed that day and put on a fake smile so the kids wouldn't begin their Christmas vacation with a grouchy mom. I wiped up the kitchen counter and looked at the stained grout between the tiles, the dirty carpet, glanced at all my belongings crammed into this small space, and said to myself, "God, this can't be my life. I just can't take it anymore."

Little did I know, things were about to get worse. After breakfast, Rose, the woman I was renting from, came in and asked if we could talk. She told me it seemed the time was right for me to move out. Eleven months earlier, she had asked me to move onto the property in the hopes of creating a sort of blended family—two single mothers, each with four kids, trying to get back on their feet. We had agreed to share the burdens of postdivorce life—child care, driving, and some meals—and I thought everything was going great. My divorce case had finally settled in New Zealand. I had been given the family home there in the division of assets and had immediately put it up for sale. Each day I prayed it would sell so we could move from this cramped space and buy something on our own, but so far the market had been slow.

I listened unbelievingly as Rose said, "Now that your divorce has settled in New Zealand, maybe it is time for you to rent something bigger." I burst into tears. Yes, I desperately wanted to move out and to have some space to move and to breathe. But the house still had not sold, and I had no money. All I could feel in that moment were the limitations that seemed to constrict my life. Rose mentioned a house around the corner that was for rent, so I went and looked at it. But it cost twice as much as I was already paying. My choices seemed limited until I had enough money to move. As much as I wanted to picture myself in a new life, I felt imprisoned by the lack of options.

Each of us faces our own set of limits on our choices. In preparing to write this book, I interviewed many women who felt hampered in their choices by lack of education or career options. "I'm a secretary. I don't have a college education, and I have two kids under eight," said Angie. "Whenever someone tells me that all I have to do is know what I want and visualize it, I want to slap them. I can't imagine how I will ever make enough money to move ahead. Even with a yearly raise, I will make just enough to cover the raise in rent. Yes, maybe when my kids leave home twelve or so years from now I might get to dream of a new life. I sure as hell am not going to count on getting remarried in order to move up in the world! I will, however, encourage my kids to go to college. I wish that I had more education so I could make more money, maybe even do something I really liked rather than typing and answering phones all day for someone else. God, my boss won't even let me go on the Internet during my breaks, so there isn't even time to gossip with my gal pals."

Often women are limited because of their children's custody arrangements. "As soon as the divorce was over, I wanted to move a few hours away so that I could live near my sister," said Patti. "My ex-husband is an engineer, so our family had to live in a pretty expensive area during the marriage since it was close to his work. Of course he can still afford to live in the area, but with what the court ordered paid to me as child support and alimony, there is no way that I can stay there. I do have a college degree in marketing and in fact worked for the same company my husband worked for when we met. When I quit, he was only making 10 percent more money than I was, but we both decided someone had to stay home and raise the kids. So now I'm stuck. We had to sell the house to divide assets. If I could move near my sister, I could afford to buy a house. But the judge ordered that I have to stay in the general area where my husband lives so he can have his visitation. I am so full of anger because I feel my ex-husband and the court are preventing me from creating a good life for myself and my kids."

Every life has limitations that put a damper on dreams. Yet, if you are willing to move past the fear, you can discover ways to expand the possibilities that do in fact exist. The possibilities arise out of the present circumstances of your life. You see, the limitations are only part of the equation. Another part is your assets and your abilities, plus your own powerful vision for your life.

When faced with obstacles that seem overwhelming, I have often found it helpful to make lists. That morning, feeling at the end of my rope, I decided to think about anything that was working in my favor. I sat down to make a list of all my personal assets, and not necessarily material ones. They included living in a safe place and making enough money to feed my kids—everything that was positive in my life at the time.

Then I realized that I had some abilities that were also working in my favor. I am a good communicator. I have tons of energy. I made a second list, writing down all my personal abilities. I started to feel a little better.

Now that I could see all was not lost, I felt brave enough to list all the limitations I felt. I couldn't afford a baby-sitter so I could work longer hours. I didn't have the time or resources to go back to school. I had four kids who still needed me. The list of limitations threatened to grow longer than the other two lists.

How could I begin to put these lists together? What did they add up to? Suddenly I remembered my jottings from the night before. There, on the paper in black and white, were my goals, a vision of where I wanted to go. Inspired by the sermon the day before, I had begun to create a vision for a life that was mine. That vision, I realized, was the missing ingredient. Vision would shape the ingredients of my life into a direction I could follow.

I sat toying with my lists, and eventually this equation emerged:

$$\text{Limitations, assets, and abilities} + \text{Vision} = \text{Direction}$$

You can find direction in your life—the courage to love again, to set out in pursuit of your own dreams—by starting where you are now and adding vision. The present circumstances of your life, both the expansive ones and the limiting ones, are the basic ingredients. Add vision to this mix, and, like adding yeast to bread dough, you will be able to take action and grow. Vision is the inspiration that moves you into action. If you simply consider your present circumstances without using your imagination, then you will not be able to act, like dough that can't rise. When you put your fantasy together with your limitations, assets, and abilities, then the direction you need to take becomes clear.

Vision

Vision means being willing to entertain any and all possibilities your life might offer. When I give myself the freedom to imagine, my heart lightens up a little, my future opens up, and I don't feel as limited by my circumstances. Instead of feeling confined to the responsibilities of my life, I begin to envision the big picture—that each day of my life is one step on a journey toward something. Then I take the time to look at my fantasy pictures and ask myself, "What would I be willing to do to create the life I saw? What little pieces of this fantasy could I bring into my life right now so I would feel like I'm moving in the right direction?"

We all live with the reality of having to pay the bills, trying to get a night off, having to provide some sort of food for our kids. Those of us who have kids know that the life of a single mom is as real as it gets. So I'm going to ask you to set aside reality for a play date. We are all going to play dress-up. Actually, we are going to try on our dreams the same way we pretended to be firefighters in preschool. For this moment, we are going to stop saying, "This is a waste of time! I have my life and I just have to accept it." Instead, we are going to picture the life and love that we want. There are only two rules. The first is that, if you have kids, you can't dream of a life without your kids. The second is that you can't imagine you just won the lottery. The purpose of fantasy play is to open your mind to new ideas, perhaps bring out a piece of your playful soul that you have lost, and to move out old beliefs in order to create the life you envision.

So here are my visions of things I would do if I didn't have to worry about making enough money to support my family. I would start a floral service where each week I'd design and deliver a new floral arrangement to private homes. The people would sign up for the service on a monthly basis. I would write steamy romance novels and have the chance to create wonderful characters who would grow into believable human beings (and who would do what I want them to do). I might start a tile mosaic business, designing beautiful scenes and then having someone else do the manual labor of putting them together. Or maybe I would teach creative writing to inner-city kids. I might buy a twenty-acre farm and design a completely different garden for each acre. I'd get certified as a yoga instructor and teach yoga classes, or at least go to yoga camps, eat vegetarian cooking, and meditate for weeks at a time. I'd get a certificate in natural medicine and learn how to grow medicinal herbs in my garden. I'd read one book a week for fun.

Women I interviewed shared many rich visions of their fantasy lives. "If I could have any job, I'd want to be a fashion designer," said Peg. "Before I had kids, I used to design my own clothes and sew them myself. I even had an interview and was accepted at a school for fashion designers, but I couldn't afford the tuition. I would invent a line of makeup, or maybe design silk scarves. Being a private investigator would be fun; I've always loved nosing my way into people's private lives! It would be so exciting to be called in to figure out a difficult case. Or maybe I would move my family up to the mountains and become a ski instructor. I used to love to ski when I was little but haven't had much of a chance in my adult life. I always admired the ski patrol who put the injured skiers on toboggans to be carried down the hill. Opening my own clothing shop would also be fun. I would go to New York and pick out all the up-and-coming fashions and have regular clientele that visit each week to check on new lines."

Isn't this fun! If I could go anywhere with my family, I would move to a ranch where we could own horses. It would be a place I could pay for out-right so I wouldn't have a mortgage payment. Some of my favorite childhood memories were in open spaces, swimming in the creek with my horse, hold-ing on to his mane, and laughing hysterically with my friends as we would fall off and have to swim frantically to catch the horses. I remember the fort I made at the very back of the woods where I would watch the trees, the flow-ers, and then look for the fairies I was sure I saw sleeping on the large petals. I would take my kids away from the stress that school and grades have become and let them learn at a more easygoing country school. We would tend the vegetable garden together and have time to talk and be close. There would be no more nights of driving to three different sports practices or games.

"If I could take my family anywhere, I would move away from the city," said Tanya. "I've lived in the city my whole life. I'd have at least one cat and one dog. I would find a place where the kids could walk to school without my being afraid that someone was going to kidnap or hurt them. Maybe I'd even open a day care center so that I could work from home and have my two-year-old with me. We would have a lawn and maybe some kind of pond. I would know the neighbors. We would go for bike rides at night before the sun set in the summer, and in the winter we'd sit around the fireplace."

"I would move with my daughter to London. I went to school there dur-ing college and loved it," said Pauline. "I was raised on a farm and for the past ten years have lived an hour away from any major city. I'd try to get a job in the theater industry, maybe in costume or set design with my art background. I only have one daughter, who is twelve right now. She loves acting, so I'm sure she would enjoy the experience. I would also make sure to take trips as often as possible to other European cities, maybe even buy a car so we could go and stay wherever we wanted. I've always liked the idea of being a gypsy-type person, not having a schedule and being free to experience life." There are so many lifestyle choices out there that we never before considered because they didn't fit in with who we used to be, but maybe they are perfect for the new women we're becoming.

It's not enough to imagine the lifestyle we want. Close your eyes and ask yourself, "What is the man of my dreams like? How does he treat me? How does he live his life, and what does our life together look like?"

When I first tried this I was afraid that compromise and desperation might have narrowed my expectations. So in order to open my mind I played a fantasy game with love that both entertained and informed me. I'd close my eyes and see myself in a relationship with an amazing man. In my mind he was devoted to me beyond belief. He listened to me, believed in my talent, thought my kids were so much fun to be around that he'd skip weekend football games to attend family outings. He was smart, witty, good-looking, and interesting. We laughed a lot. He knew how to cook, how to wash dishes, and how to clean a toilet—and he offered to do those things without being asked. He had a successful career that he was passionate about, but I always came first.

Now take your image of your own dream lover, and place him in your daily life. How does he act? How do you act? How does your life together look? Is it different from what you have experienced before? When I tried this, I imagined ordinary situations that I might find myself in, like attending a school event, trying to pick a movie for a date, or serving a rushed dinner after a hectic day. In my mind I'd watch my fantasy man play his part. I would also watch myself as if I were acting in my own movie, and I'd experiment with my responses and actions. When I look back on these fantasies, I realize that I was training my mind to anticipate, to expect, and to enjoy the possibilities a new relationship might offer.

"If I were going to picture the man of my dreams, he would be around forty-five years old, have dark hair, be at least six feet tall, and be incredibly warm," said Sally. "He would enjoy music and have a job that enabled him to travel at least four weeks a year—and he'd take me with him on these trips. I'd like him to have children of his own so that he wouldn't be jealous of the time I would want to spend with my kids. It would be great if he had money, but I'd take someone with a good, dependable job. It is also important to me that he likes what he does because my ex-husband had a problem with depression and losing jobs. I don't want to feel like a therapist, so he has to have worked on his own problems and be pretty secure in himself."

"I haven't really thought what the man of my dreams will be like, but I definitely know what he will *not* be like," said Brenda. "He will not cut down my friends, insult my family, or call me names. He will be kind and loving to my children, encouraging them to become whatever they want to be. He will attend events like school functions, my kids' sports games, and dance recitals with me, and never will he point out the mistakes the kids make during these events. He will come home when he says, won't go drinking with the guys, and will have a good job. We will be partners in all things. He will ask me questions about my job, be involved in what I do, and I'll be interested in his job. I guess if I had to visualize what he would look like, I would want him to be a little pudgy, because I'm not the thinnest person, and I'm not beautiful either. So I want someone in between who won't always be looking over my shoulder at pretty women." Sally and Brenda have taken the first step: they are thinking about the qualities they would expect in a lover.

Playtime is over for now, but you can come back to these dreams any time you want to look for new pieces to slip into the picture you are creating for your life. Now that you have played with your fantasy vision and thought a little about the limitations you face, it is time to bring the vision and limitations together to determine the direction your life might turn.

Moving from Fantasy to Reality

As I created this fantasy picture of my life, I realized that I had to find a way to bring pieces of my fantasy into my present life. There was a reason that I dreamed about moving my kids to a ranch—I love the idea of horses, a country garden, and a life with little stress. So I really looked at that picture, and, instead of waiting ten years to get enough money to make some changes, I decided to incorporate a few small parts of the vision into my life right now. It worked like this:

Vision (to live closer to nature) + Limitations, assets, and abilities
(my kids would hate living on a ranch, I do have a plot of dirt,
I can create some nature space in my yard)
= Direction (I planted mini-gardens around my house)

Take your vision of your dream life, and select one aspect of it. Write out this piece of your dream, if writing helps you. Revel in what your life would look and feel like if this vision became reality. Now go back to your list of limitations and your lists of assets and abilities. When you add your vision to these present realities, what do you see? What direction is suggested by their sum? What parts of your vision can you bring into your life here and now?

The real goal of the "fantasy to reality" process is to help you begin to lift your eyes—and your goals—up from the immediate, sometimes relentless, reality of daily life. To move from where you are to a more desirable place, you can start taking bits and pieces from the fantasy picture and decide in what ways they reveal parts of your creative and wishful soul. Then you can find ways to incorporate them into life here and now. Just because you have limitations now and can't fulfill your complete fantasy right this moment—or even see how it will ever be possible—doesn't mean it won't happen. Include your dreams in your life picture, along with your limitations, assets, and abilities, to come up with a future you would be excited to pursue.

"I made something I call my vision board," said Kathy. "I took some old magazines and began cutting out pictures that symbolized things I wanted to create in my life. I cut out words too, if I couldn't find the appropriate picture. I cut out a wedding ring because I want to be married again. There were pictures of families having fun together, because I want to be closer to my kids. And pictures of a new car and a house on a river. I included a picture of a woman dancing, because I want to start taking dance classes again as soon as I can afford them. Then I glued all the pictures onto a piece of poster board and hung it in my closet so I would see it every day."

Page said, "I came up with all sorts of fantasy ideas for my life, and then I decided which of the fantasy ideas I wanted to put on my 'life goals' list. I'm a realist, so the fantasy exercise helped me to get away from the negative self-talk that always seems to pop up whenever I get excited about what the future might bring. I hear myself saying, 'You could never achieve that; there is no way that will happen.' My goal list has become a quiet reminder that my life has many possibilities, even if they aren't being achieved this minute."

Take some time to examine your fantasy vision and see if there are any pieces that you could incorporate into your life right now. The big dreams, the ones that can't happen today, you can set out in the distance and begin taking small steps toward them.

Vision Leads to Direction

Sometimes just one goal, one area of your life in which you have a specific vision, is enough to keep you moving forward. Your vision then becomes a guide whenever you have a big decision to make. When you lose hope or feel like you can't survive another day, you can project yourself ahead and live within that picture. Just having that one picture keeps you moving in the right direction.

Your vision need not be that specific. My primary goal was to keep my kids living in the community where they grew up, but it wasn't like I had a living room with blue curtains picked out. When my case settled in New Zealand and it looked like I might have a down payment, I started looking for another house. My boyfriend, Al, and I had been dating for a year and had both decided that before considering the idea of marriage, we wanted to live together to see how our kids got along with one another. I showed him a few houses in our community, and his immediate reaction was that they were dumps for the same price as other, much nicer, homes just fifteen minutes away. Enthusiastic, I went with him to look at those newer homes. I walked through the houses with a sinking feeling. After we were back in the car, I said that I was sorry, but I would rather live in a trailer in a field than live in a place where I couldn't see the hills or a clear moon and the stars at night. I wanted my kids to walk to school unafraid, and I wanted to know my neighbors.

I didn't have a living room picked out, but I had a clear vision of what I couldn't live without! I had gone through the process of looking at my dream and adding to it my limitations, assets, and abilities. In this case, the limitations were that I needed to live near open spaces and enjoy a feeling of security in my community. I decided the direction I had to take was buying a small cottage in my familiar neighborhood. There are prices to pay for who we are, and removing myself from a place where I was happy was something I couldn't possibly do. Would I have done it if I'd had to? Yes, of course; but I was willing to live in a one-bedroom, one-bath, sixty-year-old house instead of in a five-bedroom, brand-new house because my direction was clear.

And Al eventually agreed to the same house, because his vision of our home centered on different elements. His vision just included me in it, and he was open to filling in the details that were important to me. When we bought that one-bedroom cottage, I would wander around the property and point out where the perennial garden would be, where I would plant roses, and where the lawn would go. I would draw floor plans of how we could tear down the garage and replace it with bedrooms for the kids. My vision was so strong that it inspired Al and the kids, and they started to see it too.

Not every vision is so clear or convincing, but if you do have one clear vision, hold tight to it and let go of everything that doesn't point in that direction. If you really want to go to nursing school, hold that vision in mind whenever you are faced with a choice. Before making a decision, ask yourself which alternative will bring you closer to nursing school.

So decide the direction you want to take. Get it written down or posted up on your closet door in a creative collage. Begin to make your dream a reality by starting with small pieces—whatever has the strongest pull on your heart.

You cannot accomplish everything at once, so you will have to ask yourself what you want most and then follow all paths that lead in that direction. Make sure your actions are aligned with that vision. If you want to move out of the city, only go on job interviews for places located outside the city. Too often we jump at something, anything, because we fear that nothing else will come. If you want to open a day care facility, only look at homes or areas where you could legally watch children in your home. Let all the other distractions fall away as you focus on the picture you are trying to create. Let your dreams, not your fears, lead the way.

Holding on to Your Picture in a Relationship

Once your picture of your own dreams is in place, you have taken a big step toward being ready for a love relationship. If you go into a love relationship without at least considering and spending a little time to create the picture of what you want in your own life, you may decide that the picture your partner has created looks pretty good. But you may find yourself resenting it years later when you feel like all the relationship decisions have been based on what he wanted to do and be. This is exactly what many women do in their first marriages, either because they were young and in love or they thought that was the role they were expected to play. It certainly happened to me. But I was a partner in how it played out. He never tied me down or made me go on a vacation or forced me to move; it all happened because his vision was stronger and more vivid than mine. I found myself ten years into the marriage having forgotten that at one time in my life I actually had a picture of what I wanted my life and relationship to be.

For many divorced women, part of the picture is falling in love and possibly getting married again. It is also possible that as you read this book you are already in a new relationship. You may be struggling with how to hold on to the picture of what you want your life to be when you have to blend it with another person's picture of what he wants his life to be. I've been married two years, and we're still learning how different our visions of our future life can be. It always seems to be finances that reminds us. Recently Al told me that one of his goals was to set money aside so that when he dies his boys will have something for their kids. I was shocked to hear that, since I have far different ideas about inheritance. I work very hard, and every penny I make already goes to my kids, for their schooling, their medical expenses, and their extracurricular activities. Much of the time I have to forfeit what I would like to do for myself so that they get what they need and want. I don't plan to set money aside once they are through college so that they will have more luxury when I die; they can work and create their own lives. Of course, if I have extra money, that is one thing, but I'm not willing to sacrifice enjoyment of life so they can continue to have whatever they want after I die.

Al and I argued about this because, potentially, I would want to use my money to travel, and he would not have money to travel since he would be saving his money to give to his boys. I realized that we needed to spend some time visualizing a life together. He had ideas and pictures of what his life goals were, and I had my own. What we were missing was a picture that included and acknowledged both.

This new married relationship reminds me of the bargaining process I experienced during my divorce: nobody gets everything they want! Relationship means that there is someone to consider other than you. That has been really hard for me because the best part of being single was not having to ask anyone's opinion or consent before I made a decision. I sure didn't want someone telling me I couldn't go in whatever direction I wanted to go! But this aspect of finances didn't come up until after we were married, so now we are negotiating. I love my husband, but I love me too. I want him to have what he wants from his life, but I want what I want too. The process is teaching me to be open-minded: maybe my husband and I don't have to do everything together.

If you go into a relationship with a picture in your mind of the life you want, it is much easier to determine if the person you fall in love with is a candidate for lifelong partner. If you don't know what you want, it is likely you will go along with the life he wants, only to be disappointed and unfulfilled years down the road. Sometimes women survive divorce believing that their life is over, that nobody will love them, or that things will never be easy or fun again. That simply is not true. What we all need is a new picture, new dreams, and the belief that we deserve to live the life we imagine.

The picture you create of the life you want will be accomplished only through inner healing—understanding who you are now and who you want to grow into. In the next chapter we'll look at old patterns and how they can get in the way of bringing our dreams to fruition. We'll learn that getting what we want from life requires difficult actions, which include forgiving ourselves for past mistakes and acknowledging our right to a wonderful and fulfilling life.

The gap between where you are now and where you want to be may be substantial at the moment. Let that be a challenge to you as you read on. Open your mind to new possibilities, learn how to understand yourself, and heal with each new self-revelation. Each step will bring you closer to creating a true-to-yourself outer path.

2

Who Are You Now?

I stood in the bathroom looking at myself in the mirror, just like the workshop leader had told me to do. He said to sit there for at least fifteen minutes, staring into my own eyes. I'd never done that before. By the end of five minutes I felt like I was looking at a total stranger, wrinkles around blank eyes that looked back questioningly. During that workshop, I became convinced that the marriage I was in, the relationship that was failing, was my fault. The workshop leader was a man; the audience, all women, nodded their heads in agreement at most everything he said. We all agreed that women had the power to direct the relationship, that our energy was the creative force behind our family, but the new piece of information we were all buying into was that it was our responsibility to fix it.

Who I was, as I sat and stared into that mirror, was a woman who wanted to please, who wanted to be good and beautiful in the eyes of the world. She craved a husband who would validate the importance of her role as mother and as wife. After ten minutes, I was still looking in the mirror with these thoughts running through my mind, when my face began to look a little blurry through my tears, and I could see myself as a young girl. My eyes were dancing, but they were still soft eyes that had been taught to please, to do what was right, to follow the rules, to go with the flow.

Finally I had to speak to my face, the face that my kids look at all the time, the face that I only get glimpses of when I'm fixing my makeup or looking pleasantly into the mirror. "Who the hell are you?" Through my tears I started laughing—really laughing—as it came to me that the face I was looking at had grown into a reflection of who my husband at the time thought I was. Over the years I had transformed myself into the woman that he saw. Maybe I had done it through my own choice, but definitely I had believed that I was doing what I was supposed to do—creating a marriage that worked. Of course I liked to cook—that was a valued skill for a wife and mother to have. It was my job to go out to dinner and listen attentively as my husband talked about his life. I even believed his insults afterward when he would tell me not to interrupt next time unless I had something interesting to add.

I had been interesting when I got married—at least I thought so at the time. Somehow I had become less than I was. Less attractive to myself when he found me so, less competent as a mother when he believed that I should be able to do my job without any outside help. He was not a dictator; it was just that I believed the reflection of me that I saw through his eyes. In the story of Snow White, when the wicked witch says, "Mirror, mirror, on the wall, who is the fairest of them all?" the mirror shows her the image of the angelic and sweet Snow White. I was sure that if my husband had said, "Mirror, mirror, on the wall, show me the true Sheila," he would have seen a manipulative, witch-like creature who told everyone what to do, a selfish woman who took time off for an art class instead of playing with her kids, a spoiled woman whose life had no importance in comparison with his own! The moment I started believing the reflection I saw of myself in my husband's mirror was the moment I lost myself in my marriage.

Losing Sight of Ourselves

Many of us wonder how we—the smart, creative, energetic, competent women that we are—could have lost sight of ourselves as we grew into the mother and wife we thought we should be. We believed in love, and in the beginning the reflection we saw of ourselves through our husband's eyes was one of great admiration. Over time, as the relationship deteriorated, that image might not have been an accurate picture of who we were, but by then we had lost enough of our self-esteem that we doubted ourselves. We tried harder, changed what we could to be more attractive to our partner, in the hope that somehow we could hold the marriage together. Divorce happened anyway, and we found ourselves with no mirror and no reflection for a while as we tried to pick up the broken pieces of our lives and to find this person we lost along the way—ourselves. Then we lived with no mirror and no reflection for a while, and for some of us it seemed like we ceased to exist. The grief and anger take its course—and finally we walk out of the darkness and see clearly that we have to discover the real person within us before we will have the courage to love again.

Women I interviewed spoke about the process of losing sight of their own reflection. "When I got married, I didn't know that my husband had a 1950s, June Cleaver view of what a wife and mother was supposed to be," said Samantha. "In the early years of the marriage I actually started to believe his idea of a woman's role in the home because keeping his love was important to me. Then one day I said to myself, 'Wait a minute—this isn't what my life is supposed to be!' I was a trophy wife, taken to corporate functions where I was supposed to be cute and charming. In the car on the way to the event he would drill me on family information for all the important people I would be meeting. He would tell me not to talk about our kids too much, don't say this, don't talk about that. What I really thought was obviously not good enough."

Sometimes we can become so lost in someone else's concept that who we are inside can become invisible even to ourselves. "For the first two years following the divorce, I was unable to see anything but my own pain," said Angela, the mother of two boys. "I blamed *him* for everything that went wrong in the marriage. Once we were apart and my anger began to subside, I noticed that I was still carrying with me a picture of myself that was his picture. Somehow over the years he had decided that I wasn't a sexual person. From that point forward his view of me as being uninterested in sex filtered into our relationship in so many ways. I felt sexually rejected. Over time I actually became self-conscious about sex, believing that I was unattractive or that there was something wrong with me. I had never been like that before."

Jenny also found she needed to take back her own picture of herself as a sexual person. "After the divorce, I realized that the only way to get rid of the old picture I carried around of myself was to do something to prove that picture was wrong. I decided that I was going to have a one-night stand. None of my friends believed me, but I had never in my life had the experience of picking someone up in a bar, having sex, and never seeing him again. I knew that I couldn't bring the same sexual energy and low sex-esteem I had in my marriage into this encounter or it would be a disaster. That night is still fuel for many fantasies, and, boy, did I shatter that old picture!" Both Angela and Jenny needed to change the picture they held of themselves as sexual women before they were able to enjoy another relationship.

Through work, Joanna was able to regain her picture of herself as a competent and valued person. "I transformed into someone else within my marriage," said Joanna, "and I'm just beginning to figure out how I could have let that happen. I actually went back to work when I decided divorce was inevitable. Working helped me see who I really was. Up until that point I was room mother, the coach's helper, a volunteer extraordinaire, and, of course, the perfect, devoted wife. At work my opinion mattered. When people started changing meeting schedules just so that I could attend, I started to believe in myself again!"

Sometimes what happens in intimate relationships can be a subtle form of brainwashing in which both partners participate. You hear something enough times and you start to believe it. Love, and the desire to please another person that accompanies love, has the power to change a person. There is a give-and-take in a relationship, a compromise, a sacrificing of some things you want, and a setting aside of one's own dreams. This blending of lives, expectations, and passion is part of what marriage is all about. But sometimes the blending can be more like a disappearing act, where one person willingly (but perhaps unknowingly) gives up more of what they want for the sake of the marriage. If one partner does this for long enough, they may start to believe that the other's wants, desires, and opinions are more important than their own or are actually their own. They may forget who they were before the marriage or what they wanted within the marriage. Their partner and their marriage in many ways begin to define them.

The path of healing begins when we start to see there is another way and that, now free of the ex-spouse's vision, we are free to be who we see ourselves to be.

Who are we now? That is the question that can lead us forward into a new life and a new love. Who is that person in the mirror, and how can we claim her forever so that we don't lose her again? The goal is to embrace ourselves as we really are, loving ourselves in a way we weren't able to do within the marriage, and then to hold tight to all that we have learned as we enter a new relationship.

Listen to Your Own Voice

If we are to rediscover ourselves outside of marriage, we need above all to know how to recognize our own voice. It may take some work to uncover it, for the voices of family and society all figure in. We are made up of the experiences we have had in the past, the behavior that our society supports, and the opinions we hear from those we love. I brought into my marriage certain expectations of what love would feel like, expectations built on what society teaches about marriage and what I had seen in my family of origin. I also brought my own habits, some of which were immature and self-centered. So, in order to move away from outside influences and move closer to being truly ourselves, there has to be some sort of shift. We have to stop caring so much what others think, begin listening to our own voices, and open up to the idea that we have a right to be ourselves. Until we learn to be true to ourselves, we can never really be true to another. Authentic love requires honesty, and you can't be honest with another if you haven't learned how to be honest with yourself.

A first step in being honest is to notice that the damaged reflection we carry of ourselves cannot be blamed entirely on our ex-spouse. My own ingrained expectation of what it meant to be a wife and mother contributed to my disappearing in the marriage. When I got married, I remember thinking, "Isn't it great to be *us!* I don't have to be just *me* anymore." I bought into the concept of "becoming one" and believed that we had so much more to offer the world with our combined strengths. The first year was great when we were living on campus and he was in college. It was the next year, when we moved to a new city and he took an important and well-paying job, that I began to change to fit into his new life, since I believed that was my job as a wife. When I started to have babies, there was no time to devote to myself; I was supposed to be somebody's mother.

If I believed that I changed or lost myself because of this one bad relationship or this one bad husband, I wouldn't have the courage to really take a look at who I am and what part I played in the relationship. I wouldn't be able to be honest with myself because I would have somebody to blame, an excuse for old patterns and behaviors—after all, why should I change if it wasn't my fault? Unless we are willing to look at the personal and societal structures that guided our previous marriage into being the kind of relationship it was, we will simply bring "who we were" within that marriage into the next relationship. We then replace one man with another, while we stay the same, holding the same beliefs. And given enough time, the scene will repeat itself.

Another step in being true to ourselves is to admit our own mistakes. The difference between who I was in my first marriage and who I am now can be measured by the changes I've made in my life. Some of the changes were born from the pain and grief I felt in losing something I loved and had worked so hard to achieve and sustain. The biggest changes occurred when I was willing to be honest with myself. There was such relief for me when I was able to say, "I've made mistakes in this relationship. I'm not perfect, I was at fault, too." (I have to admit that I even feel the temptation right now to type in qualifiers for that last sentence: comparisons of behaviors, explanations for choices, and degrees of mistakes!) But, in the end, and after years of healing, I know that none of that matters anymore. What matters is who I am now and what I have learned about myself, my world, and my future.

The most important step in being true to ourselves is learning to listen to our own voice. Unless we learn to recognize our own voice, the opinions of friends or family members or society around us can easily drown it out. I received so much advice when I was newly single: "The kids will do better if you move somewhere less expensive so you won't have to work so much." "It's a bad relationship model to live together if you aren't married." Some of ons I heard actually began to sound like my own voice. Learning ecognize the outside influences and filter them out was difficult.

One day after the divorce when I was trying to decide whether or not to buy a small cottage, I decided to try a new method of figuring out what I really wanted. I wrote the question I was considering in my journal and then wrote down the first response that popped into my head. I called the exercise "writing my intuitive voice."

You may want to try this with a decision you are facing right now. Simply sit quietly with a pen and piece of paper. Ask yourself the question you are facing. Notice what pops into your head first. Write it down. If you write down your own intuitive response, you have a record of what you feel about an issue before you begin to be influenced by friends and family. Once your own voice is recorded, you can ask your trusted others what they think. We all value the contributions of friends and family and want to bring their ideas into the equation. But it is important that our own voice have priority, that we hear our own voice first, and that we can still recognize that voice after we have heard everyone else's opinion. Then we can discern how we're going to respond to the situation. A creative, thoughtful, intelligent woman lives in you; it is time to let her out to begin making the choices!

Once you know how to listen to your own voice in decisions you are making, you can begin to listen to what you believe to be true about yourself. But here begins a difficulty: if you have been making your life choices based on societal expectations or friends or kids or religious expectations, how do you know what is truly you? I consider this to be the most basic human question: How do we know who we are?

Claiming Ourselves

To know who we are, we need to remain in contact with our own inner being—our own sense of what is true and right for us. I find it helpful to ask myself several questions on a continuing basis:

How am I feeling right this minute?
Am I expressing who I truly am in this situation?
Is this the decision I would make with no outside influence?
Will the actions I'm taking bring me closer to the life I want?

Getting into the habit of checking in with these questions teaches me to pay attention to my life. The answers help me to acknowledge who I am, and to get what I want. Most of my life I've been content to do more than my share of the work around the house. One Saturday, about two months into my new marriage, I was faced with a filthy house complete with dishes in the family room, backpacks thrown randomly on the floor, and a laundry room piled high with barely dirty clothes. I asked myself the question "Am I expressing who I truly am in this situation?" An angry "No!" was all I heard. So I sat with that answer and then thought, "Okay, so how would this picture look if I were being true to myself in this situation?" The questioning process allowed me to understand how I felt, to think through how I would like the family to work together to create a fair distribution of household chores— most important, it allowed me to take positive action. I was confident in expressing who I was, what I needed from the group, and in the end we were able to come up with a plan that worked for everybody (although they were decidedly happier with the past arrangement of my being the household maid!).

The only thing that seems guaranteed in my life is that tomorrow I will be different than I am today. I grow and change as I learn more about who I am right now. Why would I be open to this questioning self-evaluation that could go on and on? I like my life, things are relatively calm, and I've created so much of the life I've wanted. The continuing self-evaluation helps to keep me on track, to make sure I'm going in the direction that is best for me. I ask myself these questions because I want to check regularly that the answers I hear are my own inner voice speaking, not the outside societal or family views that clouded my thoughts in the past. If we can find a way to live true to who we are, then there is an inner feeling of contentment and success.

Who you are cannot simply be a desire or a promise or a reflection or a definition made with words; it has to be lived. If I say that I am a confident woman, then that is who I am. The first thing I need to do, then, when I walk into a room of perfect strangers is to give myself the message "I am a confident woman, and I will walk like one and talk like one." Obviously we all have good days and bad days; nobody can be completely true to who they are all the time. But the inner knowledge of who we are, maybe even the written proclamation of who we are, will influence our ability to live true to that idea.

In reclaiming ourselves, we may encounter many obstacles, and fear is the toughest one. *What will I find out about myself? What if I'm not really as caring as I thought? What if I really am what he said? What if I have to admit my failures? What if I don't look so good to people anymore if I act true to who I really am?* We may also worry that our lives will change if we are truly ourselves. *Will my friends still like me?* Each of us has the right to be ourselves, but we must claim that right, for it is easier to sit back and let someone else run the show. It will cause fewer waves if you agree with people instead of disagreeing; it will be outwardly easier if you live like everyone else instead of being an original.

Many women, after a divorce, find themselves trying to please the men they date because they believe they won't find anyone who will love a woman with children, bills, and issues. Amy, the mother of two boys, said, "I remember thinking to myself when I met this really cute guy, 'Why would he choose me with all the extra baggage and kids?' So I found myself making every effort to be the sort of woman he was looking for. I remember the time he made a comment about the way I did my hair, saying he preferred it to fall more in my face. I changed my hairstyle, and the next time we went out I did my hair so that it fell even more in my face, even though it drove me crazy. After a few dates, I started trusting that he did like me, even with my kids and my issues, and went back to my old hairstyle!"

Fear of rejection can lead us to lose parts of ourselves, as Jasmine related. "After my divorce, I went out a lot to meet guys. It was easy for me to have sex with the ones I didn't care about, and I had a great time. As long as I didn't care what a man thought about me, I was an amazing lover—a free spirit. But when I started caring about what they thought about me, and about them as partners, I lost that free spirit because I was so afraid of being rejected."

We can also lose our ability to be who we really are through being too responsible for how others are feeling. One of women's most developed skills is adjusting to the temperature of the moment, being so sensitive to what is going on with those around us that we adjust our own temperature to match theirs. Someone says he's hungry, and we jump toward the refrigerator. A friend is depressed, and we sink right in with her or try to fix it. We have been conditioned all our lives into believing that a "good woman is this," a "good wife does that," and a "good mother looks like this." We put the needs of everyone else ahead of our own. Nowhere in the feminine dialogue of my childhood or adolescent life did I hear that a good woman puts herself at the center so that the center will be strong enough to hold all the spokes.

Being truly ourselves also means making choices about what we are willing to accept or reject in our lives today. We all are searching for the opportunity to love again as our real self, fully revealed, fully accepted as an equal partner in life. It is easy to say that we are equal, that we are partners, that the sky's the limit, yet until we act on that belief, the equality we seek will not be found. I'm still working on the belief that it is okay to be in my own body, with my own pain, with my own fears and doubts, and that it is okay not to fit my preconceived ideas of what a wife, mother, or girlfriend should be.

We have to be able to say, "Hey, these are my dreams, and I'm not going to let what others think stand in my way." I had the lesson brought home to me by a woman I interviewed for this book. Laura, a twenty-six-year-old mother of two, told me she was getting her tubes tied in a week. My first reaction was to try to convince her she was making a mistake. I'd had my tubes tied when I was thirty, and I remembered the feeling of being in love in my first major relationship after divorce and how it felt to tell this man who wanted kids of his own that I couldn't have any more. When I shared this with Laura, she simply said, "I don't care if a man wants me. It isn't about him; it is about what I want in my life and what I want to do in my life, and I know that the birth of more kids would prevent me from doing it." Her inner knowledge of who she was, her belief in her goals and dreams, was strong enough that she could say, "I'm done playing the roles other people want me to play." Laura was living her convictions. She had claimed herself completely and declared her right to make her own choices.

So what does seeing, naming, and claiming ourselves look like? It means we have to hear our real desires, have the courage to stand up for ourselves, and believe that our own voices are the most important ones we will hear. It means we trust ourselves enough to direct our own lives. It means that when we fall in love the next time, we are solid enough within ourselves that we can't be reshaped into a form we can't recognize years down the road. It is most important during this time of rebuilding to choose friends and lovers who allow us the space to ask ourselves, "Who am I now and who do I want to be tomorrow?" If you get stuck with someone who wants to contain your growth or control who you are, then you might as well choose to be alone. Most of us are too old to be told who we are!

In this quest to claim ourselves, there is one last question we must ask ourselves:

Does my outwardly expressed personality match how I feel inside?

This question came up for me when, after the divorce, I was unpacking boxes of belongings that I'd put into storage years before. As I unpacked, I couldn't believe how colorful all the clothes were; by the time I got divorced everything in my closet was brown or black. Yet here were clothes that were original creations; they looked like they'd been purchased at a high-end street fair! I pulled out a pair of tumbling, chubby angels with mischief on their faces and remembered how I felt when I bought them. The most telling box contained all the clothes I had made myself. At one point early on in my marriage, I'd wanted to be a fashion designer, so I'd made some samples to take with me to my application interview to a design school. It was like I had packed away my creative self, one full of life and ideas and incredible power, and was now opening the boxes after some alien transformation had occurred. The part of me I saw in those boxes had been lost over the past five years of my life. I pulled my self-made creations out and began to drape them over me. I looked in the mirror and remembered. I started thinking about what I looked like the day I had packed these clothes, and how I expressed my personality in my daily life. I had to admit that the person contained in those boxes was the one my husband fell in love with—and she was the person I was in love with. The puzzling question was, What had stopped me from expressing it? I gained insight and a new goal that day—to drape myself in *me* again.

The Cost of Being Yourself

It is possible to become someone other than ourselves in our relationships with friends and relatives as well as with husbands or mates. Remember the last dinner party you attended where you said something that you didn't really feel just because that was the way the conversation was going? You wanted to be liked, to be invited to another party. Or what about that group of women in your community who gossip about everyone? Even though the gossiping bothers you, you decide it is better to say nothing rather than to be excluded. Okay, so we all do this; I do it too. But if we are going to be truly ourselves, some people will not like it. Friends and family are used to our acting a certain way. We may even be so used to the old way we interacted in relationships that we are afraid to push our life in a new direction.

It takes courage to be yourself with friends and relatives as well as with boyfriends and husbands. If you commit yourself to it, you will get opportunities to practice this skill every day of your life, in every area of life. Why is it so important to know who you are and then to learn to be true to that knowledge? Because if you can't, you won't be able to create an authentic love relationship. Sure, you can be true to yourself when it's just you. But when you add into the picture someone you're in love with, it can be all too tempting to morph into your vision of a woman he might love more. Yes, there is a price to pay in being truly yourself: you could be rejected. But what good is a partner who doesn't love you for who you really are? Remember, you have the right to be yourself.

Divorce forces women to take a deep look at who we are. In many cases, we are all too aware of past failures and future doubts. Figuring out who you really are is a first big step in moving from the grief of divorce to redefining your life. If you feel lost after your marriage ends, you must take the time to first find yourself before you enter a new relationship. Do whatever it takes to learn to see yourself through your own eyes instead of accepting the mirrored reflection of your former husband, your family, or society. If you skip this step, you may unwittingly bring the woman you became during your marriage into the new relationship. Then you will start the disappearing act all over again as you mold your life to please your new partner. When you learn to listen to your own voice, give yourself time to redefine yourself—to create new dreams, to set new goals, and to be open to the possibility of inner transformation—you will bring a stronger, more confident woman with you into your new relationships. From this point forward there will be no more accepting other people's reflections of you. Your voice will be the clearest one you hear, and you will be able to see yourself clearly in the mirror of your own eyes.

3

Old Patterns

When life hasn't gone exactly the way we wanted it to, we become more willing to examine our lives, to take a look at what went wrong and figure out how we ended up in the place we are today. After a divorce is a good time to look at our life patterns—old patterns of relationship that didn't work the first time around and that we would like to change.

Relationship patterns form through our earliest experiences. Each family of origin operates on certain rules of relationship, and the patterns we experienced in childhood are ones that we carry into our adult lives, including our marriages. We are comfortable with those behaviors, whether they are supportive or destructive. We are used to them. For this reason, women who were abused as children may enter into an abusive marriage. Women who watched their mothers achieve success in the workplace may decide to keep working after they give birth to their own children. Maybe when you were married you argued every night, just like your parents, or maybe because your parents argued every night you refused to engage in any conflict at all. Before you embark on the journey toward a new relationship, it is essential that you take some time to understand your own life patterns.

Are you willing to take a look at the patterns in your marriage that contributed to its failure and to identify which parts of the patterns belonged to you? Can you look objectively at your family of origin to determine what behaviors you unconsciously carry with you? What about old dating patterns that no longer fit the woman you are today? This examination of your life can be done, not with an attitude of self-blaming, but rather with the open heart of an investigator looking for clues. Of course, as in any failed relationship, our fingers can easily point out all the faults of the person, group, or institution that hurt us. But in order to move forward we must also see our contribution clearly.

Once you can identify the destructive patterns you have used in your life, you are then able to define and begin creating the patterns you'd like to bring into a new relationship. A psychologist could also help you to identify experiences and patterns in your life that may well determine how you see the world and why you respond or react the way you do in certain relationship situations. None of us really wants to do all this work to figure out who we are; we'd rather fall in love and surround ourselves with the feeling that we have found ourselves in this other person. We want to be healed by this new person's complete acceptance of us, and we want to move our thoughts as far away from past failed relationships as we can.

It takes courage to look openly at your own unhelpful patterns and to acknowledge your contribution to the end of your marriage. As painful as it may seem, the inner knowledge you gain will be your declaration of independence from your parents, from societal restraints, and from your old marriage. You will be free to start again with a clean slate. The self-understanding you gain can empower you to direct your life in a way that creates new space for a successful love relationship to grow.

How to Begin Your Investigation

There are all sorts of ways to investigate old patterns. When I began this process, I would pretend to be filming myself during the day. Before going to sleep each night, I'd run the film of the day's actions in my head and then ask myself if the person in the movie looked like the person I wanted to be. Was the person I saw that day the person I thought I was? Running the film took only a few minutes each night, but it helped me to decide if my actions were helping or hurting me.

You can get a big boost in this process by knowing that doing the work will get you what you want—a new love relationship with yourself and with another. You have to make a commitment to yourself, to learn how to pay attention to your thoughts, and then know the direction you want to go in your life. Desire is the first step, but it isn't enough. You actually have to do things differently—to think differently, to be open to reinventing who you are at this moment.

A sense of humor is a key ingredient in this work. I attended a women's meeting once where the leader introduced what I thought was a silly exercise. She told each of us to talk about a problem that was bothering us. After the person said what was bothering her, we were all to begin saying ha, ha, ha until the leader told us to stop. After about thirty seconds we were all laughing so hard we were crying. Then the next person said what was bothering her, but by then she was laughing so hard watching everyone else laughing that she could barely spit her words out. The past is painful—sometimes tragic—but there is always something funny to be found in it. Life would be so much easier if we lightened up a little!

Investigating Family Patterns

Patterns or habits are not by definition bad or good; they are just clues that define us in some way. Usually they have developed for a reason. When I first started therapy, I remember my therapist telling me that I had developed the patterns I had because at some point in my life I needed them to cope. When we investigated the patterns that led to my unhappiness in my marriage, I began to understand what she meant.

One of my biggest complaints about my marriage was that I didn't feel that my ex-husband paid any attention to me. I truly felt invisible to him. When I asked to talk with him, he acted like he was uninterested. My therapist asked me if I'd ever felt deprived of attention as a child. I said that I was sure every child would like more attention. There were six kids in my family, all born within ten years, all with a list of activities, all with needs and problems of their own. But the more my therapist and I talked about it, the deeper we got into how I actually felt as a child—how much I wanted more one-on-one time with my parents. My feelings became clearer to me. I had chosen to marry a man who was emotionally unavailable to me because it was a pattern I had experienced as a child, a pattern I was comfortable with. So every time my ex deprived me of what I wanted from him, I felt the pain, not just of his rejection, but also of the lack of attention I experienced as a child.

Realizing my own patterns, I began to panic about what my own kids had gone through—how the divorce or mistakes I'd made as a mother would play out in their lives. Would they be sitting in a therapist's office, discovering how they were deprived of attention as children? They might be; I work, run a household, and orchestrate four kids' lives, so I'm sure they wish they had more time with me. In fact, I'm sure my parents actually spent more time with me than I spend with my kids. Instead of beating myself up about this, I can look at this pattern, be aware that my kids might feel deprived of attention, and with this awareness allow things to shift. I may not have more hours in the week, but when my kids get angry with me for some small thing, I might be able to reflect back to them that their anger toward me might be about their feeling deprived of my attention. We can then have a conversation about their feelings, and their emotions can be validated. Not all the patterns we find can be changed, but awareness of them can create a shift in action.

I've also come to the conclusion that we were all damaged during our childhood in some way. To blame our parents, teachers, or community only serves to keep us in a victim mode, unable to claim the power available within us. Each of us has to move on. Part of growing up is accepting that our childhood was not exactly the ideal experience we wanted it to be. I decided to look at the patterns of my family of origin simply as a way to understand myself—I had enough to worry about without going backward to relive my childhood. And although I believe we were all damaged in childhood, I also believe that there is more right with each of us than is wrong with us. So this detective work is not just about the things that might need to change; it is also about honoring the aspects of ourselves that really work right now in our lives.

Especially if there was physical, emotional, or verbal abuse in your family, it may be important to go through the process of healing childhood trauma before moving forward. "Over the course of our marriage, my ex developed abusive tendencies that grew worse and worse as the years went on," said Allison, the mother of three young children. "At that stage in my marriage I think I was drawn to my husband because he provided a place where I could prove things—where I could fight back. I experienced a lot of abusive treatment from my dad. He would flood with anger and then lose his temper. My dad was very judgmental, critical, and insecure. Anything that didn't fit into his paradigm was very threatening. He was a survivor of the Holocaust. I created a perfect dance between me and my husband that allowed me to fight back in a way that I wasn't able to fight back against my dad. Until a friend encouraged me to attend an abuse support group, I didn't realize that I was actually being abused. I was so used to that kind of treatment. I was always on this edge, thinking my husband could change. I thought that we had so much going for us. Listening to the other women helped me put this into perspective and see the abuse pattern for what it was."

My therapist spent months helping me to look at my family patterns. As a child I remember how hard I worked to get all A's in school, to be the best at everything I did. Similarly in my marriage, I tried to do everything perfectly to get my husband's attention. In the process I felt like nothing I did was good enough. This is a pattern I'm still working on. I think in my family we defined ourselves by what we did, not who we were. Achievements were highly sought after and greatly rewarded. I remember going to a dinner party after I had my first baby and feeling I was somehow a failure when a woman asked me what I did. I felt this urge to explain my life, why I was "just" taking care of a baby. It wasn't measurable enough.

Other childhood patterns emerged in my therapy. By the age of twelve I had already been given a lot of responsibility. I knew how to cook a dinner for the whole family, how to care for other people's children overnight, and how to take care of my own younger brothers. Those childhood and adolescent experiences gave me the confidence to marry young and know that I could manage a household. It also helped me slip easily into a mothering role with my husband instead of a broader, healthier partnership role.

My girlfriend Anna recently returned from a visit with her mother and had this story to tell about a huge fight they had over a tea bag. Anna went into the kitchen to make a small pot of tea for herself. She got out two tea bags from the cabinet and put them in her pot. Her mother came in and told her she was being wasteful by using two tea bags. Anna ran out of the kitchen in tears. It took her a few hours before she could speak to her mother. She told me that her mother had made comments throughout her life about wasting things. They always had to eat everything on their plate, weren't allowed to give clothes away unless they were holey, even had to share towels to save water. Anna screamed at her mother, telling her they were no longer living during the Depression and that she would buy her more tea bags so that Anna could enjoy a strong two-bagged cup of tea on her visits home. Her mother didn't really care about that tea bag, it was about the pattern of reminding her daughter not to be wasteful, a character trait the mother obviously valued.

Our parents had the difficult job of making sure we repeated the behaviors they wanted us to learn until these behaviors became part of who we are. The problem is that the person you are in, or will be in, a relationship with also had parents making them repeat their family's patterns over and over again until it became part of who they are. Imagine my friend dating a man who on the first date asked her why she used two tea bags; she might never accept a date with him again!

Early Dating Patterns

In addition to the patterns learned in our families of origin, our early dating experiences as adolescents and young adults can set up patterns that we follow in subsequent relationships. When I was fifteen, I began dating an eighteen-year-old; the relationship lasted for three years, and it introduced me to the concept of intimacy and commitment. When I went to college I didn't know how to date someone casually, but boy was I good at long-term attachment—because that was all I knew. When something didn't feel right in my relationship, I worked really hard to fix it. The thought never crossed my mind that I could learn from one relationship and move on to something else, because I'd never seen that lived out. Kids in my high school stayed together for a long time: a year was considered a short relationship. Girls who had six-month relationships were seen as being promiscuous. That tidbit of information was stored in my brain under the definition of how good girls acted in positive relationships. We are each made up of all these random pieces that determine how we think, feel, and act.

Had I attended a high school where dating was a casual, short-term thing, I might have dated more than one person in college, but instead I met my husband the first month at university and married him a month after we graduated! Each of you has to look at your own past to determine why you are the way you are. Undoubtedly, early dating relationships, communication skills that were learned, sexual patterns, and ideas about how men and women were supposed to love each other filtered into your marriage whether you invited them in or not.

I can finally understand why my mom kept telling me that when I got married I would be marrying my husband's family—and all his friends, schools, and entire past life. I thought she was just trying to scare me. But think about it. Your world looks and feels a certain way. Then you meet and fall in love with someone whose world looks and feels completely different from yours. In the beginning that doesn't matter because the physical sensation of being in love is so yummy. Then, all of a sudden, sometimes years down the road, you find out that your husband's family didn't celebrate birthdays, at least not to the degree that your family did. You now understand why your husband looked on like you had lost your mind as you were hanging balloons and posters around the kitchen the night before each child's birthday. He was uninvolved when you passed out the hats and announced the party games the family would play. You thought he was being awful, but he was dealing with his own issues—like why no one ever did that for him when he was a kid. Then, because he didn't want to feel the pain or loss in his own childhood, he decided that you just blow birthdays completely out of proportion and that his kids would be spoiled because of this bizarre behavior. Now you have an issue that you don't agree on and that might cause you to argue as each child's birthday approaches.

There are many reasons for divorce, and each one of them includes accompanying patterns within the marriage that are extremely painful. The curse of having experienced these painful patterns with someone who was supposed to love you is that whenever something happens that feels remotely similar, you revert to your old feelings. "The other day my boyfriend told me there was a piece of old cheese on the dish in the refrigerator," said Amy. "I saw red. In that instant I was right back in my old marriage, feeling criticized for not doing a good enough job. I was so hurt by the comment that it actually made me doubt whether I was ready to be in a relationship with someone."

Your view of the world really does determine how you interact with other people, so you have to investigate your own life and actions if you want to enjoy healthy relationships in your future.

Identifying Patterns in Your Marriage

Several key areas have the potential to make or break a relationship. These are places where patterns are established early on that are difficult to break. Two of the most important ones are communication and sex, and these areas are addressed below. But you may have faced difficulty with child rearing, work schedules, finances, or personal fun time. Take some time to look back at your marriage and figure out what did not work in these important areas. After reading the questions and examples below, spend some time thinking about the trouble spots you experienced, and answer the questions. It will help you decide what you would like to understand or change about yourself as you prepare for or enter a new relationship. Once you have gathered this information, you can begin to create new behaviors in your daily life that more accurately reflect who you really want to be.

Communication

Why didn't it work?

"In the beginning of the marriage our communication seemed okay. We had a lot of fun together," said Karen, the mother of three teenage girls. "As the years rolled by I became so worried about every action my husband made, every physical look, anything that signaled disapproval. Early on my husband had an affair. He told me it was because I never tried to look attractive anymore. I had three young kids, and I admit it was hard to find time for a shower some days. After his affair, I developed this feeling like if I wasn't my best self all the time I was going to lose him. I also became incredibly controlling, wanting to make sure that he spent his free time with me. During the last two years of the marriage, he would make plans with me and then cancel them at the last minute or just not show up. I communicated how rejected I felt, and he would apologize and things would improve for a short period of time. When I look back, I can see that we didn't really talk to each other about our feelings unless it was a major blowup."

Karen realizes now that not communicating regularly about their feelings contributed to a breakdown of trust over time. Did this pattern contribute to the failure of your marriage? Spend some time looking at your communication pattern with your ex. How comfortable were the two of you speaking heart-to-heart? At what point in your relationship did you notice that communication became more difficult? Do you see any clues about why that pattern might have developed? What communication patterns from your family of origin were like the pattern that developed between you and your ex?

What you would like to change about this pattern?

Karen noticed that her communication pattern in her marriage was to not say things until she felt a huge amount of resentment. When asked what she would like to change about this pattern, Karen said, "In a new relationship, I want to be able to tell someone how I feel and have them actually care about it. I think really listening to someone is one way to show love in action, and I missed that in my marriage. It also helps to have the person who is listening value what is being said, which also comes down to mutual respect. So I guess what I want to change is to feel more confident about myself, to expect to be listened to, and to trust the relationship enough to not have to control everything so much."

How do you plan to accomplish this change?

Karen reflected on her new relationship and how she sees the old pattern sometimes trying to assert itself. "I'm in a relationship now with a man who is very caring and who does listen to me, but I can see how my old marriage patterns throw me into panic mode sometimes," she said. "A few weeks ago something came up and I was really disappointed. Every Saturday I usually spend the day with my boyfriend. One Saturday he made other plans without telling me in advance that we weren't going to spend the day together. I didn't say anything to him about how I felt. I realized that was the old me thinking that I better not put any pressure on him or he might leave me. After a day I made myself call him. I told him that I wasn't asking him to change anything but that I felt disappointed and hurt. The conversation was wonderful. We talked openly about how we felt in the relationship, and I was able to share some of the pain I experienced in my marriage and why I was overly sensitive to some behaviors. As soon as I said these words, I felt my physical anxiety actually decrease. The expression of my feelings was a release for me, and I realized the value of communication, which sounds so corny. But in that moment we were on the same team instead of him being on an opposing side. I've made a deal with myself to say things to my boyfriend as they come up instead of not saying them out of fear of losing him."

Looking at her previous pattern has helped Karen discover a new way of relating to her boyfriend. Instead of bottling things up until they become overwhelming, Karen can choose to express her feelings, not with the intention of controlling her boyfriend's behavior, but just to allow herself to be known more deeply. Her willingness to be vulnerable opens the way for her boyfriend to take a similar chance with her, and the deeper communication allows them to grow in their experience of partnership.

Sex

Why didn't it work?

"We had an incredible sexual relationship in the beginning," said Dawn. "It was all so experimental. My husband was definitely the leader as far as coming up with ideas. Over time the ideas started getting a little strange, but I was afraid not to go along with them, because sex was the best part of our relationship. One day he told me that he didn't feel sexually attracted to me anymore, which was why he wanted to try out all these new ideas—he was trying to spark things up again. The problem was that the new ideas included my having sex with another woman while he watched. I really didn't want to do it, but he convinced me that it would be fun and that our marriage would be better for it. Afterward I felt so angry and used, but I didn't say anything because he was so attracted to me and our sex life again briefly became like it used to be. There was part of me that was screaming, 'I've grown up since our experimental days. I have children and a different life. I'm not eighteen anymore!' The other part of me was feeling like I'd let him down by changing the rules, so to speak. Much earlier in the relationship, there were times when I felt uncomfortable with what he was asking me to do, but I didn't have the courage to say anything. Now I have so many sexual issues to work through before I will feel healed."

Dawn identified her pattern in her sexual relationship as adjusting her personal beliefs to fit with the person she loved. She noticed that in the early years of her marriage she didn't speak her own preferences clearly but instead went along with what her husband wanted. Over time the pattern became so deeply entrenched that Dawn not only felt unable to change the course of their sex life but also was afraid she would be acting unfairly if she did so.

What you would like to change about this pattern?

"I want to know what I want sexually before I get involved in another sexual relationship," said Dawn. "I think I went along with his sexual leadership because I never thought about how I felt about it or knew what I wanted from our sex life. I also want to be with a man who can make love with me over and over again without feeling like I have to reinvent myself to keep his sexual interest. I want to be able to set boundaries and stick to them, even if it means that the man leaves me."

Looking at her past helps Dawn identify the areas in which she would like to grow. She commits herself to knowing more about her own sexual wishes before entering another relationship. She surmises that knowing herself better will give her more courage to be herself and hold better personal boundaries in the next relationship. Noticing her pattern also helps her identify which sexual qualities she wants in her mate—a man who can retain interest in her sexually over a long period of time.

How do you plan to accomplish this change?

"I've spent a lot of time journaling on this topic, picking specific sexual experiences I had with my husband that made me feel uncomfortable," Dawn continued. "I write about how I felt, why I agreed to participate, and what I would have liked to be able to say to him about it. I'm getting my feelings out and learning a lot about myself in the process. When I write all the experiences down, it also helps me to see that my husband had an obsessive problem with sex. I'm not sure what the clinical term would be, but it helps me see that he was not 'normal.' I haven't had sex since the divorce because I'm not healed enough to trust someone yet. I have dated quite a bit, but I'm quite happy to wait until I feel I've met a man who has similar sexual ideas. I guess you never know until you get well into a relationship whether or not someone will change, but I think the stronger I am in my own ideas, the better the chance I have to stay true to my feelings."

Identifying Current Patterns

While you are working hard on knowing yourself better and identifying patterns that contributed to the end of your marriage, keep in mind that some behaviors cannot be fixed until you are actually in a relationship. It is easy to get an idea in your head and decide that you want to behave in a certain way;

it is much harder when you have a human being you love or hate standing in front of you. If you have entered a new relationship already, you are probably aware of how easily old patterns can sneak up on you.

When I was newly remarried, my husband called my attention to a pattern I was totally unaware of: I tend to begin a big project whenever I don't want to confront certain problems. When I was unhappy in my first marriage, three of my kids were those "projects"; I also built a house, remodeled another house, and moved the family to a foreign country, all to avoid facing the problems in the marriage.

I had been remarried only six months when I decided I had to remodel the kitchen. My husband asked me if there was a problem with our marriage. For a few minutes I didn't know what he was talking about. Then he reminded me of my pattern of taking on projects when there was something I wanted to avoid. This time, I realized, the relationship was fine, but I was feeling stress on many levels of my work life and struggling with some issues with my kids, and the idea of putting my energy into creating something I actually had some control over was very inviting. My pattern is in many ways a healthy one. When I feel overwhelmed, instead of turning to a bottle of pills, I shut everything out and do something that doesn't allow me a minute to think about my problems. Now that I'm aware of my pattern, whenever I feel the urge to begin a new project I take some time to look at the problem areas in my life and deal with them openly.

But we don't need a new relationship before real human beings will confront us with our patterns. Relationships with friends or children may also stimulate us to look at patterns that don't serve us in a positive way. Carol said, "I'm still working on the guilt associated with feeling that I am responsible for everything in my kids' lives: their sadness, their hunger, their homework. I feel partially responsible for it all. How ridiculous is that? I see the pattern, but it is taking conscious daily effort for me to let it go. "Just the other day I felt so proud of myself when I was able to do something different from my usual pattern. My twelve-year-old came home from school 'dying of hunger.' I put a pizza in the oven for him, but it hadn't finished cooking when it was time for him to go to basketball practice. He started complaining that he hadn't eaten anything and why wasn't the pizza done? Instead of rushing around the kitchen to get him something to eat or feeling guilty that he would go hungry to practice, I was able to say, 'I guess you will just be hungry.' He left for practice and didn't die of hunger. I had to experiment with many different kinds of responses before I found the confidence to respond differently to these old guilt patterns that have been the cornerstone of my parenting."

Amanda, the mother of four, also finds that kids provide good incentive for changing current patterns. "Now that I've gotten away from the raw anxiety I felt in my marriage, I'm able to concentrate on how I react to my kids. I'm amazingly different when I'm mindful of my behavior. I don't try to control them. Through this shifting I've been able to give each of my kids the physical and emotional space they need, and the relationship is transformed. I don't take things so seriously. I trust that my kids know my values, and I allow them to make more choices on their own. When things go wrong I'm less inflammatory, and I definitely laugh a lot more. I do lose this consciousness occasionally when I'm stressed or tired, but all in all I'm excited by my ability to transform my life with very simple behavioral changes."

Amanda says that this shift has also helped her get back into dating. "The relationship with my kids is much more open and honest, and I'm beginning to believe that I deserve to make time in my life for social outings. This attitude has helped my kids see me as a human being who has needs instead of someone whose life purpose is to serve them! It is amazing how fast the family will change when the mom shifts her own pattern of behavior. It's like they all run off your energy."

Everyday life gives us many opportunities for looking at our patterns. There are many techniques for spotting patterns and bringing them to your attention. I've gotten into the habit of looking at overall negative feelings in my life. For example, when I feel like my kids don't have time for me, that they don't appreciate all the things I do, I ask myself, "Where have I felt this before?" Paying attention to this same feeling from my past and recognizing that it is still living in my current relationships helps me to step back and ask myself, "What is really happening here?" Then I answer my own question. My kids have a lot of commitments themselves, so they don't have the time to talk tonight. That doesn't mean they never want to talk to me. I don't have to draw the conclusion that "I've wasted my life as a mother raising kids who don't care anything about me." Instead, I can say to myself, "This feeling of rejection is an old feeling, and I'm not going to be sucked into it." I can choose to see what is actually happening instead of thinking myself into an emotionally destructive funk.

Being a detective of your patterns may sound like a lot of work. It is. But it is also fascinating to observe yourself. Divorce has set each of us on a unique and difficult journey. We've been forced to accept change: a new role, a new job, a new home, and new problems we didn't have when we were married. You already have to reinvent yourself, so you might as well uncover all the rocks, pick out the weeds, keep the pretty flowers, and in general replant the garden of your mind with relationship patterns that will bring you wholeness instead of more of the same.

Start now. Challenge yourself to do one thing today in a way you have never done it before—and enjoy doing it differently. Or be very daring and ask your best friend if you can wear something out of her closet that isn't your style at all. Experiment with changing the little patterns: have hot chocolate instead of coffee, or drive a different way to school. We can all survive change and in fact may flourish in all the new discoveries we make as we uncover the person we want to grow up to be. Looking at your personal patterns and habits will make you a better lover, a better friend, a better mother, a better human being. This is time well spent. Trust me on this one.

4

Loving Yourself

Love doesn't just happen; it's an action you take. You cannot sit around and wait to feel good about yourself. You have to do something—to take charge, to embrace yourself. Confidence will not come wrapped in a package, left on your front doorstep. You will need to have the courage to fall in love with yourself—not just the shiny, attractive parts, but also the parts you think aren't so great. I'm challenging you to love yourself with at least 50 percent of the acceptance, encouragement, and nurturing attention you show your children or dearest friends or loved ones. And here's the kicker: you have to learn to do it while you're not feeling your best. Seems impossible!

What difference will it make in your life if you learn to love yourself? Each of us has a purpose in life that is ours—people we influence, children we raise, contributions to our family and society that come from us alone. When you are able to love who you are, it is less likely that you will do what others expect of you and more likely that you will do what your heart tells you to do. You will be able to stand up for yourself, declare your self-worth, stop giving excuses and explanations to everyone, and be comfortable and unafraid to be yourself. If you don't love yourself, then you miss the opportunity to add your unique contribution to the lives of those around you. In the words of my teenagers, "You become a follower!" Being a follower isn't so bad unless you are a mother, because mothers have the awesome task of raising children to be independent, self-confident, self-loving adults. If you cannot model to your children what it looks like to love and respect yourself, then they will not learn that important life skill. Self-loving also produces an array of delightful benefits in one's life: we begin to show loving action toward others, we develop a sense of balance between the family's needs and our personal needs, and we begin to forgive all that we wish we could have been and start accepting who we are.

It takes more courage to love yourself than it takes to love another person. We are harsher, more judgmental, and less forgiving of ourselves. We easily see the wonder in others yet focus on the faults within ourselves. As you begin to picture the life you want, discover who you are, and start to examine old patterns that may stand in the way of the relationship you want, you will be left with a clear idea of the woman you are—faults and all. That is the moment when loving yourself becomes the greatest step toward being ready to love someone else. It makes you human, vulnerable, and open to love in a new way. You settle into yourself as you begin to believe that you are a lovable woman whether or not a man loves you. This is important, for it will allow you to walk away from a relationship, if you have to, as a whole and self-loved woman.

The most important act of loving myself happened the day I decided to leave my husband. I stood back and took a good look at how it felt to be living my life. This time the view was filtered, not through the rosy glow of love, but rather through the gray clouds of depression, exhaustion, and despair. It was the first time I stood up and declared my own worth. That day the love I found for myself was stronger than my fear.

I had gone out to lunch with a few new women friends I'd made in New Zealand, where we were living at the time. We were talking about our lives when I said, "I'm going back to the United States and getting a divorce." They all stopped eating and stared at me like I had just told them I was dying. Slowly they asked questions—mostly, why? Many times in the past I'd thought about divorce. I had spent years complaining about our relationship to friends and family—moaning really—but I was never willing to do anything about it, to take that final step. This simple declarative sentence, delivered without excuses or apologies, made me feel that for the first time I owned who I was. In the past I'd always felt I had to explain every choice I made, make sure everyone understood that whatever decision I made was not selfish or self-serving—in other words, make sure that everyone else's needs were met. In that moment, I wanted to be me. I could actually stand outside myself and watch what I was doing, and I liked myself. I thought, *This must be what it feels like to love myself enough to be unafraid to be myself.*

I read an interview with Toni Morrison in which she said that she always wanted to be herself. That sentence alone gave me food for thought for the rest of the day. Today I really like being me, but it hasn't always been that way. I liked parts of myself during my marriage, but I liked less and less about myself the longer the relationship continued. Toni's comment caused me to wonder whether, if I had wanted to be me during my marriage and really embraced and loved that person, would things have been different?

Now I want to be me, but it took me forty years to get to this place. I don't look at magazines or movie stars and wish I looked different. I love being a writer. I love being a mother, and I'm really proud of what I have created in my home and in my garden. I wonder what the collective soul of women would have missed if Toni Morrison and hundreds of other women whose ideas have brought life and direction to all of us had decided to go with the popular opinion of who they were instead of embracing and believing in themselves enough to be themselves.

What Do You Believe About Yourself?

What a person believes to be true, and the actions they are willing to take based on those beliefs, shape every decision they make. When the United States declared independence from Britain, the founders wrote a document that enumerated the founding principles of the new country. This declaration of independence established the ability of the new country to have authority over itself.

Divorce was much like a declaration of independence for me. But independence implies some sort of authority over oneself. I don't know if it's possible to establish self-authority or self-authorship (the ability to write your own life) without the foundation of self-love.

What do you believe in, and what do you stand for? Personal beliefs are the soil that surround your seed of self-love, giving the seed a place to safely send down some roots and in time to break the surface, opening up toward the light with bursts of color, form, perfume, and grace. Right now we are all learning how to send down those roots of self-love into the solid ground of what we believe. Have you ever thought about writing down your own declaration of what you believe? I have! This is my declaration:

I believe that we are all created powerful and divine—that each of us has a right to a life directed by our own inner voices, the freedom to make choices about the paths we will walk, and the pursuit of wholeness. I believe that we all have within us the heart of a revolutionary and the wisdom to construct peace. I believe that the definition of *mother* is not that of a servant, slave, or female who is willing to put the desires of everyone else before her own. I believe that inside every woman is a creative womb where ideas, children, dreams, and spirit rest enclosed in her body, ready to be transformed into life when the time is right. I believe that the depth of love contained in the collective soul of women has just begun to be uncovered—that, as a group, women are moving toward one another and thus toward strength. I believe that each thought I have has the power to transform my actions and that my actions really can make a difference.

I could go on, but I want you to look into your own heart. Look at your life for clues about what you believe. What do you believe about yourself? About yourself as a woman? About women—and men? What do you believe about love? Take time to write your own declaration.

Knowing your beliefs is important for your journey into love, because when you are able both to act on your beliefs and to make them a reality in your life, you will be actively loving yourself. I'll show you how it works. If I say I believe that mothers are not meant to be servants yet I still act like a servant, then in that area I am not showing love toward myself. If I believe in the collective soul of all women, then I have to live as if each woman I meet is part of me and to open my heart to her accordingly. If I believe that my thoughts have the power to transform my actions, I better pay attention when my negative thoughts come up. If my goal is to learn to love myself, then I need to give my beliefs the power they deserve, not doubt my right to have them or try to change them to fit into someone else's view.

You see, it is our thoughts combined with our actions that create an opportunity to practice love toward ourselves. And so we need to be aware of both actions and thoughts that are not self-loving—the negative thoughts, the self-destructive tendencies, the absence of any time to ourselves. Once we can see clearly how we treat ourselves, in both belief and action, then it is possible to make changes that bring us closer to loving care for ourselves.

For any of us who may be drowning in negative beliefs about ourselves, our choices, our past, our looks, or our career, the process of waking up to our own beliefs is even more important. Until we can rewrite our beliefs, loving ourselves will not be possible. Sandra, a mother of four, realized only after much time had passed that she believed she deserved the abusive treatment she was receiving from her husband. "It took hundreds of experiences of verbal abuse before I even thought about divorce," she said. "When it turned to physical abuse we went to a counselor. From the beginning it was never his problem. He seemed to have good reasons why I needed to be yelled at or hit. The therapist recommended that he join a group for male abusers, but he quit the group after a few weeks. He came home and threw a schedule at me and said it was my turn to go to a group so that I could change my behaviors too. He didn't pay attention to the fact that he was sending me to an abuse recovery group! At the first meeting, someone gave me a book on verbally abusive relationships: how to recognize when you are in one and what to do about it. I can look back on this now and am still shocked that I hadn't admitted to myself that I was being abused. On some sick level I began to believe what he said about me, that I deserved it in some way. I knew I was moody and that I could provoke him, so in a sense I believed that it was okay for him to abuse me, and I put up with it for years."

It is impossible to love yourself if you are allowing other people to hurt you emotionally or physically. If you have built your belief system on negative messages that you have heard for years, it is time to create new beliefs about yourself. Many women who have been abused actually begin to interpret the abuse as a form of disciplinary love from their husbands. Don't be fooled by your past experiences. Make sure your beliefs are rooted in nurturing love, not judgments you may have made in the past. If you blame yourself when things go wrong, keep in mind that self-blame can be a way of not feeling so power-less. But, it is not a path to self-love.

Chances are, most of us have grown up with a lot of harmful messages about what it means to love oneself. Think about the words we've heard throughout our lives that describe attention to oneself. Especially if that self is a woman, the words are all negative: *selfish, self-serving, manipulative, controlling, bitchy,* and *demanding.* With these messages, is it any wonder that we may find it hard to learn how to love ourselves?

Listening to Ourselves with Love

If you are not sure anymore that you deserve loving actions in your life, it is time to sit with yourself in silence and wait. There is a power in stillness, in time spent with our own thoughts. I used to tell friends that I couldn't slow down to think because thinking hurt too much, but I've learned this isn't true. Yes, when I spend time with my thoughts there is some grief at how out of touch I might feel at the moment or judgment about whether or not I'm doing a good enough job—there are usually tears. But at least when I spend time with my own thoughts, I'm living and feeling my life in that moment, in touch with what loving actions I'm trying to incorporate into my life. When I ignore my thoughts and feelings, I get to a place where my life and my problems are so entangled in each other that I feel nothing at all. Sort of a zombie state where all the motions happen but there is no anything: no up, no down, no passion, just flatness. I used to think that the flatness was better than the ups and downs. I'm learning something different now. Lately when I sit in silence, enclosed within my own mind, away from the thoughts and influence of my friends, family, or society, I find a place where my own day-to-day experience becomes real to me.

I've chosen at times to live out of touch with my feelings, and at that point my life begins to look like a factory assembly line. Wake up, put on smile, take shower, look nice, be nice, make lunches, kiss good-bye, straighten house, hold on, no time to process, no time to listen to myself. The product created on this factory line is predictable, and it doesn't break down, but it also is not very self-loving. The product I get when I sit still and listen is unpredictable—a flood, a burst of insight, a change in direction, and a knowing that has the potential to shock the family and social system. I've stepped off the assembly line and into myself, so all the machinery in the factory now has to shift to accommodate my movement toward acknowledging myself. This is what it means to root your self-love in the soil of your beliefs: you step off the assembly line and into the silence of your mind; then you begin to believe you matter.

Removing Obstacles

There are things that stand in the way of reaching the goal of self-love, like not trusting that our feelings are valid, our past negative experiences, and self-judgment. Sometimes my feelings scare me. I seem to have no control over them—they just appear out of nowhere and take me wherever they are going. You can't really measure feelings. Nobody can tell you if my sad is worse than your sad or if someone's anger is great enough to kill somebody. So this world we live in, filled with technology and scientific explanations, has given feelings a wimpy backseat to the measurable processes. Feelings may not be measurable, but they are visible every day in the behaviors each person acts out in our world. No matter how much knowledge, self-control, or desire we have, feelings of depression, desperation, and love can easily override all of our thinking skills and can hijack us. A feeling of intense anger might cause someone to hit another person. Feelings of betrayal may cause a woman to leave the home she just built. Feelings of failure might cause a woman to become self-destructive. Sometimes the negative feelings we have are directed at ourselves. When that happens, self-love has no chance to sneak through.

Negative feelings like depression, anger, loss, guilt, and fear—which often lead to negative thoughts about ourselves—have a tendency to take up more mind space and require more attention than love and other positive, uplifting emotions. It is like the kid who gets more attention from mom when he misbehaves; as women we usually put more of our energy toward fixing what is broken or who is hurt than toward basking in the glow of what feels good! "The feeling of fear seems to creep into my life more often than the feeling of love," said Tamara. "I'm afraid I won't be able to pay all the bills, that I've screwed my kids up for life, and that I'm going to be alone forever! I want to be able to feel good feelings, but the bad ones seem to rule my thoughts sometimes. I have a friend at work who is a single mom too, and she is such a positive person. She told me that she is trying to befriend her negative feelings. I've actually tried her little game and it works. She says that when a bad feeling comes up (like being scared that her boss will make her do a report over again) she says, 'Hello, fear, it is nice to meet you. My name is Alexis, and I am confident in my ability here at work, so I don't need what you are selling today!' It's a childish game, but it helps me to acknowledge the feeling and then say something positive about myself that helps me to remember that the bad feeling can come and go without having control over me."

Another obstacle to self-love is a negative experience in the past that has convinced us that we aren't worth loving. "When I was in high school, I was not very pretty," said Deb. "I was a little on the chunky side, not in the popular group, not really in any group. There was this guy in our class who I thought was gorgeous. I was sure he had no clue who I was, but he was in my biology class, and one day we started talking and he told me about a party that night. I never had much going on socially so I decided to go to the party with a girlfriend. When I got to the party I noticed that there weren't very many people there, and then I saw the guy. He came over and kind of apologetically asked what I was doing at the party. I didn't know what to say because I thought that his telling me about the party in biology class meant that it was a party that was open to anyone who wanted to attend. I left immediately and felt so humiliated. That one experience seemed to solidify my belief that I simply was not lovable in any way, and I'm still working on getting rid of that assumption."

Self-judgment can also stand in the way of self-love. "I fall into that category," said Dani, the mother of three young boys. "No matter what I do, or how well people tell me I'm doing it, there is a little voice in my head that tells me it isn't good enough. When I think about it, I probably have had that little voice my whole life. My older sister was great at everything she did, or at least when I was younger it looked that way to me. Now I realize that there were many things that I was really good at, probably better than her, but nobody really took the time to point that out to me. I make a huge effort now to point out all the talents my boys have. Whenever I point out positive things to my kids I think about all the compliments I wish I could have received from my family and teachers when I was growing up. I guess it isn't too late to start believing positive things about myself now, even if I am the only one. I know for sure the negative judgments aren't helping, so why not try something new?"

Balancing Self-Love with Love for Others

As women in our society, we have learned so well how to love others, to sacrifice for our children, husbands, families, and jobs in a way that we won't sacrifice for ourselves. I make sure my kids have healthy food, I help them with their problems, I get them to bed on time so they get a good night's rest. I drive them to self-improvement classes, sports practices, speech therapy appointments, drum lessons, and dance classes so they can become the best people they can be. I don't bat an eye or think twice when asked to drive my daughter someplace that will take me forty-five minutes round-trip, but I don't love myself enough to say no or claim that same amount of time for myself to practice yoga. Worse yet, if I do tell my kids I can't do something for them, I feel like I owe them an explanation. I would never dream of telling them I can't attend a basketball game because I need some time to take a nap, even when I feel like I can't take one more step without sleeping. I will get myself to that game. I also know that I'm not the only mother who feels guilty for focusing on her own needs. It would be great if there were enough time in each day to focus on ourselves as well as our kids so that everyone's needs would be met. But if you are a single mom, that isn't always realistic.

Trying to find a simple way to bring more self-loving actions into my daily responsibilities is a real challenge. It can mean something as simple as noticing when we set aside our own desires for those of others. The other night when I was making dinner, I asked myself, *How can I love myself in this moment?* I'm a vegetarian, but I cook dinner each night for the rest of the family, who all love meat and chicken. Each night as we sit down to dinner, I eat the salad and whatever vegetable I've prepared for myself. I never look forward to eating unless we are going out to a restaurant. So when I asked myself while cooking how I could create more balance, the answer was really clear: I'm going to cook at least two vegetarian meals each week. My kids may not like them as much as spaghetti and meatballs or chicken stir-fry, but then I don't like the food I make for them. Love is partly about giving yourself worth, taking your desires into account, allowing your wishes to have equal weight with the wishes of others. I have a hard time doing that, and so do most of the mothers I know!

For my birthday last year, my new husband, Al, gave me a beautiful Italian cookbook and told me he would cook one meal every month from the cookbook for the family. I forgot about his offer until he pulled the cookbook off the shelf and told me he was cooking something special. He chose a linguine pesto dish that had potatoes and green beans. He passed over many recipes that looked delicious, saying he wanted to make something that I could eat.

He loves me. In moments like this I realize how little weight I give my own desires compared to those of others.

In each activity of our daily life, we can ask ourselves, *How can I love myself in this moment?* I remembered to ask myself this last night as I was putting my kids to bed. My little voice (the one I hear silently in my head) said, *You have been so tired lately, why don't you go to bed early tonight?* So I told my son that I could either put him to bed early or say goodnight and allow him to put himself in bed since I was tired. He had no problem with putting himself in bed; in fact, he looked thrilled with the prospect.

Every day we look into the eyes of our children and see that they are hungry, need rest, are upset about something, and we nurture what needs healing. We would never let our children run their lives the way we run ours. I'm discovering that if I can see myself through a mother's eyes, as if I were the child, and can then nurture what I see, it will be a giant step in the direction of loving myself and balancing my needs with those of my children.

Sometimes it's hard to paint a clear picture of what this nurturing love might look like, especially if we don't have money to burn on child care, massages, dinner out, and weekend getaways. "What do you do if nurturing yourself means coming home from work and falling on the couch that night but you can't afford take-out food?" asked Paula, the mother of two toddlers. "Sure, I know I need a vacation, but that isn't possible. My family doesn't live near me, and I don't want to burden my friends with baby-sitting for my kids. I can't afford a baby-sitter more than once a month, so I'm stuck."

In some ways we are stuck, at least for the years our kids are at home, with the responsibility to raise them. But there are ways to create balance without money. It is more about how we see ourselves, what jobs we think just have to get done, and the standards we set. It may also be about getting the kids to take more responsibility for themselves, be it dishes, laundry, cleaning their own rooms, or helping their siblings with homework. It might mean that two nights a week everyone has to go to bed one hour earlier and read or play in their rooms so that mom can have private time to roam around the house. You can also learn how to say no to children's requests for rides or teachers' requests for volunteer time, and you can serve cereal for dinner once a week. Lowering the standards can be an adventure for the whole family.

Magazines usually paint the picture that taking care of oneself looks like a long soak in the bath and a cucumber facial. But what I'm talking about is a complete mind-shift. It means learning how to put your needs on equal ground with those of the rest of the family and then actually setting up family schedules and activities to reflect that mind-shift. Develop some healthy self-nurturing patterns, surround yourself with women who make you feel good, and phase out friends who bring you down or take your energy. Instead of running around your home touching base with each of the kids, sit yourself down on a chair in the middle of everything and let them come to you. Schedule your free time on the family calendar so the kids know when the chauffeur is off duty. Use your imagination: What would your life look like if you started to give yourself the nurturing love you freely give to others?

I recently joined a women's group. At the first meeting, the group leader taught us an exercise to help us see what parts of our life felt out of balance and what parts were going well. She told us to ask ourselves the following simple starting questions:

- How am I feeling mentally?
- How am I feeling physically?
- How am I feeling emotionally?

My first response to the three questions was, Tired, tired, and tired! Then I decided to try harder and began to get some answers. I kept repeating to myself each question until something came to mind. Mentally, I was feeling overwhelmed because I was thinking all the time about my writing, my kids, my future. Everything swirled in my head—what would I write, how would my life turn out? Next I focused on my physical feelings, and I could feel the ache behind my eyes from not sleeping well. My body felt stiff and out of touch with itself. For months I had been too busy to exercise. Then a voice stepped in and added that I felt grateful for my health and the fact that I looked pretty okay for not taking care of myself. Finally, I focused on my emotional feelings. It felt good to be sitting with these women, attending to my emotional self for the first time in weeks. I wasn't sure what she meant by emotional self, but she told us to search for one word that described our emotional state at that moment. We went around the circle and I heard the words "perky," "sluggish," "excited," so I jumped in with the word "open," thinking it fit in. After we answered the three questions, she gave us one more instruction:

- Ask your higher self if there is anything you need to hear.

Skeptical, to say the least, I was wondering when we were going to start working on the group goal of becoming more balanced in our lives. I was looking for information! Yet as I turned inward, a clear picture came into my mind of a painting I'd seen at the Uffizi art museum in Florence, Italy, of naked women coming out of the earth reaching upward and angels in the sky reaching down. Then I heard what I guess was my higher self saying, "You cannot save everyone." Let me now assure you that I am not a visionary: I don't read minds, and I can't predict the future. But we all have the ability to look within and to pull out some amazingly right-on directions for our own lives. We simply haven't learned how to trust or to acknowledge these feelings, beliefs, intuitions, and thoughts as valid sources of information. We haven't learned to turn inward to check how we are balancing our lives.

Forgiveness

Loving oneself requires forgiveness—looking at the mistakes, the bad parts of our lives, and then accepting our choices and letting go of the regrets. I met a single mother who was still stuck in grief three years after her divorce, and I asked her what she thought all the looking back would accomplish. She said that she would understand what happened to her marriage and then be able to forgive herself. I wanted to say to her that some disappointments and tragedies in life cannot be understood; they can only be set aside or moved past.

Many women look back and tear themselves down with negative images, thoughts, and explanations, with no healing direction in mind. Forgiving and letting go will allow you to love who you are today and to begin life in the present moment. It happened to you, it is over. Forgive yourself and your ex, and get on with your life. Love and accept yourself even if you feel you don't deserve it. That is the beginning.

It is easy to say we need to move on, let go, and get rid of that negative energy. Most of us would agree life would be a much friendlier place if we could. The question is *How?*

In the true sense of the word, forgiveness is when we are able to set a grievance aside and feel compassion for ourselves (if the mistake was ours) or for the person who has hurt us. But is it really possible to feel compassion for someone who has cheated on you or, for that matter, killed someone? A year ago a single mother named Laura told me her heartbreaking story. She received a phone call one day from a woman who claimed to be having an affair with her husband. Laura didn't believe it was true. She had been married for thirteen years and thought she had a wonderful, loving relationship. She called her husband at work and confronted him. He said that he would be right home. Three hours later police were at her door with the news that her husband had killed the woman he was having an affair with. Of all the women I've talked with, I thought that Laura would have the most forgiving to do, so I asked her where she was in the process of forgiving her husband (and herself for feeling like her phone call led to the murder). She sent me the following letter, which she gave me permission to share with you:

> When I first came to forgive Pete, it was after many, many months of steaming in my hatred for him, my anger, my bitterness, and my sadness. I cut him out of my life and told the children we were no longer going to communicate with their father because he was not good for our lives anymore. He hurt us deeply. He is now in prison for fifteen years to life. . . . But, as time went on, I felt myself changing. The hate was zapping my energy, making me feel weak and sick. I'd blow up at my kids, at other drivers on the road—I had no joy or zest for life anymore. I got so miserable that I entertained the thought of suicide. It seemed the only way out. It was selfish, I knew, but when a person hurts so badly that death is appealing, selfish is okay. I went to bed one night and prayed to God to help me out of my pain. I wanted His permission to kill myself. The next morning, I woke up with such a light feeling inside. I truly believe God spoke to my spirit for the very first time in my life. . . . I heard Him tell me that the only way to free myself of this pain was to forgive. I was shocked. For one thing, I wasn't a God person or even used to praying. I did so out of desperation. But He answered me so clearly in a way I didn't expect. I immediately went to my children and told them that we were going to buy Daddy a card today and mail it to him telling him we forgive him.

Laura sent Pete a card in prison saying, "You hurt us very badly, but what hurts worse is not having you in our lives and not forgiving." It opened a channel of communication between them that had been closed for over a year. They began writing back and forth, and Pete slowly explained that he had a sexual addiction, a sickness that had destroyed everyone he had ever loved. Laura then faced the difficult challenge of forgiving herself as well.

> I kept thinking there was something I should have seen, something I should have done differently, and I kept thinking of this dead woman I had spoken to on the phone that day. What I can tell other women is that forgiving is not a favor to the one who hurt you. It is a gift to yourself—a gift of freedom from bitterness and fatigue and depression. It doesn't mean what the person did was okay and you will just overlook it. It says that what they did was *not* okay, but that you refuse

to hold on to it and let it make you sick. You are forgiving so that you can go on with your life, heal and move forward, not stay stuck in the past. There will be times when you think you're crazy because you forgave this person after all they did to you. There will be times when you feel that the difficulties your family has to face is all your fault. That's when you have to remind yourself that forgiving is the only way to heal, move ahead, and be free.

Laura confesses that she still struggles to this day with leftover feelings from being betrayed by a man who cheated on her, murdered his lover, and left his family in poverty. "I want to hate him and hurt him back," she says.

But then I remember that he isn't the same person anymore. I'm not the same person anymore. He has changed, he is living in his own hell after all the hurt he caused, and he has been truthful with all his secrets so that the slate can be washed clean. I had to do this with my own guilt about this whole thing too, to try to forgive myself for mistakes I've made and to give myself the chance to start with a clean slate.

Learning how to forgive is really about freeing your mind from the attachment you might feel to the pain that has happened in the past. It is not about condoning a behavior or letting the person go free without any consequences. It is about freeing yourself.

We hold on to past hurt for some good reasons. After my divorce I became aware that I was holding on to all the mean things that my ex-husband had done to me rather than forgiving him. Then I realized those hurts were useful to me. They gave me excuses to act the way I was acting, and friends felt sorry for me. People expected less of me because of the pain and difficulty I was experiencing. If I let go of those hurts, I might have to look at my part in the divorce drama or leave the divorce behind entirely and get on with my life. Blame—the energy it takes to hold someone else responsible for your situation—is incredibly draining, and it leaves that person emotionally attached to you by your own choosing. When I realized that not forgiving my ex was actually hurting me, I started to make forgiveness a priority.

One side of forgiveness is forgiving others. Often the more difficult exercise is forgiving yourself. "I was miserable in my marriage, so I had an affair," said Stacey, the mother of five teenage children. "I felt like I'd spent my life tending to my husband and the family, and I couldn't stand it anymore. My kids thought we had a great marriage; they were stunned and hurt, but at the time I didn't care because I had a man who was crazy about me. I hadn't felt loved for so long it was like feeding a chocolate bar to a starving child. I know that I broke my wedding vows. I let my family down, and it was hard to forgive myself for that. Then I started thinking about how I loved my kids throughout their lives. I loved them and forgave them when they picked a fight at school, got bad grades, stole something from the grocery store, or called me names. The forgiveness was immediate, and a month down the road I didn't think about what they had done. Then I looked at this mistake that I had made, and I wondered why I had to be a hundred times harder on myself. I was actually much happier out of the marriage, but I still felt responsible for making their lives more difficult. Then I looked at how difficult raising five kids had been for me, how much I had sacrificed, and how unhappy I was. Somehow this open-minded looking at both sides of the situation helped me to see that I needed to love myself the way I loved the kids, and to forgive myself."

Forgiveness and acceptance go hand in hand. To love ourselves, we must have an awareness and unconditional acceptance of who we are. That doesn't mean we don't try to change and grow; it just means that we are aware of our human failings and have made a conscious decision that we can live with them. Along with this acceptance needs to come a sense of gratitude for all that we are, even if it isn't all that we want to be.

Think about the purest form of love you know, the way you feel about your kids. Are you going to be less accepting if they aren't the smartest, the prettiest, the most athletic, the most successful? No, more likely you will love them most when you see their weakness. When we can make an effort to accept, love, and forgive ourselves with the same encouragement and enthusiasm we offer our children, then self-love will become a reality.

5

Our Sexual Soul

Each of us has a sexual identity, a part of our personality that records past sexual experiences, registers rejection or abuse, and remembers tenderness and passion. When a relationship falls apart most of us are left feeling either massively rejected or like complete failures. It is almost impossible for sex to survive as the marriage disintegrates. So chances are that many of us, for quite a while, have been in sexless or passive sexual relationships where sex doesn't have the intimate love connection we want. We feel rejected, betrayed, too old, too wrinkled, or too angry. We doubt our lovemaking skills, are afraid we will never have an orgasm again, and are sure there are no men out there interested in a woman with children. From this place of pain, uncertainty, and self-reflection, we are trying to gather the courage to love someone intimately again.

Sex is important in a love relationship. As much as we want to talk about communication skills, having similar life goals, and being friends, we all know that sex is what attracts couples and it can be the glue that keeps them together. But before you get to that place where sex becomes a passion-filled opening of yourself to another human being, your sexual soul has to be strong on its own; you have to know what you want from sex and how you feel about yourself as a sexual woman.

Our sexual identity when we leave the marriage influences the kind of relationships we choose and the standards we set for ourselves. If you don't take the time to do the inner work, look at your sexual identity, and be willing to work toward creating the sexual woman you want to be, then you might attract a man who is exactly where you were at the end of your marriage. "When my marriage ended my husband hadn't slept with me more than two or three times over that year," said Sandra. "I didn't know at the time that he had been sleeping with other women, but even after I found out it didn't change my feeling of sexual inadequacy. I kept thinking that if I had been enough he wouldn't have screwed around: I should have lost the weight after the baby faster; I should have been a better lover. Even with all the exposure to and understanding I have of women's issues, being a nurse, something primal took over that I seemed to have no control over—this belief that I was just not a sexually desirable woman. It is really hard to be faced with the prospect of dating from that starting point."

Sandra tried gamely to pick herself up after the divorce and prove her husband wrong. "The first man I was with was wonderful in many ways, but he was impotent. It didn't really bother me at the time because I felt safe not having to prove my sexuality. But I realize now that I was attracted to someone as wounded as I was. When I started to feel better about myself, and my sexual identity became clearer and more healed, then his impotence wasn't acceptable. The next man I went out with was grossly overweight. That relationship was a mirror of the feelings I had toward my own body being overweight and not taking care of myself. I thought that was the best I could do." Sandra is now in a relationship with a man who fits with the beliefs she has about herself. She didn't commit to the first few postdivorce relationships because she was aware that she hadn't discovered all the aspects of her sexual soul that she had lost over her marriage.

That doesn't mean you sit back and wait until you are completely healed before you dip your toe back into the dating pool. So much of relationship is about practice. Yes, we all carry baggage from the past and hold ideas that keep us too afraid and full of self-doubt to try again. We don't want to feel rejected, criticized, or judged. Perhaps, as a way of showing self-love, we'd like to shed those postdivorce pounds before giving dating at try. The problem is that it is hard to heal many of the sexual ideas we have about ourselves on our own. We can work on our sexual identity by examining where our beliefs come from. We can determine that our bodies really are beautiful. We can decide that we are going to be proud of our bodies as we undress during our next sexual encounter—but until someone is actually looking at us as we disrobe we won't know if we have the courage to live our new beliefs.

The goal of this chapter is to gain knowledge about our sexual experiences and beliefs so we can become the kind of sexually expressive women we want to be in the new relationships we create. To do that we need to examine our sexual history, what beliefs we have about ourselves, and how our sexual relationships have contributed to those beliefs. With that information it is possible to move forward, to change what we believe, and to create sexual relationships that are free of past mistakes, past feelings, past doubt, and past self-criticism.

Sexual History

What we believe about ourselves as women, or about a woman's role in a relationship or in society, for that matter, determines the kind of relationships we create. If we can understand where the ideas we have about our bodies came from and identify how those ideas affect us today, we can begin to let go of the beliefs upon which we have built our past unsuccessful relationships. Then we will be ready to discover all the possibilities that await us as sexually aware and powerful women.

The historical accounts of sexuality in our society provide clues about why women today feel the way they do about their bodies. One day I decided to imagine how it would have felt to be a woman living during a different time in history. For fun I imagined myself acting the way I'm free to act today within a society where I would have been expected to call my husband "master." As women today we cannot really imagine some of the treatment our great-grandmothers put up with. I often wonder what my granddaughters will be saying about our social beliefs. I began to see how each society's beliefs about women, whether goddess or slave, affected the behavior of men toward women, and of women toward men. For the first time I truly understood how women moved from being sacred and honored to being sold by their fathers and brothers in exchange for more land. Investigating the history shows just how deeply, in our culture, sex is rooted in power, and it makes sense that women have faced an uphill battle in trying to regain their rights both sexually and personally. When I became acquainted with some of this history, I started to see how much of this history had trickled into my brain through social conditioning.

Some societies have incorporated a healthy respect for the feminine into their daily lives. When I look at how women in native American Indian tribes gain a sense of connection to themselves and their sexuality through menstruation rituals, I feel I've missed out on something life changing. I know I'm not the only woman who started bleeding one day and was handed a pad and a belt. For me, there was no bath filled with rose petals, massage by a wise woman who then braided my hair and dressed me in a beautiful white-beaded gown. There was no race where I ran with the other girls in front of the village as everyone cheered my athletic prowess. I wasn't set in a hut alone to meditate on what it meant to become a woman. There were no ceremonies where the people of my tribe came to touch me, believing they would be healed by the power my first period represented. No man in my family acknowledged this event. Instead, it was hidden and messy. I had no idea that my period meant anything; I was just disappointed that I couldn't go swimming. I felt embarrassed, not honored.

Women in our society aren't encouraged to honor their monthly cycles or their bodies. We don't connect them to nature; we don't give ourselves inward space when our periods arrive. When our PMS comes, we are more likely to consider antidepressants and feel out of touch with ourselves. We *are* out of touch.

So how do we get more in touch? How do we establish a connection with our sexuality? How do we create rituals of our own to honor the changes that may accompany our monthly cycles, which are necessary to create children? How do we cast aside the historical and societal constraints in order to create a wellspring of sensuality based on freedom of choice and respect for the female body?

More important might be how we can learn to re-create ourselves as sexual women on our own terms, knowing what we know about our own assets and limitations. Again, we will start with vision, the picture we create of the sexual woman we want to be. Then we need to look honestly at the assets we have—the positive ways we already express our sexuality—and our limitations—the insecurities or negative feelings we would like to change. The more you can pinpoint the place you are starting from, the easier it will be to know where you want to go and how to get there.

I am the mother of two daughters, so I'm conscious of the current sexual beliefs—the ones that lead girls in epidemic proportions to eating disorders, hoping to change their bodies into acceptable sizes and shapes. Fifteen-year-old girls have told me that oral sex isn't really sex and that sex really isn't a big deal—it is just a physical activity. As adult women and mothers, we have to sit back and listen to the young girls around us, for we are their wise women. Somehow as a society we have to turn this around and find a way to honor our girls and our women. We all need to know that we are beautiful and powerful just as we are, without the implanted breasts and the size six pants. But we can't preach to the world; we have to lead by our actions. And that is why I've bothered to talk about history at all. If you don't know what is happening within yourself, what is unconsciously influencing your thinking, then you can't be inspired to change.

Sex isn't meant to be something that you let happen because you don't want to cause an argument. It isn't something you give a man in exchange for a gorgeous necklace he just gave to you. Sexual expression is truly the greatest gift of creative expression and healing available to us. It is supposed to be like a playground—a place where you can laugh, tell secrets, dream together, and relax in this rejuvenating exchange of energy.

Personal Beliefs

On a recent trip I was discreetly reading an article in *Redbook*, "12 Amazing Sex Tricks He Secretly Wants You to Know," making sure to bend the pages of the magazine so the man next to me couldn't see the title. Then I started to laugh. I have a right to read anything I want to read. Why was I embarrassed? The article did get me thinking about women's sexual experiences and how lovemaking in that magazine was boiled down to "amazing sex tricks" or "ways to drive your man wild in bed." Is sex really about how we rub a lover's testicles or anus while licking his ear? I admit to learning a few new tricks from this article: where a man's G-spot is, some great ideas on how to share fantasies, and the importance of masturbating in front of your man. But I couldn't help but wonder how many women are comfortable enough with their sexuality to actually perform the designated activities. Or was this just another place for women to internalize their feeling of inadequacy, believing that other women are out there stripping to music before lovemaking while they can barely manage taking off their makeup before falling asleep? The fact that so many women read these articles means that we really do want to get to that place of fully enjoying our own (and our partner's) bodies, openly expressing our desires, and sharing this intimate connection with another human being.

I know one thing for sure: any woman can be an incredible lover. Rubbing, sucking, and licking—these are basic skills that anyone can do! The part that the sexual how-to books and articles miss is that these are not simply physical actions; they are creative expressions of who the person already is. When I was married at twenty-one, I didn't have a ton of sexual experience, and neither did I have the confidence or trust in that relationship to allow sex to be a place where I flowed with the energy I was feeling. I was afraid to be judged. I couldn't figure out how to move from discussing the kids' summer camp options to seducing my husband by whispering in his ear that I was hot just thinking about him. I believed that sex was a part of the relationship that my husband needed, but I never put my creative soul into it. I never really showed up able to be completely vulnerable and open one moment and dominant the next.

I have learned so much over the past twenty years about myself as a sexual being. I've listened to hundreds of women talk about sex in their lives, and I've discovered that what keeps women from fully living their lives as powerful, creative, sexual women is what they have been programmed to believe about themselves. It has absolutely nothing to do with one's physical abilities as a lover. It starts with the messages about our bodies that we hear as little girls. Then it moves into our actual sexual experiences. We are so influenced by society's pictures of what sex is and how sex should be and what it means to be attractive or unattractive that we can't tell what comes from our conditioning and what comes from our own sexual souls. It is rare to hear a woman say that her sexuality is a complete expression of her creative center, that it gives her energy, that it is a place to allow every part of who she is to show up in the presence of another. But that is what sex can be—and you don't get there by teaching your tongue the right technique. You get there by understanding why your sexual beliefs are what they are and then creating a new sexual model that works in your life.

After interviewing many now-separated or -divorced women, I can see similarities in their lives that involve the loss of creative expression, loss of self, loss of self-esteem, and lack of confidence in their bodies especially with regard to sex. A majority of women seem to be greatly affected by social beliefs that have woven themselves into the fabric of our female brains. "I've always believed that the way my body looks determines whether or not I'm sexually appealing to men," said Samantha, an accountant with three teenage daughters. "You need to be thin, attractive, and fashionable to attract a man's attention. I've also read in various articles that men like women who are self-confident, even if they aren't beautiful. But I'm fifty years old, my husband left me for a more attractive thirty-eight-year-old woman, and somewhere along that path of rejection I lost the image of myself as a woman who was filled with sensuality! The outcome of those beliefs in my life is that I don't live fully in my body, don't really appreciate my body or honor it the way I should, and I certainly haven't found the confidence to share my body in a sexual encounter. I would love to be able to come from a place of embracing myself, accepting my larger-than-I'd-like-it-to-be butt, and throwing my creative energy into the world unaffected by people's views—but I don't really know how to do that."

"This belief goes way back to eighth grade," said Jamie, "that good girls act certain ways. To this day, whenever I see a buxom woman with a low-cut top or any woman flaunting her sexuality, I immediately jump to the conclusion that she is a slut. Two things come to mind as I'm saying this. The first is that somehow our society has set it up that women judge one another and feel they need to compete with other women to be the prettiest or smartest. In judging others or putting them down for their choices, we then see ourselves as better. The second thought is that women who are able to wear what they want, and in other ways flaunt their feminine qualities, threaten the moral structure of our society."

Jamie continues, "I don't really believe that there should be a moral judgment placed on self-expression. In fact, I wish I could be more like those women because I admire their freedom. But I think I've had this belief about good girls acting a certain way for so long, because girls who stepped out of line were presented to me as such dangerous hussies. Just think of the questions women get asked when they are raped: What were you wearing? Did you do anything to lead him on? As if there could be any reason that would make rape an acceptable outcome. So as women I think we live with this inner fear of looking too sexual or acting too sexual because we could be raped, hurt, or misjudged." Both Samantha and Jamie have been influenced by our society's belief that women need to look a certain way to be attractive and that there are consequences for both living up to and not living up to expectations or social rules.

Women also learn very quickly to judge themselves harshly in any area where they might not be the best. "I'm always hearing that women have this great creative force within them, but I haven't seen any real creativity within myself or my life," said Becky, a dance instructor with two toddlers. "In my family you had to be really good at something in order to say that you could do it. If you only painted pictures in art class you were certainly not an artist. I love to dance, but to proclaim myself a dancer I'd have to be in a dance company. In our society, I think that in order to declare yourself a creative person, you have to be really good at some recognized artistic endeavor like painting, writing, or music. Because of this feeling, that I have to be really competent, I find myself too afraid and self-conscious to really express myself."

Becky says she is working hard to become aware of and let go of those unhelpful beliefs. "Since the divorce, I've spent a lot of time with my own thoughts. I'm trying to shift my beliefs about creative expression to include everything—from the way I dress to the way I talk to my kids, make dinner, arrange furniture, write thank-you notes, and even in the way I make love. I'm trying to see my life and choices as an expression of my creative power." Becky's experience shows that society's beliefs can influence us strongly only when they become the acceptable norm, when we as a group buy into their "rightness."

Think about what you believe about your own sexuality. Have you set up rules for yourself that keep you from intimacy? Do you feel confident in expressing your true sexual soul to yourself or to another within a relationship? It is amazing what you can learn about yourself if you are willing to take a look.

Try making a list of your beliefs about women and sex. What do you believe about your body and your sexual capacity? What do you believe you can and can't do with regard to sex? Is initiating a sexual relationship off-limits for you? Mine your own experiences for any strongly held ideas about how women should behave sexually. Try to identify your beliefs for what they are—beliefs that either help you to be truly yourself or keep you confined to someone else's, or society's, view. Once you make a list of your beliefs, see if you can identify when each belief started and where it came from.

Prior Sexual Relationships

There is something to be learned from every sexual relationship. It is possible to go into a sexual relationship with strong convictions about what you would do in this case or what you would do if that happened, but it isn't always easy to hold fast to those views while in the act of making love. Both the pleasant and unpleasant experiences have wisdom to share, although we may not be able to look at the unpleasant parts until we have moved on in our lives and can view them with fresh perspective. When we look at our prior sexual relationships, we have an opportunity to think about both the bad and good things that happened. The good experiences are positive things we can use in creating a new sexual relationship; they inspire us to try again. The bad experiences offer clues about what we need to process and then let go of so that our old feelings or experiences won't live on in our new relationships. All our prior sexual experiences influence the choices we make. They can hold us back from letting someone fully love us; they can solidify our confidence or tear it to pieces.

When I look at my own sexual history, I remember how I felt in the beginning of my first marriage. There were just the two of us. I had so much creative energy, and sex was good. I was excited to be married and beginning my new life. I wasn't afraid to take hold of my life and follow whatever direction my heart pulled me. Twelve years and many nights of lovemaking later, I found myself filing for divorce. Every disintegrating relationship experiences a collapse of sexual, sensual, and creative life, and mine was no different.

At the end of the marriage I remember waking up aching for sex. It had been months since we had made love. A few months earlier the discomfort I felt while sleeping next to him had finally become overwhelming, and I had moved to a separate bed. I wanted to feel sexual toward him, yet the anger, arguing, pain, and loneliness dulled my sexual feelings. Logically, I could look at him and see how beautiful he was, but whenever he touched me I cried almost instantly from a burning and tightness across my chest. Neither of us had made any real move toward divorce yet. We were separated within our own home. I had said many times that we were getting a divorce, and we had even discussed dating others, but it was like we were stuck in the life we had created, not sure how to move from that point. Some part of me still harbored a small hope that things might change for the better, that therapy or some conversation, experience, or revelation would open up our relationship and allow healing to begin. But another part of me knew that there was too much space between us—that even a miracle couldn't put our love back together. It didn't matter how sexual I felt inside. I couldn't make love with him emotionally."

Women I interviewed also remembered the unhappy sexual demise of their marriages. "One time during our separation I tried to pretend that he was someone I had met in a bar, a one-night stand that I would never see again," said Norma. "I took a bath, drank half a bottle of wine, and asked him to sleep with me in our bed that night. I kept my eyes shut and tried to use my imagination. It was a love scene from a recent movie I visualized, and it was working until he asked me if I had bathed. Not that the question in itself was wrong, but the words carried with them history, and that history for me was feeling that my husband didn't like my body. During the years of my marriage, I lost the confidence I once had in my sexuality. I was rejected many times. When I asked why, the answer was varied: 'You come to bed every night in your old nightgown; why don't you wear something sexy?' I'd get my courage up a week or so later and wear something sexy, and he'd turn over and go to sleep. Then a few days later he would feel sexual and I was still too hurt to respond. Each time we discussed sex, he would give me a different reason as to why things weren't working: I wasn't responsive enough, I was nursing a baby and the milk bothered him, I needed to exercise, I didn't know what I was doing. Over time I forgot how fun sex could be. I forgot that I did know what I was doing and that men had been attracted to me in the past."

Norma acknowledges that the image she saw of herself was the one reflected in her ex-husband's eyes. "I can understand that in trying to please him sexually, I gave him incredible power to influence how I saw myself. It was like looking into a mirror: he was my mirror, and the reflection I saw seemed real to me. If I could have taken a snapshot of myself at the time, I would know it was me by the outer looks—but it wasn't really the person I felt inside. I didn't notice my sexuality leaving bit by bit . . . until it was gone." Like many women, Norma internalized her husband's view to the point of believing it herself.

Unhappy or abusive sexual experiences from our early lives can cement in us a story about who we are sexually—a story that we make the mistake of believing is true simply because we've never experienced anything else. "I was sexually abused when I was ten by a twenty-four-year-old cousin," said Lauren. "I remember how guilty I felt when he started touching me, because it felt good even though I knew something was really wrong with it. I thought he was cute, and I was pretty mature for my age. Because it felt good at the fondling stage, I started believing that I was allowing it to happen. Then when it became painful, I believed I deserved to be punished for liking something I knew was wrong and dirty. That abusive relationship ruined all my sexual relationships, including my marriage. I needed therapy, and years of it, to learn how to let go of those experiences in order to build my sexual identity. I really had to start from scratch as if I were hearing about sex for the first time because every other sexual thought had guilt or pain attached." Lauren recognized the power abuse had on her ability to have a healthy sexual relationship, and she chose to get help in telling a newer, truer story about herself and her sexuality.

Sometimes the limiting story we tell about ourselves begins with just a few words from someone whose opinion we value, like a mother or a boyfriend. We internalize that person's opinion and allow it to grow into a lifelong belief. Donna said that when she started to look at her beliefs, she was shocked at how many of them could be traced back to an opinion someone had once expressed to her. "I remember my first real boyfriend making a comment about how boobs were perfect if they filled a man's hand. Well, mine certainly didn't fill his, and from that point on I became self-conscious about breast size. I was always looking for sexy bras that made my breasts look bigger, and I did everything I could to keep my bra on for fear that my breasts wouldn't measure up!"

Happily, Donna found her freedom as an adult and realized she no longer needed to hold on to those outdated stories. "One of my greatest triumphs was when I fully acknowledged my right as an adult woman to make my own sexual choices. I didn't need to hear my mother's voice telling me my actions were good or bad. I didn't need to listen to that first boyfriend or husband after that to decide what breasts should look like or how I should make love. The freedom I felt was so exciting! In that moment I knew that sex could be whatever I wanted it to be. And it wasn't just my sexuality that shifted. All my thoughts went with it, because what I was letting go of was the societal structure I grew up with and was still unconsciously living by." Often, just acknowledging where a belief came from and how it became embedded in your mind can free you from that belief.

Identifying our negative beliefs about ourselves and our bodies is terribly important because, left unacknowledged, those negative beliefs can keep us so bound up in fear that we are unable to move forward. "My second child was one month old when my husband left me for another woman," said Keri.

"One day when he was visiting our six-year-old, I started yelling at him and he said that at least his girlfriend didn't have saggy tits and purple stretch marks all over her stomach. I was so devastated by that comment that I couldn't bring myself to date for years after the divorce. I still had the saggy breasts and stretch marks, and that was obviously what turned him off. I didn't have the self-confidence to let any other man see my body. I started to believe that men were all pigs who could only see the physical body. When I began to date I couldn't make love with the lights on."

Keri found she could move forward only when she was willing to leave behind those old, limiting beliefs about herself. Finding a more trustworthy man helped her confidence grow. "When I did fall in love it was with a man whose wife had died of cancer. He told me about how much he loved her and how he had to take care of her. I started thinking if he could love his wife, and accept her bald and with all the physical changes she went through, that just maybe he could accept my stretch marks. I was right, he loved my body. It wasn't an issue at all for him."

Just as bad sexual experiences can influence us for years, so a good sexual experience can overturn an old negative belief and free us forever. "My husband used to tell me that oral sex with a woman was disgusting," said Marti. "Of course, he thought that giving him head was appealing and that I should enjoy it. I had many experiences with past boyfriends where I received oral sex, and it was really the only way I could have an orgasm. I talked to my husband about this, and early on in the relationship he tried it, but he continued to tell me how disgusting it was. Over time I stopped asking and started to believe that he was right. After all, I knew I wouldn't want that job!

"My first lover after the divorce absolutely loved oral sex. He said there was nothing as sexy as a woman who was willing to be licked. It took many months before I felt comfortable with it because I would hear my husband's words in my head. I was so thankful for that experience because it gave me back a piece of my sexual soul that I had lost during my marriage." Marti was able to take that good experience and use it to set higher expectations for getting her sexual needs met.

Letting go of negative experiences that have marked our lives is a difficult task. We will look in the next section at ideas for creating a new sexual identity for ourselves, but, before moving on, let me reiterate: the patterns in our marriages and prior love relationships that cause women to put a man's needs first, to feel less important, or to feel like we have to make a man happy, are all learned beliefs. They do not originate from our own sexual, creative center. Just acknowledging that can free up our minds to imagine a different sexual self.

Creating a New Sexual Identity

The goal in creating a new sexual identity is to take your sexual soul out of the control of past beliefs and experiences and put it into your own hands to mold and create as your imagination sees fit. You have the freedom, at this moment, to create something completely original, a new idea of what you want your sexuality to mean in your life. It is up to you to put the sexual, creative power back into your life in a way that allows you to be the kind of lover you want to be.

Taking control of your own sexual soul is easy as soon as you claim the right to determine who you are today. Even though this chapter is about sex, structuring our lives in a way that honors our sexual identity doesn't start with the act of sex with another person. It begins with the way we think about ourselves as powerful, creative, and deserving women.

Thinking About Ourselves in a New Way

Try this exercise. Take a piece of paper and write at the top one of your good sexual experiences. Then list under it all the good sexual experiences you hope to have in a new relationship. Listing the sexual experiences you hope to enjoy helps you create a new vision for your sexual self. And vision, as you recall from chapter 1, is the magic ingredient that, added to the realities of our lives, moves us forward in a positive direction.

Add to your list of positive sexual experiences your vision of the sexual partner you would like to become. Will you need to think differently about yourself in order to make this vision a reality? Will you need to let go of any outdated beliefs to make your hopes real in your everyday life?

We can free ourselves to be great lovers, first in the way we think about ourselves. "I went into most of my past sexual relationships excited to see what kind of sexual partner the man would be," said Sandy. "I didn't go in with a real sense of the sexual partner I wanted to be or with many thoughts about letting my desires direct the relationship. I guess I liked the idea of the man being in charge, or maybe I just thought I should like that idea. Now that I've been divorced for three years and have had many lovers, I can see how powerful it is to really know who I am as a sensual woman. Now I go into the relationship open to new experiences but at the same time solid and comfortable with my sexual expression. Lovemaking is now more of a joint project, with both of us architects, rather than the man creating the building and me living in it whether I like it or not."

Creating a new sexual soul means taking time in our lives for our own desires. When there is no space in our lives for our own needs, then it is impossible to create anything new. As Toni said, "I know that I've bought into this Superwoman-Martha Stewart-at-home-and-sex-kitten-in-the-bedroom myth. And, as a result, there are days when my life is spinning out of control because I simply can't be all things to all people. But inside I feel like a failure if I can't manage it all. There is no space left in my busy, responsible, overwhelming life to dip into the well of anything but survival." If creating a new sexual identity is the goal, then you have to set some time aside to feel sensual. Try the simple pleasures, like lighting a candle, taking a bath, and reading a little erotica.

Keep in mind that creating a new way of relating to our sexuality does not mean taking a month-long spa retreat away from the kids. It means, instead, finding the simple ways to attend to our own sexual needs and desires in the middle of our responsible lives. Remember the question we asked in the previous chapter to increase our self-love?—*How can I love myself in this moment?* To think of ourselves as creative and sensual women, we need to ask ourselves in our everyday lives, *How can I claim my sensual self right now?*

Take a look around your bedroom. Do you like the feel of it? Is the color, texture, and ambiance right for you? What about the way you dress? Do you allow your sensuality an avenue of expression or are you wearing clothes to fit an image you have held in your head of what you should look like? Be willing to experiment a little. Instead of wearing straight skirts buy a flowing one, or vice versa. Listen to new and different forms of music until you find something that feels sensual to you. Start wearing the perfume you already have that you usually save for special occasions. Let each day of your life become a special occasion where you feel comfortable expressing the new you.

Honoring Our Bodies

Once we begin to think about ourselves as sensual, creative, and powerful women, the next step is to begin to honor our bodies. For some women that means taking a look at diet, exercise, and sleep patterns. For others it means accepting their monthly cycles and the changes that may be part of the process. Some women will need to do serious healing work if they have been battered or abused, in the form of individual or group therapy. Others will honor their bodies by accepting their imperfections as they walk away from a relationship where those imperfections are pointed out daily.

"One way I am beginning to honor my body is by making time in my schedule to hike with a friend each week," said Paula. "I'm really out of shape, so walking is the only aerobic exercise I can manage right now. But instead of avoiding any exercise and beating myself up about all the wasted time and how fat I feel, I've decided to get out there and do something about it. I get to watch the wind blow across the tall brown grass, listen to the birds, and talk with my closest friend. I'm honoring my physical, spiritual, and emotional body whenever I make the time to get out of my old pattern of self-destructive thought and move in the direction I want to go." As Paula found out, small steps in the right direction can be huge steps toward the goal of honoring your body, especially if you have spent most of your life feeling negative about it.

Expressing Our Sensual Selves

The more in touch we become with our sexual souls and the more we honor our physical selves, the more likely it is that we will begin to express our sensuality in the outer world. I remember clearly the day I looked at my bedroom and decided I couldn't sleep one more night in it the way it was. I hadn't changed anything about it since the day we had moved into it. There was no insulation, no carpet, and all redwood floors, ceiling, and walls, so it was very dark. Each night as I fell asleep I would look up at all the spider webs and imagine what might fall on me in the night. The tiny room was stuffed full with a king-size bed, huge antique cabinet, and two dressers. There was no room to walk around. In the winter it was so cold I could see my breath. I had hoped we would be able to remodel that end of the house, so I didn't want to waste money making permanent changes. I couldn't feel sexual or sensual in this space any longer because nothing about it was an expression of who I was. When my husband was gone one week I completely transformed the room. I had the walls plastered and painted white, I ordered carpet for the floor, hung old scarves up as drapes, bought a bed frame at a consignment store, and changed the bedspread and pillows to shades of blue. I painted two old tables, used old earrings as knobs for the drawers, then placed candles on the tables and around the room. My husband and I both love our new room; it is a much better expression of who I am and who we are as a couple.

Whether you express yourself in the way you dress, arrange your home, cook your food, or play with your kids, you are becoming outwardly what you believe about yourself inwardly. You don't have to spend a lot of money or remodel or move; you may find yourself simply acknowledging that you need more color in your life, livelier friends, less stress, or more laughter. Expressing yourself means opening your heart to life, as you would like it to be. From this open place sex is much more likely to become a healthy, enjoyable, and natural part of your everyday experience.

Relying Less on What Others Think

The more we allow ourselves to express outwardly the person we are becoming, the less we will let ourselves be stopped by what other people think. I've heard older women say that one of the greatest things about getting old is that you stop caring what people think. You are no longer as beautiful as you once were, people expect less from you, and there is no longer anything left to prove. You finally have enough life experience to trust what you think and who you are more than what other people think. You have found a place within yourself to be content with your looks and your accomplishments so you aren't living each day with the goal of proving you are "someone."

The real question is, How do we get to that point sooner in our lives—like today? Many women find that the overwhelming challenges of divorce push them toward placing more confidence in themselves and relying less on the opinions of others. "I believe that the less influence society has upon us, and the less we care about what people think of us, the more honest and real we can become," said Gale. "This kind of self-acceptance has been one of the big challenges for me in the divorce process, and it took a lot of inner work to reach a place where I was willing to let the past go. It also took a long time before I felt any real hope for my future. One of the most painful aspects of my divorce was that everyone seemed to know all about my life, including the failure of my relationship. When I got to a point that I didn't care what people thought and was able to judge myself from the inside, I felt I'd made a huge step toward healing."

"I still see my divorce as the biggest failure of my life so far," said Tina, the mother of two teenagers. "But the divorce has also been my greatest triumph. It let me feel reckless abandon toward myself. I started thinking, *Who cares what people think about me now?* I had nothing left to lose, and other people already had their opinions anyway. I learned how to let go of my judgments: about myself, my life, my choices, as well as other people's choices. When I let go of things, I found there was so much extra space in my life. I had room to create new ideas on my own, and I found myself so much more open-minded. When you don't have this need to please other people, then you can please yourself a little. I was also able to bring this attitude into my dating life, which was great because I wasn't so afraid of being rejected."

Daring to live a life in which self-direction and self-approval are more important than the opinions of others is like pruning all the unwanted branches off a tree that has been blocking your view for years. You will begin to see clearly the view from your own window. Decisions become simpler. Honest relationships begin to happen when you are able to show up as yourself. You become more confident and more comfortable in your own skin—instead of feeling that the world is controlling you with its opinions, you feel a sense of control over your own thoughts and direction.

Rewriting Our Beliefs About Sexuality

Women can set the stage for how sexual expression happens within a loving relationship. No matter how bad your marriage was, or how low your self-esteem is now, it is possible to rewrite what you believe. It is possible to change how you act.

It is time for all of us as women to honor ourselves by writing a new set of personal beliefs. I'll start by writing mine! These are some of the commitments I make that help me understand, accept, and express my sexual soul.

> Every part of my body is beautiful and clean. I will not be ashamed, and I will make no excuses for imperfections.
> When I feel like making love, I can freely and creatively make my desire known.
> Desire is a good thing.
> I will also honor my lack of desire.
> When I don't want to make love, I will say so without feeling guilty.
> I will not stay in any relationship where I am not respected, appreciated, and honored.
> In my daily life I will put my own sexual needs first 50 percent of the time.
> I will not be afraid to let my full sexual power out, and I refuse to be less than I am just so others will feel more comfortable.
> My sensual dreams and desires are equal to my husband's.
> I will trust my inner voice above all others.
> I will believe in my ability to make good sexual decisions, and I will stand alone in those decisions without fear.
> I will celebrate my creativity, my feminine qualities, and my connection with the earth regularly through rituals I create.

You have done all the hard work of examining beliefs and claiming a new sexual self. Now you might be wondering, What kind of results will I see in my life? Your sexuality will become a natural and integrated piece of your personality. You will no longer feel the urge to modify your sexual expression to meet the needs of somebody else, whether those of the man you are sleeping with, or those rules for relationship that were preached by society. You will feel grown up, in charge of yourself, and free to play by your own rules. You will begin to feel a woman emerging who is separate from her children and her role as a mother. Your creative center will begin to grow as you retain the power you used to give away in your life. Making love will become an expression of self-love as well as an offering of love to another.

6

Expectations

My grandmother once told me that in her day it was easier to stay married because a woman knew her role and what was expected of her as a wife and mother, both within the family and as a member of society. Nobody sat around wondering if they had good communication in their marriage, if they were raising their kids according to *Parenting* magazine, or how their sex life compared with the neighbors'. They didn't question everything; they simply lived life and accepted their fate.

My mother, on the other hand, received her college degree while raising six children. She lived with the idea that it was possible to fulfill herself as a person, work, raise her kids, keep an orderly house, host big holiday parties, be beautiful, and still serve a warm breakfast in the morning with a smile on her face. My father's life was not so different from my grandfather's: he worked to support us, and he played with us in his spare time.

I picked up where my mom left off, believing it was my job to do everything she had managed to do. On top of that, I believed that if I did everything well enough, my husband would see me as an equal and valuable partner in life. I would respect his job, and he would respect mine. He would contribute to raising our kids and keeping the house. We would play together. We would be a team. Those were my expectations, but they didn't come to pass the way I thought.

Expectations are those personal beliefs that define the life we think we should be living. They are the standards we expect from our homes, our jobs, our kids, and our lovers. When we set reasonable expectations that spring from a balanced place, then those expectations can help guide and direct our choices. If the expectations we set cause us to be unhappy, feeling that we aren't good enough or that our life isn't the way we need it to be, then they work against us, causing us to feel unhappy and unfulfilled. When a love relationship has failed there are certainly expectations that were not met—some might have been reasonable; some might have been the kind that weren't possible to meet and therefore caused sadness, stress, and conflict within the marriage.

Floating around in the mind of anyone whose relationship just failed is the question of how to set reasonable expectations for the new relationship they would like to create. We all stand at the end of something painful and at the beginning of something a little scary, but exciting too. We have looked at who we are, our old patterns of dealing with life and relationship, how to love ourselves in a more nurturing way, and how to claim our sexual souls. Now it is time to really look at what we expect from the future and to be sure that our expectations are built on a foundation of self-love and healthy relationship patterns.

Setting Expectations Now

Many of us set expectations for ourselves now that are based on how our lives were at one time, usually when we were married and could share financial, parenting, or career burdens. Rarely in the years following divorce is there time to reevaluate the way we develop expectations—what they are based on or where they came from. We are all too busy trying to grieve and heal and do all the things that have to be done now that we have more responsibility. Annie confessed, "I *have* to be therapist, gardener, cook, handyman, plumber, teacher, breadwinner, lawyer, and mom. I can't afford to pay someone else to do those jobs. So you would think that I would be realistic and expect to be exhausted, short-tempered, and sad at times. Instead, I expect to feel the way I felt when I had less responsibility than I do now. I'm really disappointed with myself when I begin to feel depressed." Annie is afraid to expect less of herself. The more she demands of herself the more she feels she is moving forward and getting to a new place in her life. Many of our expectations aren't bright flashing lights that announce themselves; they are quiet, underlying beliefs that may have been present in our thoughts for a long time.

Expectations need to be flexible and change as we enter different stages of our lives. "I had different kinds of expectations right after my divorce," said Kiley, "that I would make it, I would not fail my children, and I would find a way to take care of the family's basic needs. I expected to be superhuman, and for a time I was. But now I realize that I don't need to function out of survival mode anymore. I did make it; I have a lovely home, a career I'm good at, a new relationship, and two kids who are doing well. I think the problem is that my expectations—of what I need to accomplish to get my family settled into a life with the financial benefits they are used to—have remained in survival mode. I haven't taken an honest look at how my expectations might have to change if I ever plan to live a more balanced life. I find myself sad and overwhelmed way too often, guilty when I don't have enough time for my kids, frustrated when I can't meet work deadlines, and judgmental when my ex-husband can't take on more parenting responsibilities so that my life is easier. My daughter told me that you have to set your expectations high or you won't achieve anything, which may be true, but I'm struggling to set expectations that bring me happiness instead of ones I cannot fulfill."

I identify with Annie's and Kiley's quandary. Even though I've come a long way toward seeing my life more realistically, I'm still surrounded by my own expectations of what my life could be if only I had this, if only my kids would act like that, if only my husband did that. I look at my bookshelf and see all the "simplify your life" books that I've been too busy to read! I can only imagine the look on my kids' faces were I to tell them that I've decided to lower my expectations and simplify my life. With a content smile on my face and a novel in my hand, I would announce plans to discontinue taxi and catering services so that I might have more time to enjoy life. I suspect it wouldn't go over well.

Simplify, expect less, say no to new commitments, live in the moment—I know all this is important. I also know that to do this I need to shift my thinking and my actions out of survival mode and learn to set obtainable and realistic expectations based on my current life instead of the life I wish I had. If balance is to be found, an inner shift is required.

Each of the previous chapters has given us some healing tools for creating balanced and appropriate expectations. When we pictured our lives in chapter 1, we shaped our direction for our future by taking into account our present assets and liabilities as well as our vision. In examining who we are now in chapter 2, we found we needed to look at the person we expected to be. Looking at old patterns from our families in chapter 3, we discovered how much our expectations of what a married relationship should be were based on the relationships we lived with or observed. Deciding to love ourselves, the theme of chapter 4, led us to notice that our lack of love comes from the expectations we carry that we should or could be better—more beautiful, successful, or engaging. In endless ways, expectations can infiltrate and rule our lives.

Yet we would not want to let go of *all* our expectations, because it is the power of those expectations that can motivate us when it seems impossible to take one more step toward our goals. It all comes down to one word: *balance*. Somehow we have to identify what we do expect from our lives and our relationships and then find ways to modify expectations so that we can have fun, find time for a new relationship, and then enjoy what we have worked to create. To help us think about balanced expectations, let's look at a few examples of expectations that work against us and those that work for us.

Expectations That Work Against Us

Expectations that are either too low or too high can make us unhappy. In neither case do the expectations spring from a balanced place inside, where we are in touch with our strengths and content with who we really are. As you read each story below, think about what piece of balance is missing for the woman speaking—and for ourselves when we fall into the same traps. It might be lack of self-knowledge or fear of not being good enough or not accepting the limits of our present life. Any one of these can lead to forming expectations that work against us and make us unhappy.

Setting No Expectations

Setting no expectations can cause as much unhappiness as setting unrealistic ones. "I went into marriage simply on the wave of love," said Carla. "I didn't think about the practical things about living with someone. I didn't care who was going to cook or take out the garbage or get up with the kids in the middle of the night. I believed that we loved each other enough to work it out. Then the kids came, and with their schedules I wasn't home a lot. He started asking me where I was all the time. If he called home from work and I wasn't there he would get upset, so I began to feel like I was living on a short leash. I really thought that love would be enough for us to weather whatever came up in our lives, but the intensity of our love faded. We still loved each other when we got divorced; we were just too tired of putting up with each other's lifestyle choices. We had such different expectations of what the relationship would bring to our lives. Things that weren't important to me in the beginning—like his opinions of my friends, his lack of participation in household chores, and his addiction to TV—became very important to me the longer we were married. I learned that love is definitely not enough to keep two people together for life. There has to be some shared vision of what that life together is going to look like."

Accepting Less from the Relationship Than You Want

Sometimes women lower their expectations because they are afraid they will be alone for the rest of their lives. "I was talking with a friend after my divorce, and she said something that really hurt me," said Pam. "She said I couldn't be so picky if I wanted a man in my life; after all, I had three kids. I had been on a few dates that she and her husband had set up for me—all with men who were not my type at all. When I complained to her about her choices for me, she said she didn't think many men would be interested in coming home to a house full of kids that were not theirs. After this conversation I started thinking if I would be willing to take less of a relationship, less of a commitment, or less than what I wanted all around just to be sure I wasn't alone for the rest of my life. Would I feel so grateful to any man who would love me with my kids that I wouldn't feel entitled to expect any more than his presence in my life? I don't know those answers because I haven't found someone yet, but I can tell you the conversation made me wonder how many of us single mothers are accepting less because we see ourselves as having less to offer." Accepting less than what we really want can only lead to feeling unfulfilled down the road. Settling for something we don't want does not lead to a balanced life, and it does not spring from a balanced place inside. It grows out of fear that we have too little to offer. Over time, unhappiness will set in.

Expecting Dating to Be Easy

One expectation that leads to disappointment for many women as they approach dating is thinking that it should be easy to fit a new relationship into their life. But for single mothers especially, the new demands and challenges can often make it difficult to manage the dating process. "The first man that asked me out was a man I met in the self-help section of a local bookstore," said Diedra. "I was immediately attracted to him and thought that he was just what I needed to get my energy back and my mind off all the issues in my life. We did go out, really hit it off, and ended up wanting to see each other again. But fitting the relationship into my life wasn't as easy as I expected it to be. I didn't want to introduce him to my kids, so we went out on weekends my kids were away. Sometimes he traveled, so we would go weeks without seeing each other. It took some real adjusting on my part because my life was certainly different, not as glamorous or carefree as my prechild dating experiences. Yet, when I was able to let dating be what it was for me at this stage in my life, I really began to have fun with it." Diedra wanted to love again, be in a relationship that fit in with her life, but she needed to set new dating expectations based on the reality of her life.

Expectations That Work for Us

Expectations that work for us spring from a balanced place inside. To form reasonable expectations for our new lives, we need to accept who we are and what our lives look like now. When we are honest with ourselves in this way, we naturally form expectations that work for us and lead to happier, more fulfilled lives.

An Equal Partnership

Many women view a new involvement as a chance to build a relationship on an equal partnership, where their needs are valued and they retain the right to direct their own lives. "I made a deal with myself to wait two years after my divorce before I started dating," said Deb. "I was married at twenty for fifteen years, so I hadn't had any time on my own. We started having kids right away, so my life was more about who I was as a mother; I never had time to contemplate who I was as a woman. For me a relationship with a man is very much about who I am as a woman and how I enter into that love as an equally important and significant human being. That wasn't present in my marriage, so one of the expectations I have for myself is to hold true to who I am no matter what direction the relationship goes. I would not have been able to do that had I begun dating right after the divorce because I was a mess and my low self-esteem would have led me to an unequal partnership. Having those two years set aside for myself gave me the space to think clearly about who I wanted to be and what I wanted out of a new relationship.

"It does start with your own knowing," Deb continued. "If you are really clear what you expect to give and get from a relationship and you are able to voice it, then neither person gets hurt." Deb uses her expectations for what she wants in a relationship to help her decide which men to date. "I've just started dating—five dates, to be exact, but no two with the same person. I wrote a list of my relationship expectations before I began dating. When I date someone I look at the list, and if the person doesn't meet at least half of them, it isn't worth my time no matter how attracted I am. I would never have been that clear after the divorce. I probably would have grabbed the first guy who showed me any attention." Many women share the expectation that the relationship they will build the next time around will be based on an equal partnership, where their needs are valued and they retain the right to direct their own lives. But to build an equal partnership, we need to be clear what our expectations are and be ready to communicate them.

The Ability to Communicate

Once we have done some healing work so that we know ourselves better and can communicate our needs more easily, it is reasonable to expect that a partner will also have good communication skills. "By the end of our marriage I'm not sure I ever really listened to what my husband was saying," said Ellen. "I had already built up resentment and anger that kept me from being a good communicator. One of the top priorities for me now is to use all the new communication skills I've learned through classes, therapy, and my women's support group to do a better job communicating my feelings in a new relationship. I do expect to be listened to, and I expect to have a discussion without being screamed at. I expect my opinions to be valued, my ideas to be important, and my life to be of interest. I've also made the commitment to myself that I will get help if I fall into old patterns of not talking when my feelings are hurt." Tuning up our personal relationship skills, looking at areas of past relationships that were weak, and determining what is important for us to focus on will all help us in setting reasonable expectations for the future.

Making the Relationship a Priority

"When I was married, we never once made the relationship a priority," said Jan. "We focused on the kids, the house, our jobs; there was never time to devote to us. I want to do it differently this time around. I know I have responsibilities, but if I'm going to be devoted to someone, I want him to be devoted to me too. I've also spent time working on that concept within my own life, so I have an idea of what it will mean to me to make the relationship a priority. Things like having a weekend together without the kids at least every six weeks, taking one night a week to go out together, possibly spending twenty minutes at the end of each day sharing what happened that day. It may mean that a few nights a week the kids go to bed early or put themselves to bed so I have time for the relationship. I know how quickly a marriage can fall apart when the relationship is not a priority, and I don't want to go through divorce ever again, so this is a very important expectation for me." Relationships take time and commitment to become a priority. For women who are raising children, working outside the home, and trying to rebuild their lives, it takes effort to determine how to make a relationship a priority.

A Relationship Designed to Work

When I was remodeling my kitchen recently, I thought about how we might spend months meeting with a specialist to design one room in a house that the family might live in for ten years, yet most of us spend little time designing a relationship we may live in forever. Granted, finding a man is not as easy as shopping for tile, but some design guidelines are clear. None of us would put brick on a kitchen counter because it simply isn't counter material, yet we decorate our lives without much thought to function or design. I'm not trying to belittle the physical love and chemistry involved when you fall in love, but I think there needs to be a little time spent determining whether the man you have chosen fits into the life you are designing. When love and chemistry are in full swing it is easy to forget that you can feel physical attraction for many men. Realistic expectations and an honest look at who the man is (not who you wish he were) and what kind of team you make together is a step toward creating a lasting relationship.

There are many ways to go about designing such a relationship. We can look to successful friendships that have lasted over the years to direct our love choices; we can make sure we discuss our sexual expectations before having sex; we can look at the reasons we are in the relationship to begin with; or we can make a list of the character traits we want our partner to have. The most important thing to remember is that we have the right to design the relationship we want.

Take a Cue from Friendship

The first place I'm going to look in creating a relationship that works is to my successful and long-lasting friendships. I've had many of my friends for more years than I've had a husband. My friends and I love each other; I tell them everything in my heart; we value and respect each other. The only thing we don't share is sex and financial debt.

I can learn about what expectations in a relationship are reasonable by taking a cue from the expectations I have with my friends. One morning recently I planned to go on a hike with a friend. She called at the last minute and canceled because she had to go to her son's classroom and talk with the teacher. I wasn't hurt, I wasn't mad, I completely understood, and we rescheduled our hike. A few days later my husband called from work and said he would have to cancel our dinner date because he forgot that his son had a baseball game. I was hurt, and I felt like he was putting me at the bottom of his priority list. I began to ask myself, *Why do I have one set of expectations for lovers and another, more forgiving one, for my friends?* This again boils down to expectations. My husband is married to me. He signed on to my life forever, so he needs to act a certain way for me to feel valued. In my mind, husband equals slave to my wishes! Friends, on the other hand, are appreciated for whatever they offer because there is no obligation; they're just friends.

I am able to stay more independent in my friendships, thinking whatever I want, doing what I want with my life, and making my own choices. I don't expect my friends to fix my life or drop their lives to help me. I forgive my friends when they disappoint me, and I'm able to tell them how I feel. I have fun with my friends. We don't spend our time fixing the relationship; rather, we enjoy the time we have. I do expect my friends to listen, to be there when I need them or when I ask for help, and to respect and support my life choices. The relationship seems to survive without daily interconnectedness. I feel close even if I don't know everything that is going on in a friend's life. I want my friends to be happy even when I disagree with their choices.

What characterizes this list of friendship attributes is a sense of independent thinking and an acknowledgment of each person's right to be who they are. There is an absence of neediness: friends don't have to do anything for me to feel loved. Yet I know without a doubt that if I called any of them at 3 A.M. and said I needed them, they would be there without asking one question. I've begun to use this information in my marriage. Whenever I feel judgment descend or disappointment that my husband isn't doing something I want, I ask myself how I would behave if he were just my friend.

Discuss Sexual Expectations

Of course, making a love relationship last has other components on top of friendship. First of all there is sex. Discussing our expectations is key to a more fulfilling sex life this time around.

Sally related how making her expectations clear with her new boyfriend enhanced her enjoyment of their first night together. "When we began the relationship a year ago I was very clear in communicating all the ways I was disappointed with sex during my marriage. I told him how selfish I thought my husband was for never caring whether I had an orgasm or not. That he never made an effort toward romance—no candles, whipped cream, or massage oil ever showed up on his bedside table! And my husband loved to receive oral sex but never seemed to return the favor. I actually told him all this before we ever made love, so I'm sure he was scared to death that he wouldn't live up to my expectations. But I really think it helped to talk about our sexual expectations before we made love. When I arrived at his house that first night there were candles on the dinner table, a bowl of strawberries by the bed, and a bottle of champagne." Clear communication about expectations smoothed the way for an enjoyable sexual experience. Perhaps even more important, however, is that Sally's expectations and those of her new boyfriend were similar. If you are with a man who is very shy, and you can't wait to pull out the handcuffs, then you may have a problem!

Be Aware of Your Reasons for Entering the Relationship

Two people can enter a relationship for completely different reasons, so discussing what you are looking for in a relationship is a good place to start. The other day my husband sent me a small article off the Internet that claimed women get married for security and men get married to have a constant sex partner. Maybe those aren't the exact reasons we get married, but I do think that men and women get married for different reasons. Taking a look at what those might be is important before starting another long-term relationship. "The biggest argument I have had with my boyfriend is about how much weekend time he spends golfing," said Toni. "I want him to do things with me and the kids, and he says he loves me but he wants his days off work to be his own. He does spend at least one weekend a month doing things with us, but in the long term I'm looking for a man who wants to participate in family life. He is perfectly happy seeing me twice a week and sleeping with me the weekends the kids see their father. I'm the one who wants more out of the relationship, so I guess it is up to me to decide what I want to do about this." Toni's boyfriend is looking for fun, companionship, sex, and occasional family activities, while Toni is looking for a life partner to share every aspect of her life. For the relationship to last over the long term they will have to understand and come to terms with each other's reasons for being in the relationship.

Know the Traits You're Looking For

Being aware of the character traits we are looking for in a partner helps us choose a person who fits with our own expectations for our lives. As Brenda related, this can be accomplished in a fun and lighthearted way. "When I began dating I really wanted a man who had a sense of humor," she said. "Everything was so serious in our marriage. If there was an issue or a problem, it grew into a huge ordeal. If I hadn't gone to the grocery store, he made it seem like we would all die of starvation by the morning. So I wanted a fun way to discuss how we each wanted the relationship to go. I decided to write a relationship contract—kind of like an employment contract—where I outlined chores, responsibilities, vacation time, sick days, and pay schedule! I exaggerated it so we could laugh a little and have a way to talk about the hard things with a sense of humor and lightness. I think it made both of us really think about the day-to-day things. It was kind of like a test to see if my boyfriend could be lighthearted and look at difficult relationship issues with a sense of humor."

Sandy said, "I made a very simple list of character traits I was l̲
in a man. They weren't any great accomplishments—simple things ̲
honest, kindhearted, and funny. I also made a list titled 'At What Po̲ ̲ ̲ Do I
Move On?' I would check the list whenever I felt hurt in the relationship. If
there were more than five things checked, then I made an agreement with
myself that I was going to end the relationship. I found this helped me to let
go without making excuses for him or believing that I could make him better
with time." At least think about the kind of person you want to spend time
with before allowing the physical attraction to rule your decision-making
processes. You don't need a list a mile long; just pick your top three character
traits and be content when you find a man who has them.

Setting Reasonable Expectations

Reasonable expectations are self-loving. They come from a kind place within
us, they let us blossom in our lives, and they give us gentle guidance. To be
reasonable, an expectation needs to be within reach. Many of us in the past
based our expectations on our limited personal experiences or on the ideas
we'd inherited from our families. Maybe we haven't taken the time to evaluate
or discard expectations that no longer serve our purposes. Here is our chance.
In the rest of the chapter, you'll find eight suggestions for setting realistic
expectations. Following these tips will give you a better chance of recognizing
specific relationship expectations—which ones will leave you feeling unfulfilled and which ones spring from a balanced place inside.

1. *Expect less and let life surprise you more.* The expectations that direct our
   lives show up in little things. "I expect my kids to come and eat breakfast
   when I call them, and I expect them to show gratitude for my effort in
   making their breakfast," said Davida. "I expect my boyfriend to take the
   time to listen to the activities of my day. I expect myself to have the
   energy to comfort my kids when they are sick. The list goes on—so
   there are many chances each day for me to feel let down when my
   expectations aren't met. A friend said last week that the most enjoyable
   moment in her day was going to a coffee shop and sipping her coffee
   all by herself. She said when the first taste slid down her throat the
   issues that were bugging her slipped away. I found myself wishing that I
   could find something as simple as drinking coffee to make me feel that
   all was well. But her words hung with me that day through my work,

after-school carpooling, kids' homework, the hectic dinner hour, and getting my kids in bed. Then I made a cup of hot chocolate in honor of her, sat on my couch, and sipped it, imagining that the first sip was washing my troubled thoughts away. I didn't expect much, which is probably why it worked!" It is easy to miss the little moments of happiness in our lives when our thoughts are focused on bigger and better accomplishments. When we are able to relax a little and set our expectations aside, life often offers priceless moments of joy.

2. *Be kind and accepting toward yourself when life is a challenge.* Instead of pointing out all the mistakes you are making, look honestly at the situation you find yourself in and acknowledge that you are doing the best you can. The more I listen to working mothers, which all of us are in one way or another, the more I see that many of the standards we have set up for ourselves cannot be reached.

   "When my husband left and the reality set in, I fell apart," said Susan. "I knew my husband was having an affair for a year before I asked him to leave," she said. "I was afraid of how my life would change if I were a single mother. My youngest was three and I had just started working three mornings a week at a friend's dress shop. I wanted to make sure that I was strong enough to be a good mother through the divorce process, but that wasn't the case. I don't think my kids really saw it because I put on a great act whenever they were around; I kept up the family routines and made sure the kids' needs were met. But it was so hard to be a good mother when I was going through a personal hell. At least a third of all the tears I cried were because I felt I'd failed at my mother job." Susan felt like a failure, but she wasn't taking into account the difficult place she was in. She kept being harder on herself when in fact what she needed was a huge dose of kindness and self-love.

3. *Don't let anyone make you feel guilty for your choices.* Mothers especially are prone to guilt trips since we feel responsible for our children's welfare. But remember, you love your children, and that is all you owe them; the rest is a gift. "I have pretty high expectations of myself as a mother," said Janet. "People tell me all the time that I do a really good job, but somehow I don't feel that in my heart. I miss so many of the kids' events and performances, usually because I'm attending another child's event. I actually keep a running list to make sure that I get to an equal number of activities for each child, and still I feel like what they are going to remember is the time I wasn't there. It hurts me when my kids say, 'You never go to anything!' I feel this need to defend myself and go over everything I do in their lives. It becomes a running list of explanation for

why I can't be the mother I want to be. I really want to move from this place of feeling disappointed into a place where I can acknowledge all the ways that I am an excellent mother." When we set expectations for ourselves out of guilt that we aren't meeting the expectations of others, we begin to feel that we owe explanations to everyone for why things aren't going as planned. Janet felt like she owed her kids an explanation because she set expectations of being the kind of mother who could attend every event, when in reality she had too many responsibilities to meet that goal.

4. *Let life happen on its own.* Don't work so hard! Sit back and let events happen without feeling that it is your responsibility to fix, maintain, or change them. I tried an experiment the other day while picking my daughter Brooke up from high school. Instead of trying to use all the time we have in the car to talk, I decided to say nothing but "Hi, honey, how was your day?" and see if she started a conversation on her own. I could barely stand it. The whole time I kept thinking that we were wasting time, that I have so little one-on-one time with her that we really should be using it. I couldn't resist trying to begin the conversation a few times, but she answered in short sentences and continued to listen to the music. We drove the whole way home without talking. At first I felt sad about this, thinking she didn't care about me at all. I always work so hard to keep up a good relationship with each of my kids, trying to spend individual time doing something they like, getting to know their friends, encouraging them to share what is on their minds, but they don't put forth the same effort. It made me think about what they really need from me. Maybe it is enough that I am here for them, that I give them food, clothes, and lots of love. Maybe my success as a mother isn't determined by the standards I set and try to control. Maybe it is my idea of the good mother that makes me feel that we have to have so much time together, when in fact they don't need it or appreciate it. This experience taught me that too much of my energy goes into fixing the relationships in my life. When I stop trying so hard I feel less stress.

5. *Learn to see your personal needs as equal to other people's needs.* "I'm experimenting with being a selfish bitch!" said Julie. "All my life I've been the one to say yes to everything. Whatever I can physically do, I will do for anyone who asks me. I'm finally learning what it is going to take to make space in my life for my own needs. I also think that when I do put time into my needs I'm a better mother, better lover, and a more attentive friend. It is impossible to nurture others if you have nothing left to give, which is how I started to feel a few years after the divorce. Especially

when the kids were going through a rough time, I felt like I had to be their rock, but now I'm beginning to change my expectations around that and see myself as really important too." Julie has learned what many of us do after the first few postdivorce years: we can focus on everyone else for only so long before falling apart. At some point the expectations within the family have to shift so that the mother's needs matter.

6.   *You do not have to rock the world to make a contribution to society.* Work is just something you do to make money so that the people you love can have a good life. When what you do becomes who you are, it is time to step back, take a day off work, and answer this question: "If I died today, what would my kids say about me?" Debra commented on the unreasonable sights we set for ourselves: "I remember the day I realized that if I didn't accomplish one more thing in my career I could be happy with my accomplishments," she said. "I'm not sure how many people in our society could say that because we are all trained from little on to keep achieving until the day we die. We have this mind-set without ever stopping to question where it is getting us. Are we happy? Not really, but we sure as hell are moving up, getting paid more, and becoming someone. I do care that I can support my family, but not at any cost. My current employer is great; she understands that I have kids at home and need to get home at a decent hour, but my last one fired me when I wouldn't stay until eight two nights a week." When Debra was able to believe that she had achieved enough in her life already, she began to reevaluate her expectations and her life choices.

7.   *Make sure the expectations you are working hard to meet belong to you and come from your heart instead of from those around you.* "I worried in the beginning about being a working mother," said Mandy. "I was afraid I wouldn't find a career I could be happy with and that I would fail financially. Really it was everyone else's expectations that were too high. My husband's attorney put in a request to have me either begin working right away or to have income attributed to me based on my college education. I had been a substitute teacher during the last years of our marriage, but they wanted me to get a full-time teaching job right away. I wasn't ready for that—I was still grieving the loss of the marriage and needed time to put my life together. I also wanted to be available for the kids just as I had been throughout the marriage. I expected things to go on as they had been going with me working a few days a week, but their expectations were for me to work much harder. In the end we compromised and I began a full-time teaching job a year after the divorce." Sometimes we become sad, feel we have failed, or think we need to make another choice in our

lives because of someone else's opinion. When that happens, take a moment to step back and ask yourself who and where the expectation is coming from. If it doesn't belong to you, give it back to the person who gave it to you.

8. *Begin to like who you are today without the future accomplishments you dream of achieving.* Maybe that is what living in this moment is about—doing what you can, doing the best you can, and then forgetting about it. "This divorce has changed me so completely—I've finally learned how to appreciate and admire myself," said Samantha. "I do a dynamite job given all that I have to do. It certainly isn't easy, but I like the challenge. I do have my down days, but I have this ritual whenever I feel overwhelmed. I make myself repeat all the accomplishments I've achieved since the divorce to remind myself how far I've come. The journey is hard enough without dwelling on all the problems that never seem to go away." Most of us spend too little time acknowledging all the great things we already have in our lives and within ourselves. We really need to learn to like ourselves—all of ourselves—before we can enter into a relationship with another person.

My husband and I have a saying taped to a picture hanging on our bedroom wall: "Love is less about the perfect moments and more about how you handle the imperfect ones." To me this means that love is less about creating and checking off a list of expectations and more about how you deal with the disappointment that is inevitable when you are in a long-term relationship with a human being who has faults. However, if you begin the relationship with a clear idea of what you really want and what you are willing to give, then the relationship has a better chance of growing into the love you imagine.

Make a plan, however you envision it. Then make a pact with yourself and stick by it as closely as you can. Examine your plan for unrealistic expectations, and then create realistic expectations for yourself personally and for your relationship. The love you find after doing all this hard work will be based in reality instead of the happily-ever-after fantasy. You will be in love with a real, flawed human being instead of an idea. You will become softer and easier on yourself, and your measure of success in relationship might actually be within your reach.

7

The Courage to Act

You might have begun this book lacking the confidence to begin a new relationship. By now I hope you are feeling a sense of excitement, possibly mingled with fear, and readiness to embark on the outward journey of welcoming love back into your life. The first six chapters of this book focused on the inner journey of finding out who you are, what expectations you have, which patterns need work, and what you want your life to look like in the future. They gave you the tools to figure out who you are and what you want from a relationship. However, no matter how much self-knowledge you possess, how many patterns you have been willing to look at and change, or how well you know what you want, if you aren't willing to take charge of your life and actually make it what you envision, then all you have is new inner knowledge. New inner knowledge is great, but knowledge doesn't necessarily change your life unless you learn how to use it in some meaningful way.

This chapter is the sendoff party for the journey into creating that new, special relationship. In this chapter we will take the inner knowledge we have gained through the first half of the book and convert it to usable actions. This chapter is a bridge to the second half of the book, where we use the knowledge we have gained on the inner journey to claim the life, career, and relationships we desire. But to get to that place where loving becomes a free and confident choice, we need to develop the courage to act.

We'll begin by asking, "What does a woman in charge look like?" Then we'll look closely at three areas in every woman's life that could use a little attention: finances, personal power, and family organization. Once those big responsibilities are in line, we'll move on to our love relationships—how to enter them whole, healed, and ready to love again. Finally, we will celebrate all that we have gained from the inner journey that results in our determination to take charge of the lives we want to create.

Women in Charge

In 1848, the first women's rights convention was held in New York. Elizabeth
Cady Stanton read her Declaration of Sentiments, a manifesto that began, "All
men and women are created equal." It listed eighteen legal grievances and
called for major reform in suffrage, marriage, and inheritance laws. In 1851
Stanton and other women took on the issue of dress reform. They were trying
to pass a law that would make it legal to wear bloomers! In 1860 doctors
declared that reproduction was the most important function of the female
organism, and they warned adolescent girls that they could damage themselves by pursuing intellectual interests. Women of the time were advised at
the onset of menstruation to take up a passive life. In 1907 the American Society for Keeping Woman in Her Proper Sphere was formed. Women throughout history have had to fight for their right to be in charge of their own lives.
Now that we have won many of those basic rights, what are we doing with
them?

We've talked a lot about the roles we either consciously or unconsciously
agreed to take upon ourselves within our marriages and how familial and
societal ideas strongly influenced us as we grew into the women we are. In
order to take charge of your life, much of what you learned might need to be
set aside for a time, for as long as it takes to get a new picture up on the screen
of your mind. That doesn't mean you leave everything behind; it just means
you agree to approach this new phase of your life with an open mind, willing
to redefine what a woman in charge looks like and imagining how you might
become one. The goal is independence because only from that place can we
be in a position to choose love.

Every woman I know loved the movie *Erin Brockovich*. Why did we love
it? She was a woman in charge; she didn't care what people thought of her—
no soft words to manipulate her way into getting people to do what she
wanted. She knew what she wanted, and she was willing to take action to
make it happen. At some point during that movie each of us was right there
with her, especially when she told her boyfriend all the things she had always
given up for men. I loved it when he said, "What do you expect me to do all
day, just sit around watching the kids, waiting for you to come home?" But it
wasn't just the role reversal or the fact that she was fighting for a great cause
or that she defeated a power that should have squashed her and went on to
become rich. What drew me to her character was her inner power, the power
every woman has access to when she claims who she is and decides to live as
that person. I use Erin as an example because many people would have found
her rude, uneducated, and unladylike. Yet these are exactly the kinds of judg-

ments from others that can stand in our way if we let them. Erin didn't let them, and so she makes us want to be like her.

All around you are women who have taken charge of their lives; they will be your best teachers. You can ask them how they did it. You can observe them, see them struggle, and watch them get knocked to the ground, dust themselves off, and keep going. Ordinary women can be heroes too. One day when I was feeling discouraged that I hadn't found a corporate sponsor for the workshops I wanted to create for single mothers, I decided to ask for help. I e-mailed all the women on my mailing list, announcing that if they would organize a workshop in their hometown, I would come and lead it. After sending the message out I felt a little foolish, like I had handed off my job or somehow admitted to failing. But to my surprise, within twenty-four hours I had twenty responses from women who said that they had never organized a workshop but they would do it, whatever it was that they had to do. Each response moved me to tears. For nine months I had labored over how to offer these workshops at low cost in small communities so that single mothers could meet one another and form support groups. Now, in twenty-four hours, I had answers from all across the country.

Sometimes we feel all alone, as if there is nobody to watch and to learn from. But I communicate weekly with hundreds of divorced women, and we are a pretty powerful bunch. We just need refueling sometimes; we have a lot of responsibilities, we get tired, and we don't give ourselves enough time to recover. When we fall down and get a little dusty or discouraged, it helps to have a friend to pull us back up to our feet, dust us off, and push us back out the door proclaiming, "You can do this!" We need to do that for one another. We have to start picking each other up when things don't go as planned and remind each other of the big picture, the goals we have set, the direction we are going. We need to reflect to the women around us the strengths we see in them.

It isn't always about being loud or charging ahead. Sometimes it is the small steps we take over time that allow us to take charge one piece at a time. "I'm an Indian woman living in the United States, but I was raised in India until I was betrothed to an American," said Nimah. "I never saw the man I was to marry until we faced each other on my wedding day. In my country, the position a woman holds in the marriage is so different than in the United States. I remember thinking that women here were so bold and disrespectful toward their husbands. I would watch what women wore, what they said, and how they acted in public, and it made me think about how I had been raised. My husband was quite a bit older than me, and I never learned to love him as my mother had promised. I stayed married to him for twenty-two years, even though I was miserable, because I had no idea how to take charge of my own life. I had no formal education and didn't believe I could make it on my own."

When Nimah's children left home, she found the courage to make one small change that turned out to have long-lasting effects. "My husband discouraged me from meeting many people or taking classes, but finally when our last son went to college, I decided to take a pottery class at a local community college. I was drawn to a woman in my class who was so vibrant. When this woman laughed, her whole body almost fell off the potter's stool. She was not pretty. She dressed in mismatched, brightly colored garments with different and unusual jewelry draped over and around her. I didn't even talk to her much, I just watched her, and watching her changed me. I wanted to laugh and express myself any way I could. I ended up leaving my husband and getting a small townhouse with the assets from the divorce, and now I work in a clothing shop. I know that doesn't sound like a huge success story, but I claimed my life and began living it the way I always wanted to, and I am so happy." Sometimes the way we take charge expresses itself in our ability to validate our desires and act on them in small ways.

What we accomplish with the rest of our lives is completely up to us. When women really get that concept, they can transform from people who expect to suffer and sacrifice for others into fierce warriors, fighting for their lives. Part of what keeps women from taking charge of their lives is an acceptance of the certain way their lives have always been. One day I took a mask-making class at our community recreation center. I was doing it to spend some quality time with my ten-year-old daughter. The masks we made were of our own faces. When they were dry, the teacher told all the kids to paint them however they wanted to paint them. Then she came up to me (I guess since I was the only adult taking the class) and told me to look at my mask and ask it what part of my personality I was missing that I needed in my life right now. I thought she was kidding, but I did it anyway and was surprised that when I shut my eyes I saw a face with warrior paint on it. I really hate conflict. I avoid all arguments and usually make choices based on what will cause the least problems for others. I immediately understood why my inner voice answered with a warrior face. I decided to paint my mask like a warrior.

Around that time I faced appearing in court for a support hearing. I usually gave in to my ex-husband's demands just to avoid conflict. Before I went into the hearing, I held my warrior mask in my hands and asked it what I needed to do. It helped me to go in there, to set my timid personality aside, and to remember that there is a warrior within me who wants to take charge and get what she wants. Aspects of our personality may have defined us in the past, but things can change—and they do change—as soon as you begin to pay attention. Ask yourself what parts of your personality might need to change or to grow if you want to become a woman in charge.

Being a victim will not get you the life you want. You don't have to suffer to prove a point or sacrifice your wishes so that other people are happy. It is much more fun to play with the abilities you've been blessed with and take charge of your life. Taking charge doesn't mean that everything will always go the way you want it to go. You may fail at winning custody or picking the right house or choosing a career, but if you sit back and do nothing, life and the living of it don't belong to you. Put on the warrior mask, and push yourself out the door.

Taking Charge of Your Life

Divorce can throw every part of life into disarray. We may be pitched immediately into survival mode, taking a job we hate just to put food on the table or picking up all the household jobs simply because we don't have time to supervise or to teach the kids how to do the housekeeping themselves. We have less time to relax, since there is more to be done than there is time in the day. In most cases the family assets have been divided in half, which leaves both parents with the challenge of living on half the money they are used to spending. We may need to take our careers more seriously, knowing that in a designated period of time we will have to be supporting ourselves. If we have children, we have to take charge just to get the kids out the door each morning in time to get to work. Taking charge seems to be a requirement, and we may feel we have little choice.

That is the problem. We can't take charge if we feel that our lives are running us rather than the other way around. So the bigger question is how to take charge of your personal life, your career, and your finances in a way that puts you in the driver's seat. How do you do what has to be done and still feel that you have some choice in your life?

Taking charge in your personal life means that you make a commitment to be true to how you feel, that you say what you need to say, and then you do whatever you have to do with the outcome. Not taking charge means you sit back and let your fear decide what you say or what choices you make. Fear and rejection are two feelings that keep women from setting personal boundaries that would help them feel more in charge. "There are some things my boyfriend does around my kids that I really hate," said Alexis. "He is very sarcastic, so he says things to them and then says that he is kidding, but I can see by the look on my kids' faces that they are confused and hurt. I'm afraid he will think I'm overprotective if I start complaining or set rules about his behavior around my kids. I feel it is insulting to have to tell an adult how to act, or that he will not be interested in a relationship with me if I start telling him how to behave. In the long run I want the behavior to stop, but I haven't decided if it is worth the argument we might have." Alexis is afraid to take charge of the situation because her boyfriend might respond in a negative way.

Sometimes we don't take charge of a situation because we know that there is nothing we can do to change the outcome. "I had this fight with my mom, and I really wanted to tell her how I felt," said Stacey, "but I knew that it wouldn't change anything even if I did tell her. I thought about it for a while and decided to go ahead and tell her how I felt, because it isn't always about changing someone or making them do what you want. Taking charge is also about being true to yourself, even when you know you can't change the situation or the person's opinion." Every time we hold a feeling inside out of fear or don't express how we would like things to go, we are giving someone else the right to take charge of our lives. Just because you say how you feel does not mean the person will agree with you or will do what you want. But the act of expressing your thoughts or standing up to others' opinions teaches you how to take charge of your right to feel a certain way. If the person doesn't agree with you, you then have the right to make a new or different choice, even if the choice is simply to leave things as they are.

There are times when we sit with our life for months at a time and feel miserable but do nothing about it. Then something goes off inside of us and we just get it; we know what we have to do, and then we are ready. We may surprise ourselves or others with our choices. "After the divorce, when things settled down," said Gayle, "I had the house and a job, the kids were doing okay, but I was still miserable." Gayle realized the life she was living was not exactly the one she wanted. "I hadn't created an environment where I could thrive as a person. So I quit being the mother I thought I was supposed to be and started mothering like I wanted. I quit my anxiety-ridden friendships and started friendships that weren't so needy. Everything—religion, job, career path, house, community—I blew into smithereens in the process of creating something new. Every aspect of my life, of my existence, was gone. What remained was a frank discussion with myself: *What are you doing?* Some of my friends might now diagnose me as schizophrenic, which may be how it looks from the outside, since I have made these very different choices from those I made in the past. But from the inside I have begun to take charge of the life I wanted to live." Becoming a woman in charge may look radical to the outside world. Some may think you have lost your grip on reality. But others will stand back and marvel in awe at your sheer determination to own your own existence.

Work, Money, and Power:
The Glory of Financial Independence

No matter what society says about women's work at home being equal, in our culture the person who makes more money in the relationship has more power. I wish that statement weren't true, but it feels true for me. I've been remarried now for a year, and it is becoming clear to me what a difficult position I'm in. I want to maintain my financial independence so that if the marriage doesn't work out I won't have to learn all over again how to support myself. I also want to believe that if we blend our financial assets I won't be fighting over the division of them ten years down the road. I need to take care of my kids, and make enough money to support them, while living with a man who isn't the kids' father, so technically he doesn't really have any legal responsibility for them. I don't want to depend on my husband because I did that once, and it has taken me five years to be able to stand on my own two feet. Now I have the power and equality in the relationship that come partly from financial independence, and I refuse to give them up.

But I also want to trust that this marriage will last forever. I've been told by my friends and family that I need to learn how to trust again, to work together with my husband to blend our financial future in a way that benefits both of us. I see everyone's point, but I haven't been able to do it. I'm still scared to be that connected, even to the man I love and trust. I don't want him to tell me what to do, how to spend my money, or how to live my life.

Once you live through the divorce process, as you find the parts of yourself you lost in the marriage and begin to take charge of your own career and finances, it is hard to be vulnerable again. "I've been thinking of living with my boyfriend," said Sandra, "but I'm afraid to buy a house with him that I couldn't pay for on my own. I like knowing that I can manage the life I've created. Right now I can pay every bill; it isn't always easy, but I find a way. If we were to live together, we would need to buy a bigger place, since he has one son and I have two daughters. Then we would have to combine our money each month, figure out who owes what, and deal with financial issues that we haven't begun to address as boyfriend and girlfriend. He also makes more money than I do, so he could afford more than I could. There is something about living within my means that brings me great comfort, so I don't know what I'm going to do."

We all want to fall in love again, to live happily ever after, but in order for the relationship to succeed, you will need to make significant financial contributions to gain some financial independence. Besides, no man is sitting around thumbing through the personal ads looking for a woman he can support. It's your job to make your own decisions and to take charge of your own financial success. If you have come from a marriage in which you were the primary caregiver and you didn't work outside the home, this can feel overwhelming. However, if you can manage a home, you can certainly manage any other career that may interest you, so don't get discouraged. "I went back to school four months after my ex walked out on me," said Frances. "I got a government loan to pay for tuition, and it left me some money to live on each month. I made this decision to live on practically nothing because I believed I would do much better once I got into my field as a computer programmer. The greatest thing I did was to return to school even though my baby was only fourteen months when I started. I was so excited, so thrilled to learn. I was thirty-three at the time and the only mom in the class. When I first got to school, I felt like I had been released from prison. I was so grateful that people were speaking to me and treating me like I was an intelligent person. I wasn't the person my husband thought I was, not even the person I believed I was. I was so much better and stronger. At my graduation party I realized all the things I had accomplished during that year and a half. Now I have a great job and believe the sky is the limit. I'm so happy to have a career with a financial future I can count on." There is a great sense of accomplishment and personal pride when you take charge of your career and create a financial future for yourself. Even better is the knowledge that although you may want a man in your life, you don't need one to support you.

However, at no time does financial independence mean letting an ex off the hook for child support. The father of your children is just as responsible for their welfare as you are and should be footing his share of the bills. Your financial success means rather that you have the freedom to make choices about your own life that would not be possible if you depended on someone else for support. Like Sandy, we are better and stronger than we think we are, and an independent source of income can be a mainstay of our self-esteem.

Family: If You Don't Take Charge, Who Will?

Divorce changes the structure of the family, pushes rules and traditions off balance, and usually creates two households where both adults must work harder. A mistake many single mothers make is trying to keep the family running the same way it was running before the divorce. "I remember the month after our divorce was final, there was a huge rainstorm and the roof started leaking," said Erica. "My husband was the one who usually fixed everything, but there I was up on the roof trying to attach sheets of plastic so that my walls wouldn't be ruined. All of a sudden I was mowing the grass and calling a car dealership to figure out when my car was supposed to go in for service. At the same time I was looking for a job, mourning the loss of my marriage, and trying to assure the kids that I could handle it, nothing for them to worry about. The problem was that I felt too guilty to ask for the kids' help after what we had put them through. And yet I desperately needed to take charge of the new family structure and to assign new responsibilities."

Erica kept up this pace for six months but then decided that she needed to rewrite the family script. She called a family meeting. "I told the kids that we were going to start having family meetings each week. At the first meeting I talked about how much my life had changed since the divorce and that I had too much responsibility taking care of the house. I was sorry, but their lives were going to need to change too. I assigned jobs that included cleaning the house, doing the laundry, and cooking our meals. The kids were not enthusiastic at first, but I told them the only other option was to move out of the area to a smaller house so that we could afford to hire someone to do my jobs. The biggest shift had to take place within myself. I had to stop feeling like the divorce was my fault and that I owed the kids something for failing in the marriage. When I came forth with a new plan, and honestly described how overwhelmed I felt, my kids were right there with me." The new script Erica wrote was one in which she took ownership of her predicament and accepted the changes that had taken place in their lives. She created a fair division of labor in the family that made her life easier.

Sometimes we get the idea that taking charge means getting everyone in the family to do what you want, gaining complete control of the kids' discipline, and determining how the household runs. For Jessica, taking charge of her family life didn't look exactly the way she wanted it to. "I had to move in with my parents after the divorce," Jessica said. "There I was at forty years old, depending on my parents like I had at eighteen! I wanted to create a lifestyle where I could be at home with my kids but also make a living. I began to teach piano lessons and write part-time for the local newspaper. Establishing clients was going to take time. For a while I felt almost hostile toward my parents because I resented the fact that I needed them. But we talked about it, and my parents said that this was a family problem, that we would work on it together. And soon I would be back on my feet." At first glance it may look like Jessica gave up control of her life in moving in with her parents. But her decisions in fact show her taking charge of her life because she is going in the direction she believes is best for herself and her kids in the long run. She wants the freedom to be able to work during the hours they are at school but also to be available for them when they need her. She has made choices that take into account the present circumstances of the family and that give her the support she needs to create the life she wants for her family.

When you have become accustomed to a certain style of living for years, it may take time before you can step back and determine what fits the new family arrangement. "For the past ten years of my life, I lived in a house that could have been on a home tour every day," said Ellen. "Everything was white because my husband loved white. And here we were with a five-year-old, spending every moment washing his hands and keeping him off of everything. My friends told me after the divorce that they were afraid that one day they were going to come over and find one of those red velvet ropes, marking off the rooms they weren't allowed into! Now my house is full of candles, pillows, blanket throws, and all sorts of things that would not have measured up to my former husband's expectations of what a home was supposed to look like. There are toy trucks in the living room and popcorn on the floor, and I like it that way." Ellen took charge of her family's surroundings as she decided what kind of home she wanted to create.

As we weather the years following a divorce, many of us don't take the time to measure how well we are doing. Perhaps we are more in charge than we think we are, even if we haven't yet accomplished everything we want to do. One day when I was complaining that I hadn't accomplished anything for my family, my therapist had me list six things I had done well over the past year. I thought about this for a week, and then I made this list.

Bought a house
Funded a retirement plan at work
Began an educational IRA for my daughter
Adopted a dog
Got a raise and promotion at work
Helped my daughter start school

By the end of the assignment I thought, "I've done pretty well!"

Try the exercise yourself. Make a list of all the little things you have done well recently, all the ways you've taken charge of your life and your home. It may include little things you do for your family, or it may include ways that you take charge of your own life so that you can be more present with your family. Then pat yourself on the back for a job well done.

Take Charge of Your Relationships

Many of us may not yet be in a new relationship, so we may wonder what it means to take charge of our relationship if there is no man on the scene. I used to wonder this myself, until a friend gave me a clue. She told me I was looking for men I could be committed to for life instead of men I could enjoy for an hour. Typical of my way of thinking: set the goal of wanting to get married again and then decide that 99 percent of the men I met were unqualified for the position. That's when my friend said that I was looking way too hard at this problem, that I needed to lighten up and use dating as a chance to practice the skills I had been working on. I needed to try out my relationship ideas on a real person, to experiment with being myself instead of trying to change to fit the man I was interested in. One small detail many of us forget—the relationship is for us! We are not interviewing a man for the role of father or breadwinner. We are looking for a partner, an equal human being who adds joy to life.

Many women have told me that they have enough hassles in their lives without adding the problems that a new relationship will create. They say that dating is awkward, finding the time is impossible, and that one fractured heart in a lifetime is all they can bear. In fact, dating is challenging, especially for single mothers. Dates don't appear at the front door with flowers in hand, having heard that a woman lives there who needs a night on the town. There doesn't seem to be enough time in a mother's day to nurture relationships outside the family, especially in the years just following divorce, when it can feel like the kids need all the emotional support a mother can muster. Most new relationships take some sort of action or, at a minimum, a decision by the woman that dating is the next desired step.

Before taking that step, it helps to answer the following questions:

* What do you want from a relationship?
* What are you willing to put into the relationship?
* How do you want a new relationship to fit into your life?

It also helps to write down, in reasonable detail, the qualities of the person you're looking for before you begin dating so that you have something concrete to look back on that will remind you of what you wanted in the first place. Of course that list might grow and change with each new date, but at least it makes you pay attention to the qualities you desire in a partner.

Set Your Intent

Once you have a fair idea of the kind of person you are looking for, it is time to set your intent. You are ready to love again. Then make that intent known to everyone who cares about you. That way your intention goes out into the world and has the best chance of becoming real.

As you think about beginning to date again, open yourself to the possibility of meeting many different kinds of men. Who knows, the nerd you have always avoided might be perfect for you, but you won't know until you give many types of men a try. If you approach dating as if you are on a fact-finding mission to determine what type of man you are interested in at this point in your life, then you won't care as much whether they like you or not.

When excuses fill your mind, like, "I'm too fat, too busy, too uninteresting, have too much baggage," recognize them as fears that are trying to make decisions for you. Don't decide what a man might think of you before you even try. Instead, be willing to get out there and experience the dating life. Somebody will be interested in you, I promise. You may not be interested in him, but you are in charge of deciding if you like someone or not. If you like him but he doesn't like you, then shake it off and try again on the next date.

And above all, as you take your intention out into the world, be open-minded, confident, and clear about the way you expect to be treated. Don't accept less than your heart's desire. There are plenty of available men, and someone who is right for you is someone who will treat you in the way you want to be treated. Taking charge of your relationship life means refusing to settle for anything less!

Establish Respect and Partnership

Relationships that are fulfilling are relationships where partners enjoy a sense of equality. So before you begin dating, set your intention to find relationships that embody respect and equality. This is not a relationship in which partners measure whether each person is working, cooking, cleaning, or driving kids an equal number of hours each week. It is rather a relationship in which equal value is placed on each person's right to pursue their own dreams, to choose and to manage their own career, to engage in their personal enrichment, and to set their own goals. "I fell in love a few months ago with a great guy who has also been divorced," said Renee. "Right off the bat, I told him I was looking for an equal partnership. He said, 'Good, does that mean you are paying for our dinner?' He has a great sense of humor. The one thing that has been so important to me is to really stick with and be clear about what I need. I want to express my feelings and be heard and respected. In my marriage, I let some of the things I needed or wanted slip under the rug just to avoid conflict. It didn't work. I feel so much more determined now to say what I need or feel. Otherwise I think it actually weakens the relationship. If the other person can't accept that, then you have a clear sign that you aren't in the right relationship. Once you can communicate openly, it makes partnership an obtainable goal. He makes me dinner, values my work as much as his, and takes care of himself so that I can keep taking care of myself." The equality you seek in a relationship will not happen unless you communicate openly, right from the start, about the things that are important to you.

"I think my marriage was unusual in that we did have an equal partner- ship in the household tasks," said Maria. "I had an established career when we met, used my maiden name when we got married, and he did the cooking and shared the parenting. We traded off with the grocery shopping. But he had a big issue with spending money. I was a convenience person, picking up take-out food on the way home or buying expensive gasoline so I wouldn't have to drive to another station. He went crazy over things like how I swept the floor and was critical about everything I did, so I was always on the defen- sive, trying to prove myself. So even though there was a sense of equality and partnership in many areas, there was also this underlying criticism that made him judge everything I did, and that behavior made me defensive." *Equality* and *partnership* are both words that describe an inner respect for another per- son, putting equal value on another's experiences and view of the world. It is important to begin dating with some sense of what kind of partnership you are looking for. You cannot take charge of something unless you know what it is you want.

If you want a man to see your career or home life as important, and he monopolizes the conversation by talking only about his career, then taking charge means you have to bring this to his attention and begin talking about your own life. If he seems uninterested or can't stop talking about himself, then cross him off your dating list. Maybe you want to feel partnership in a different way, or maybe you like it when men take charge of parts of the rela- tionship. Whatever it is you want, just be clear about your expectations, and don't be afraid to share them with the men you date.

What We Gain When We Take Charge

On the wall in my office hangs my favorite quote from Gandhi: "Be the change you want to see in the world." When we begin to take charge of our lives, we become the change we want to see in our lives. We embody it; we act out the direction we want to go, and in doing so that desire becomes a reality. By watching us, our children learn how to manage difficult times in their own lives, how to take charge of situations and be true to themselves. And what is the benefit of being true to yourself? You learn to follow the direction of your heart. You won't get lost in someone else or his ideas. You will not become a reflection of someone else. You will be yourself—an original! You will also learn how to deal with the feelings of loss and disappointment if everything doesn't go exactly as planned. As we take charge, we also learn how to let go, because the more we put ourselves out there, the more chances we will have to succeed and also to learn how to deal with disappointments.

You're now ready for the outward journey that includes another person. From this point on, the most important choice you have to make is whether or not you have the courage to be yourself. Will you be able to stay true to what you have learned about yourself as you begin to build a new love relationship? If you understand that the relationship you seek is meant to make life more enjoyable (not present more problems), and if you can be truly yourself, being an open, honest, and equal participant in the creation of the relationship, then you will experience love in a new way. It is time for me to push you out the door and say, "Go on now, get out there, don't look back. You can do this, *and* it is going to be fun!" You have done a lot of work on your inner journey. Trust that you are ready to reach out to love and to embrace all that you already have become.

Part Two

The Outward
Journey

8

Dating

What force is strong enough to push us from our cozy cocoon of single life into the world of relationship with men again? Could it be that our bodies, souls, and minds need to feel like we are not alone? Most of us long for companionship and the sharing of our days with someone who cares about us and listens to us. Maybe we are bored with our own lives—the problems, stories, and experiences—and are ready to be entertained by someone else's tale. We don't want to cuddle a body-length pillow and masturbate to romance novels for the rest of our lives! We want to feel desirable and in turn to feel the power of desire, the way it takes over our thoughts, replacing pain and self-doubt. Strongest of all is the urge within us that makes us crave a man, his scent, the rough feel of his skin, his body pushed against ours, as he holds us to him, moving together. The directness of his gaze looking past us and into the rhythm of our thoughts, sending heat into our stomach as we ache to feel him inside us. We want to fall in love again, to jolt ourselves back into the world of sensual awareness, to begin new and fresh with hope for the life we want to create. Mostly we want to share our lives, our days, our worries, our greatest joys, our dreams and wishes with someone who loves us.

Dating is the first step toward acknowledging that you are willing and open to feel the sensations, both good and bad, that go along with loving someone. You've licked your wounds, healed the best you can, and are ready to feel the beat of a man's heart next to yours. Dating allows us to meet men, to observe how they act, to hear about their past, to see if our life goals are similar, to check out values, character, and life ambition, and to feel if there is any chemistry. Dating is the interview process before you sign on for a longer commitment, and it is the vehicle that makes falling in love possible.

The goal of this chapter is to get you excited about the prospect of dating and confident enough with yourself to try your hand at love again. We'll start by looking at the preparations you might want to take before actually meeting a man. Then we'll set some dating goals so you have an idea of the direction you're headed. After that, we'll hear all sorts of creative ways that women have found to meet men. From there we'll hear about a few dates and figure out what works and what doesn't work. We'll end by talking with men about dating: how the process works for them, their own insecurities, and what they are looking for in a new relationship.

Prepare to Date!

Remember eighth-grade science lab, when you mixed a little of this with a little of that to come up with who knows what? Dating is like that—one continuous science experiment. You mix a little of your personality with a little of his, and you get something that either deserves a write-up in the lab book or a trip to the trash bin. This is your big chance to experiment with relationship styles before settling into a long-term romance. You have undoubtedly changed since your divorce, so you may learn things about yourself that surprise you. The type of man you were attracted to in the past may not fit the person you are today. You may be looking for someone with better relationship skills than you experienced in your marriage, but you may not be sure how to measure if a man actually has the skills you need. Dating is your opportunity to pay attention to the reactions you have to different men, to how they treat you, whether or not you like their personality, and to begin to recognize what turns you on or off. When you feel a negative reaction to a man, what he says or how he acts, be sure to take the time to ask yourself why, and remember it as you consider other men.

It is also important to decide why you are dating and to determine what you want to get out of it. Some women just want to get out of the house once in a while and have fun, while others are seriously looking for a new partner. "I'm dating to have fun, fun, fun!" said Stacey. "Sex is too intimate for me to share with 'dates,' and remarriage is not something I have any intention of doing. I just want to have interesting conversations, go places with adults, kiss and cuddle a little, and not get attached or feel needy again."

"I do want to get married again sometime in the next five years," said Janet. "Even though my divorce devastated me, I still believe in lifelong commitment. I don't want to grow old all alone with nobody to share the memories of my life with. But I'm also not going to evaluate every man I date to see if I could marry him. I'm trying to enjoy the attention, and if something clicks, if I feel drawn to a man, then I date for longer and possibly have sex, but I don't rule anyone out right off the bat. However, if I don't enjoy a man's

company on the first date I politely decline a second—no need to lead anyone on, even for a free dinner!"

"I can tell you this because nobody will know it is me who is saying it,
but I date for sex," said Maryann. "I was married sixteen years to the person I
lost my virginity to, and I swear I feel like a teenager who never had a chance
to experience her sexuality. I've never had the chance to feel how men
respond to me or understand what a powerful experience sex can be. I don't
sleep with men on the first date, and I make sure to check out a few personal
things about them so I know they aren't criminals, but once I picked a man
up at a dance club. I do insist on condoms. My husband left me with my self-
esteem in shreds; these sexual encounters have helped tremendously to make
me feel that I am sexy, beautiful, and desirable."

"I am dating for fun and for sex," said Briana. "I'm not banking on remarriage and not completely ruling it out. I do know what a passionate relationship is like, and I won't settle for less. I am at a point in life where I am
content with myself and with my ability to provide for my family. And I know
exactly what I have to offer a relationship as well as what my needs are. If you
don't like a man the way he is today, then leave him alone. That is the main
thing I've learned. There is a man out there for me. One who is all grown up
long before I show up in the picture, with whom I can take my shoes off and
tell him that I am tired. Who makes me laugh and who laughs at my jokes."
Every woman has her own agenda when it comes to dating. Some women
tell their date the agenda immediately, while others wait a while until they
decide whether or not they like someone. Knowing why you are dating and
what you want to get out of the process will help you to navigate your way
toward a relationship that fits your life and needs.

Bring to each date a practice piece of the woman you want to be in your
life and in the relationship. If you wished your marriage had more humor,
introduce humor into the dating relationship and see how it works. Don't
pretend to be anyone but yourself, but also remember that there are parts of
yourself that may have grown and changed, so allow yourself the freedom to
play a little with your personality to see what feels right to you at this stage in
your life. This can be hard to do when you've been dateless for months and
really want someone to like you. "I have lived my life as a very timid person,"
said Gina. "Hard to imagine how I managed to raised three strong-willed
boys. I didn't mind all those years when my husband controlled most of the
relationship decisions, because I liked not having to worry about them. He
left me and tried to push me out of the way when we were dividing our assets
so he could take more than his share. That is when I learned how not to be

timid, and I really liked that new piece of my personality. I used to think it was attractively feminine to be timid, but now I don't sit around wondering what might be attractive to men. Instead I've decided to be myself." The truth is that your date will find out who you are sooner or later, so you might as well put all the cards on the table at the start. Then if things don't work out, at least you'll both know before you've invested too much of your time or your hearts.

Make a commitment to begin the relationship the way you want it to continue. If you want honesty, be honest. If you are looking for an outdoorsy person, plan a hike within the first few dates. Set the expectations and the mood right from the start, and you won't have to waste energy trying to fix or explain things later. Casey said, "I don't want to be stuck in another relationship where I spend half of each weekend competing for attention or convincing a man that it would be more fun to go on a bike ride with me than to watch sports on TV. I wouldn't mind if he watched one game a weekend, but if he turns down an invitation to a fun wedding because of a game, then I'm done with that relationship."

"My girls are really involved with volleyball, which means they have tournaments most weekends for half the year," said Ashley. "It is important to make it clear right up front that my kids are a priority in my life and that I have to schedule my social life around their sports, school, and social schedule. Some men don't want to deal with feeling second to anyone, but other men completely understand and have similar commitments to their own children. I guess the older I get, the less willing I am to waste time on a relationship that would need a ton of work just to get through the everyday things." In order to begin the relationship the way you want it to continue, you need to have some idea of the kinds of activities you would like to do on a date, how you see yourself spending your free time in the future, and how a relationship might fit in with the responsibilities you already have.

As you prepare to date, keep in mind that the probability of finding the right man increases when you know who you are looking for. It also helps to believe that there is someone out there who is capable of loving you the way you hope to be loved. "There is this couple at the dance club I joined," said Victoria. "They are old. Been married for the better part of fifty years. I love watching them dance. He was an army officer and she was a professional dancer who was diagnosed with MS a few years ago. He drags her out dancing every week so her muscles won't atrophy. Every time I see them, it brings home to me the fact that I may never find someone who will love me that much for that long. So I will settle for someone loving me that much for only a short time. In the meantime, when I'm at the dance club, I stop whatever I am doing and watch them glide across the dance floor. I feel privileged to witness their commitment to each other and hope that I will be as lucky."

Set Dating Goals

Most of us are used to setting goals in our lives: how much weight to lose, what we want to own by the end of the year, the job we will have five years from now, how well behaved our children will become after we take a new parenting class. But it isn't often that we set goals for our love lives. Yet, as we found at the beginning of the book, having a vision for the future helps us find the direction for getting there. Hopefully, once you know the direction, then you can take small steps to make that goal a reality. A good way to set dating goals for yourself is to make a list of what you want to accomplish during the dating process. Maybe you want to start trusting men again, to feel more attractive, or to discover what kind of man you are really looking for. Only you can determine what your goals are. Here's a peek at other women's dating goals:

1. *Learn to trust again.* When relationships fall apart, the first thing to go is usually trust. Part of the dating process is getting to know someone and then deciding whether or not you can trust them. Sometimes that decision is overshadowed by past experiences. "It has been hard," said Paula. "I have one guy that I have dated solely for the past few months, and I find myself frustrated with my inability to trust that he will tell me if things aren't going well in the relationship. He promises to tell me if the relationship begins to feel different or he finds someone else he wants to date, but I question him all the time. He actually hasn't given me any reason to distrust him. I think that is what frustrates me the most about my divorce—how my ex-husband's behavior affects my trust in every new relationship." If Paula's goal is to learn how to trust, then she needs to give trust a try with small aspects of the relationship. She might want to make it clear from the start that she has a major problem with trust, so she will need to hear the truth no matter what. Then she needs to make some agreement with herself about what would cause her to end the relationship—one lie, forgetting to call her, missing a date—and if that event occurs she needs to move on.

2. *Enjoy the dating process, meet many men, and take some time before committing to a serious relationship.* "I want to go out with lots of men before making any commitment," said Jennifer. "I have a tendency to become attached

to men very fast. I see all their good points, ignore their bad ones, and am so thrilled that someone likes me that I almost make myself fall in love more with the idea than the person. So this time I've decided that I have to go out with fifteen men before I'm allowed to stick with just one." Carrie echoed her words: "I fell in love with a man right after I separated from my husband. I was really surprised when he told me he thought I should date many men before settling on him. He knew that I had experienced only three relationships in my life and was sure that I'd regret missing the opportunity to be with a variety of men later. At first I was hurt, but now I understand—it was man number eight I really fell in love with." Don't rush to jump into a committed relationship. Enjoy the wining, dining, and meeting of new people.

3. *Be open to men we might not have been attracted to in the past.* "I need to discover what type of man suits me at this point in my life," said Toni. "I'm not really interested in a man fitting a physical description. I'm more in tune now with how I want to feel in the relationship. I'm looking for someone who enjoys going to a kids' Christmas show and who wouldn't be embarrassed if I began wildly waving at my daughter on stage. I need someone who needs me in his life. I don't want a man who is so completely on his own that he doesn't need me for anything. I want someone to sit with me and have coffee and ask my opinion. I'd like an equal partnership with someone who is in touch with people, a kind man who isn't cold or empty. My man needs to know who he is and what he wants in life. He can't still be looking for himself." The best thing you can do to find out what kind of man is right for you at this point in your life is to have a general list of attributes, and then, with that list in hand, approach all men with an open mind.

4. *Learn how to move on when a relationship ends.* "I'd like to learn how to deal with rejection or disappointment in a positive way," said Cindy. "It is never easy to be the one left wishing the relationship was still going on. My casual boyfriend decided he needed a year to himself with no distractions (which means me, I guess). I was not heartbroken because I didn't love him, but I did feel as though I had been dropped off a high ledge. I dealt with it by making a list of all the things I didn't like about the relationship, telling myself it was better to find out it wasn't going to work sooner rather than after I had fallen in love, and going out for a fun evening with a girlfriend. I felt much better the next morning, like I was ready to let it go and open up to the dating process again." Rejection of any kind hurts. Think about the strategies that have worked in your life when dealing with disappointment or rejection. Remember, if you have

a mind-set that you are out there dating as a way to discover the relationship you want, then it becomes easier to let go of relationships that don't work. It may also help to go into the dating process acknowledging the fact that you may be hurt more than once before you find someone to love.

Meeting Men

All the good men are not taken, they are just busy living their lives. So how are you going to meet one? Let's think about what busy men do: go to kids' sports games, work out at a health club, take weekend trips, go to concerts, walk their dog, grocery shop, and wonder when they are ever going to meet a woman who wants them!

I met my husband when I least expected it. My girls were participating in a musical sponsored by a local church. It was my turn to watch the youngest cast members during rehearsal while they waited to be called onstage. I heard the music that signaled my daughters' dance number, so I looked through the glass windows to watch her. As I stood there a man who was in the play walked up and introduced himself. I felt instantly attracted, but I wasn't sure if he was unattached. One of the kids fell off the play structure, so I had to run and resume my job. Half an hour later he came and talked to me again, mentioning the fact that he was also going through a divorce. I wasn't sure what to do with the energy that moved through me. I was trying to remember how to flirt as I thought about asking him out! We talked about the musical and where we lived, and then he said something about my two daughters being very talented. At that point I said, "My two sons are talented too," just to see if he fainted on the spot. A look of shock did cross his face, but when he left to practice his scene in the play, he did ask me to meet him for lunch. There are all sorts of ways to meet men. Once you decide that you're ready to begin dating, you'll be surprised how many available men show up in your life.

Many women are taking advantage of today's technology and searching for men on-line. "At first I was hesitant to send my profile, because I was afraid that someone would contact me back," said Angela. "Then if they did contact me, I was afraid of responding. I got past my initial fears. Right now there are twelve men in my mailbox. The response has been amazing. The first thing I do is read what they write and talk about. A lot of people go for the catchy titles: "I'm one handsome stud!"—things like that. I told myself that I had to make my profile down to earth and honest so I would have a better chance of weeding out the ones who are looking for someone that I am not.

All the men who have responded have been polite and well mannered. Talk about a self-esteem booster when my ex left me for dead! So you know what I have to say to my ex now? 'Tough luck, buddy, this girl is hot!'"

Nancy too is shopping on the Internet. "I know—now—that I am a very young fifty, in good shape, and half decent looking. I first contacted eight men, but they all fizzled out for one reason or another. One would have married me on the spot, but I tried very hard to be sensible and caring at the same time. I enjoyed reading their profiles, their wants and needs. Some made me hoot with laughter! For one area in New York City and Connecticut I put in my requirements and had 500 hits! I hung in there with one guy who was really nice, and his picture looked great. I planned a trip to New York to see a friend and then meet this man for dinner. I can only describe him as [British comic] Benny Hill's double! He turned out to be everything I dreaded and more. The date lasted all of two hours, and it was hard work! I was disappointed because we had such a good time writing back and forth, but he wrote many things that were completely untrue about himself, which I guess is one of the problems if you meet a man on-line. I'm now writing to a great guy and will be meeting him soon. We'll see if he has inflated himself. It really is a fun way to meet men!" To go on an Internet "date," you don't have to get dressed up, find a baby-sitter, or waste an evening checking out the men at a local club. All you have to do is turn on your computer as you sit in your pajamas, sip tea, and read descriptions. You immediately know their ages, what they like to do, how many kids they have, and what kind of relationship they are looking for. That is, if they're telling the truth!

Other women prefer to meet men "live," within their own community. "I think the best place to meet men is while doing things you already like to do in your own community, like going to concerts or art galleries," said Jackie. "That way you meet someone within the elements of activities you already personally enjoy. I met my boyfriend at an outdoor concert. We both love music. After the concert, we found out that we had mutual friends, which is another benefit of hanging out in your own community."

"The year after my divorce I went to a blues bar every Thursday night from April to November," said Jill. "I decided that I couldn't judge my success on one night, so I decided to pick one place and stick with it so that I would feel safe and comfortable. This was also the only fun place near my home that seemed to have an older group of people. It was there that I met the first two guys I dated. I loved the music and would close my eyes and drift away, relaxing in that time away from my kids. I'm so different from anyone in there, but I'm trying to have an open mind about people, to make new friends, and to take one Thursday night out at a time." Attending events that interest you is a good way to meet men with similar interests and to enjoy the personal time you've been able to free up.

Another way to find single men is in the personal ads found in most local newspapers. You can read an ad and then listen to a greeting recorded in a private voicemail box. "I met many men through the ads," said Suzanne, "but none I wanted to see more than once. Then on Valentine's Day, I heard a voice that I was sure I could listen to for a while. His name was Brad. We talked on the phone a number of times, and then we met a few weeks later. He was tall, lanky, and really not the type I'd been attracted to in the past. Had I just seen him somewhere, I probably wouldn't have taken a second look. But there was definitely chemistry, and he began flirting with me. We ended up dating for two years."

"When my marriage ended I used to read the personals just for a laugh, or maybe to convince myself that there were adults out there trying to meet each other," said Joan. "At first I was discouraged, because it seemed that most men wanted a woman quite a bit younger than themselves. But out of every week's paper I seemed to find at least five men who sounded interesting. It was very strange the first few times I left messages, but after a while it was something I looked forward to." Contacting a man through the personals in your paper may be a good way to avoid a long-distance relationship. You also get to hear the person's voice!

The scariest date (or most exciting, depending how you look at it) is the blind date. Your best friend calls you and says that she has the perfect person for you, a man at work who just got divorced, who is interested in skydiving, who is funny and attractive—all in all, a great catch. She talks you into it, so you arrive at the coffee shop and see a man sitting alone. A jolt of terror runs through you—that could not be the man she described. You are thinking about how you are going to disown your friend when another man walks in, more your age, seems sort of the skydiving type, but he walks past you and joins some friends. As you look back at the first man with dread, a man you missed, your blind date, catches you off guard, says your name, and introduces himself. So, relieved that the meeting ordeal is over, and even though the man isn't half bad, you swear never to agree to a blind date again.

The problem with blind dates is that a friend is setting you up with someone whom they believe would be perfect for you, but they haven't seen your dating goals or the list of qualities you are looking for in a man. To be on the safe side, if a friend wants to set you up, you might meet the person together with your friend or go on a double date. That way at least you have your friend to enjoy the evening with if her taste in men doesn't meet your standards.

The Date

My favorite game as a girl was the dating game. You go around the board landing on squares that determine your outfit, say where you are going on the date, and all sorts of other tidbits as you travel on your way to the final move of the game—opening a plastic door to find out if you got the gorgeous hunk in a bathing suit holding a surfboard, the preppy cutie with a polo shirt and loafers, the nerd with big glasses, or a dirty bum. Although now that I think back on it, the men all had the same face and body, just different hair, clothes, and accessories! So you have met a man, probably talked a few times on the phone, and now you've decided to meet in person. From here it is pretty much like my board game: time to figure out what to wear, where to go, and who the man really is behind that plastic door.

Only a few words of advice. Times have changed since you dated five, ten, twenty, or more years ago. It is completely acceptable for you to call the man and ask him out. You can suggest places that you would like to go. You can even be in charge of planning the entire date. You can direct the conversation and ask pointed questions about his goals, what he believes, and whom he has loved in his life. You might even ask for his views about sex and discuss your preferences before you even consider kissing him. Things may go faster than you remember. You're older and know what you want, so you may decide to cut right to the chase with honesty and intimacy. It is all up to you. There are no real rules in today's dating world, certainly not for grown women who've already spent most of their youth following other people's rules. Enjoy this stage. Play with it. Let whatever happens delight you, and know that it is your right to walk away from any man or behavior that is unappealing.

My first date with Al, the man I met at the musical, was a quick lunch at a local microbrewery restaurant. I thought hard about what to wear and chose a short, white, V-neck linen summer dress. My goal was to convince him that although I had four children, I was still a very sexy and appealing woman. We had talked on the phone almost nightly for a few weeks, so I felt relaxed and excited to see him in person. Our conversation centered on religion and psychology, the two subjects I had studied in college. It was evident to both of us that we were attracted to each other, so there was this sense of urgency to get to all the important subjects as soon as possible. That way we could either go forward and possibly fall in love or be disappointed by things not working. Neither of us wanted to be hurt again or to be heartbroken by finding out, after a long, drawn-out yearning, that our life pictures were too different to ever love each other. When we left the restaurant he hugged me, which was a disappointment; I wanted a kiss. A few days later we met at a park for lunch once again, and as I got out of my car, he handed me a dozen red roses and kissed me softly. After our picnic lunch, we sat on the grass and kissed for a long time. That evening he called and asked if I felt like a game of backgammon, so he visited my home for the first time and we played—but not backgammon. Two weeks from our first date we were professing our love.

Sometimes love happens really fast. You know what you want, and you recognize it in a man. Sometimes it takes a string of good and bad dates, embarrassing moments, and indecision, with you going back and forth to yourself: "I'm attracted, but he is a little rude. His smile is nice, and he did call three days in a row, but he has three kids under six!" Have the courage to build the relationship you want. Be willing to open up and have fun while you're doing it. If it isn't happening with this man, move on and make space for the relationship that you have envisioned.

To jump-start your creative date-planning ideas, here are some of the best dates from the lives of real women, including single moms. "We were driving out to the ocean," said Amy. "I thought we were headed for a restaurant to watch the sun set when he pulled off the road by a secluded path. He took out a picnic basket stuffed with a catered dinner, wine and dessert, battery-operated plastic candles, and a radio. We walked down to the beach, spread out the blanket, and were serenaded by the waves. It was the best date because I know how much effort it took. It wasn't easy for him to get everything ready, to buy the food, to pack the car, and to do something out of the ordinary. I'll always remember how special I felt."

"The best date for me was a county flower show," said Amelia. "We met at a nursery where I was buying tomato plants for our vegetable garden. I hadn't planted tomatoes before, but my daughter grew a tomato plant at school and was bugging me to get a vegetable garden going. I didn't know there were fifty kinds of tomatoes to choose from! I must have looked lost because he came up to me and asked if I needed any help. We talked and I told him that my hobby was flower gardening. His hobby was vegetable gardening, so we decided to go out. The date was so easy because we were both in our element, talking about the plants, general landscape ideas, admiring the bridges, ponds, and outdoor furniture. We didn't have to sit and stare into each other's eyes and think of what to say. We just talked as we walked and afterward went to a wonderful and romantic restaurant for a big piece of cheesecake with strawberries."

"My favorite date was a trip to the drive-in movies," said Anna. "I know that should be a common experience, but I had never been to one before, which I mentioned to him during one of our phone conversations. There were no drive-ins in the middle of New York, so we went on a late afternoon drive, had dinner at a mom-and-pop restaurant beside a lovely river. And then he surprised me afterward by pulling the car into the drive-in. Halfway through, he said it was traditional to get into the backseat and neck. I laughed and told him he should have brought me to a bad movie because I was too into the plot to climb into the backseat!"

Other best-date ideas: a local art and wine festival; a jazz or blues concert; the state fair; taking a windsurfing class together; horseback riding on the beach; bowling and inviting your closest friends; a night at a comedy club.

There are great, fun dates and then there are romantic dates that take your breath away. "The most romantic date I've ever had was with this guy who played in a band," said Kim. "He invited me to come and listen to the band and then go out with him afterward. I thought I'd feel embarrassed sitting there sipping wine while he played the guitar and sang, but when he dedicated a song to me about a woman with brown hair and sexy eyes—I do have brown hair but never thought my eyes were sexy until that night!—I thought I was going to melt. The way he looked at me when he sang was right out of a movie. During one of his breaks he asked me to dance. I think part of the romance was being able to observe him, to admire what he was doing, to wish he were touching me and then have him hold me in his arms as we danced. We didn't talk much until afterward, but it was all in the eye contact and the gestures."

Sherrie said, "I used to think romance was overrated, unobtainable, and a sure sign that all the man wanted was sex, but I changed my mind when I was invited to a fund-raiser at the city zoo. We arrived, ate our appetizers, drank a little wine, and then began to walk around looking at all the animals. I realized once I got there that my date was the head of this fund-raising committee. He talked about the animals like they were his children and was so excited about a baby white tiger that had just been born. When we approached the tigers, he took out a key, opened the door, and pulled me into the building where the baby tiger and his mother were resting. There was a little table, one candle lit in the middle, with boxes of Chinese food all ready to eat. It felt sort of forbidden and intimate to be locked away where nobody could find us. I also felt honored that he would share his passion with me and that he would go to the trouble to find a way for us to be alone."

Other romantic dates without the details: a night sailing trip; a visit to a planetarium; dinner at a Moroccan restaurant with belly dancers; a night walk in the summer under a full moon; taking a ballroom dance class; going on a hayride; the man making dinner.

Dating Mistakes

Along with the stories of great dates comes a list of dating mistakes that women have made. "I began dating way too soon after my divorce," Jessica said. "I had two relationships right after the divorce, and both were bad. The idea was to get out there and have a little fun. I had just gotten a new job, which demanded focus. The kids really had a bad year with all of us running to counselors, and I was unhealthy and kept getting sick. That is how I started dating. I was still processing, grieving and not feeling solid within myself, feeling very vulnerable. Little disappointments with these two guys shook my foundation and made me believe I could never fall in love again. After both, I felt devastated and hurt. I think these experiences ultimately made me put off dating for two years out of fear of being hurt again."

"The biggest mistake I ever made was giving this man I went out with one time too much information," said Elizabeth. "He seemed nice enough when we met for coffee, so when we started talking about where we worked and lived I was open to telling him. By the end of the coffee I knew I wasn't attracted to him and that I wasn't interested in seeing him again. He was very attracted to me and began calling me every night. I had my number changed because he bugged me so much. Then I noticed he was driving by my house, sitting outside, and watching my kids and me. Once he even showed up at work with flowers for me with a note about how he couldn't stop thinking about me. It scared me to death. I ended up having my brother call him and tell him to leave me alone or I would get a restraining order and have him arrested for stalking. I guess that scared him, because he stopped driving by."

Planning too long of a date before meeting a man is another mistake. "I met this guy on-line, then we talked on the phone and planned on meeting for dinner," said Tina. "My friends told me to meet him for coffee in the afternoon first so I wouldn't be stuck with him all evening, but I was excited to go on a real date. He was good-looking enough, but I swear, all he did was talk about himself. He never asked me about my life, my kids, what I did—nothing. Since that date, I never plan a first date to last longer than an hour, and I always meet at a public place for something light and friendly, nothing romantic or costly."

Dating married or attached men is also a mistake. "Six months after my husband left me, I heard that a neighbor I had always found attractive had also left his wife," said Linda. "We became friends and after a while started going out. We had so many things in common. We were both healing from a divorce, both had kids, lived on the same street, and shared similar interests. I began sleeping with him, and then he started saying he wanted both of us to be able to date other people, that it was too soon to commit to anyone. I was heartbroken, especially when I noticed the same car in his driveway every day for two weeks. I asked him about it, and he said it wasn't serious. We slept together a few more times—I hoped to lure him back into the relationship. This went on for a few months, until he told me he was getting married in two days! In the meantime, I fell in love with him, and now I feel like I'm going through the grieving process all over again. He has actually called me since he came back from the honeymoon, telling me what a mistake he made in getting married and asking me to still sleep with him. Now I've decided to wait a while and to focus my energy on getting to know myself before I jump into a relationship. I also have a rule that I will not go out with any man who is still attached to someone else in any way."

Sometimes we make choices in our love relationships that we know are mistakes because we don't see a better option. "I let someone walk into my life and I painted the picture that he was my savior, capable and willing to take over things that I was too emotionally distraught to deal with," said Kathy. "When I was first separated, I had this guy friend for years. He was familiar with my life, liked my kids, and he said he would be there for me, which I really appreciated. Over time, we switched from friends to lovers. I let him make all the decisions, called him with every problem, let him help me parent the kids, until one day he told me that he didn't want to see me anymore because I wouldn't let him move in and be Daddy. He didn't like it when I started healing, because when I became stronger I didn't need him as much. He barely talks to me now." Kathy didn't have any time or space after her divorce to consider other options. Instead, she grasped onto a man who was willing to take control of her life for her. But as time went on and she became stronger, the relationship fell apart.

"I'm not sure if this is a mistake or not, but I'm in a relationship with a man I don't love simply because I need his financial support," said Elaine. "Sometimes I feel like I do need to keep this man in my life just to survive. If I pay all the household bills, I'm left with only $150 per month to feed my four kids and me. We can't support ourselves. It seems many men get to go off and do anything they want while the mothers are left with the responsibility for the children. I have mixed feelings about needing this man's help, and sometimes I feel so dishonest because he thinks I love him. But I can't seem to figure out any other way to keep me and the kids in a house and out of a homeless shelter."

There is no way to get through the dating process without making mistakes. The goal is to be aware of how you feel and to know that the choices you make lead you in a certain direction. Make sure that direction is the relationship you really want. Mistakes teach us many lessons. They give us new relationship skills and in most instances a better understanding of ourselves.

Men Talk About Dating

Women are not the only ones who experience heartbreak and loss in love relationships. We are all wounded in many ways throughout our lives, and those wounds emerge in full force in intimate relationships, especially when those relationships fail. Many women find the courage to reenter the dating world because they hope they will find men out there who are different from the man who hurt them—men who want to be in committed, loving relationships, men who want to share their lives and their dreams. We all think that men and women are so different. Volumes of books are written discussing this difference. Comedians make jokes about it. Yet when it comes to love, we are very similar. Men want to be appreciated. They want someone to laugh with, someone they can count on—and yes, the comedians are right . . . sex is very high up on the list!

I interviewed a number of men in the process of writing this book, and here is what they had to say about the dating process. "I didn't feel very attractive after my wife dumped me for another man," said Thomas. "I wanted the marriage back—or, more truthfully, the picture of this perfect family. I didn't particularly want my wife back. I didn't date for the first eight months, and when I began dating, it was because I was lonely and missed having sex. Dating was fun and helped me feel better about myself. The first three women I went out with were younger than me, had never been married, and didn't have kids. I thought it would be easier to have a relationship with a woman who had no children, but I found out that we didn't have that much in common because they didn't understand parenting or what it's like to love my children. It took me quite a while to realize that women still did find me attractive, which was a welcome surprise."

"I guess one thing that seems daunting in the dating process is all the money I have to spend to take women out," said Dan. "I'm still pretty traditional, and it makes me uncomfortable to sit at dinner fighting over who is going to pay the check. On the other hand, I don't have money to waste on a woman who may not be interested in me at all, so I'm pretty up front with my agenda. I would also appreciate it if a woman tells me when she isn't interested so I don't make a fool of myself calling repeatedly. If we are attracted to each other and haven't begun discussing the big life questions by the third or fourth date, then it might be time to move on. I want to know: How do you feel about more kids? Where do you see yourself in ten years? Would you consider a longer-term relationship, not necessarily with me, but is that in your plans if and when you do fall in love? How would you parent someone else's kids? How would you expect a boyfriend to be with your kids? What do you believe? I don't want to waste my time with a woman whose basic direction is not the same as mine. I guess I'm just the type of person who likes to be faithful and involved in a long-term relationship. Also, if we aren't at least tempted to have sex by the fifth date I wonder if there is enough chemistry between us to keep going."

"I know pretty much right off the bat if a woman is right for me because I have very specific likes and dislikes," said Jared. "It is very attractive to me when a woman is sure of herself, when she voices her own opinions. I like it when she intends to live her own life whether she is with a man or not, when she pursues her own dreams, but also that she lets me know when there is something about me that she is interested in and likes and wants. This attitude of being sure of herself needs to include her liking how she looks. I absolutely hate having to assure a woman that she looks good. It is such a turn-on to see a naked woman who wants you, whether she is twenty pounds overweight and has stretch marks or not. What turns me off is women who hide under sheets, need the room to be pitch black before disrobing, or complain all the time that they shouldn't eat this or that. Maybe women should take a lesson from men. There are many of us who have beer guts or aren't in the shape we were at twenty-five. That doesn't get us down or keep us wrapped in sheets."

Men do their own preparation for dating, and they probably have their own list of dating goals, even if they don't write them in a journal! They are creative and come up with wonderful and romantic dates. But they also make mistakes and do things that they regret. They feel hurt, self-conscious, un-loved, angry, and sad just like we do. Women and men alike are searching for that special person, to make the desire stir within us, to love, protect and share our life with. So get out there and find the man that is right for you!

9

Sex Esteem

It was about the third date I had with Brett," said Emily. "Sometime during dinner he looked at me, and I began to feel that slow creep of desire begin again. This was the first man I'd been with since my divorce—I never cheated on my husband for the fourteen years we were married, even though he admitted to many affairs. During the first few dates with Brett, I was too nervous to settle into my feelings; instead I was trying to be talkative, funny, and interesting. But the way he looked at me for just those few seconds made me sure that he was sexually attracted to me. I took a chance after dessert and told him that I was beginning to have feelings for him. He said that he was beginning to feel something for me too. As we got in the car to drive home, he reached out to hold my hand and then turned it over to kiss my palm. That was the first kiss. In my head I kept thinking, "Don't take me home; ask me to come to your house." My kids were with their dad, but I didn't want to ask Brett to my house, which was a complete mess. I had promised myself to be outgoing, to take charge of the sexual relationship if I wanted to, and now that I wanted to, I couldn't force the words out of my mouth. Finally, I said out loud what I was thinking, 'Do you think we could sleep together without having intercourse?' He chuckled and said, 'Probably. Do you want to try?' I said, 'Yes, but it can't be a probably. You are the first man I've been with other than my husband in fourteen years, and I'm not ready for the whole thing yet.' He promised.

"We arrived at his apartment, and I was tingling, anticipating his touch, feeling unsure of how to begin things, when he took me by the hand and led me into his bedroom. There were a few lights on, which made me nervous. Total darkness had always been my preference when making love, especially after I had kids. He took my face in his hands and began to kiss me. We kissed until I felt like ordering him to strip! But he slowly guided me to a sitting position on the bed and began to take off my shoes. He kissed the top of my feet and then asked if he was allowed to remove any of my clothing, or if I'd be more comfortable sleeping with my clothes on. For some reason his tenderness and understanding of how I was feeling made me much braver, so I told him he could remove anything he wanted to. With that he knelt on the floor between my knees and began to unbutton my blouse as he kissed my stomach. By the time he got to unlatching my bra, kissing as he went, I had felt more sensations in those minutes than I had over the last five years of my marriage. He took his shirt off, then put his arm under my legs and slid me onto the bed.

"For at least an hour we kissed and touched before he even went for my pants, and by then I told him I wanted to take back what I had said in the car. He told me that a promise was a promise, that he wasn't going to take advantage of me. *Damn. No, please go ahead, take me!* was screaming in my head. He slid off my pants, then lifted my hips and began licking. When I started to moan, he smiled and said, 'This isn't intercourse, is it?' I had an orgasm in less than five minutes. In my entire marriage I had maybe twenty orgasms with my husband, and never had he used his mouth! I pulled him up to me and begged him, trying to get his pants off. But he wouldn't let me, so we started wrestling, laughing, and pulling at each other. God, it was so much fun. This was the first sexual experience in my life where I was the one who was being given to. I wasn't the one doing what my partner wanted, following someone else's desire. In those few hours, this man changed me forever simply by showing his intense desire and tenderness at the same time. He opened up a sensual space inside of me that I would never let close again. I did end up falling in love with him. We were together for two years. But in the end, our lives went different directions."

Sex is the simple connection of two bodies, but it can be so much more than that. I began this chapter with Emily's first sexual encounter after her divorce because it carries the honesty, sensual feeling, desire, insecurity, courage, openness, and the ability to be given to that we are all trying to reach. It shows the struggle she had with her inner voice, which remembered everything she learned about her sexual soul and the kind of woman she wanted to be, and also how insecure and afraid she felt, expressing what she really wanted when she finally had a man next to her. We aren't all as lucky as Emily to have a man like Brett for our first postdivorce sexual encounter. But it is possible to significantly improve the chances of having these kinds of sexual experiences if we are in touch with our sexual souls and are willing to push past some of our fears to the kind of sex we can so easily imagine in our minds. The goal of this chapter is to help you remember what you have learned about your sexual soul, to find a way to draw out of yourself the sensual woman you want to be, and then to become that woman in real-life relationships.

If all you want from sex is a few minutes of kissing and a little genital touching followed by intercourse, then you might as well skip this chapter, because you can get that from any man with no effort at all. If you want to experience your sexuality as a way of life that spills over into the way you act with men, then you have come to the right place. In this chapter you'll discover ways to create new sexual visions in your mind to replace old sexual experiences. You'll learn how to begin the foreplay with the first telephone call, whether you are interested in sex or not. Then when you do have a man you want to make love with, we'll talk about ways to make sex happen the way you want it to happen.

Create New Sexual Images in Your Mind

The sexual experiences we have had throughout our lives live on in our memory. They form the foundation on which we build our understanding of what sex is meant to be. The only way the pattern of your thoughts or memories will change is if you consciously work to create new thoughts and then find experiences in which you can build new memories. Remember, this is a new chapter in your life. You have to take advantage of the one benefit of divorce—you get to create a new starting point, not just with a new partner, but first with yourself. Start daydreaming, have a few fantasies, reread the love scenes in your steamiest romance novels, and get out those books of erotica. We all need some material to create new sexual images in our minds. These new images can then begin to replace the old experiences as soon as we make them real by living them.

Ask yourself a few basic questions when creating your new sexual images. How do you want to be treated in bed? Are you the soft-caresses type who wants massage oil rubbed over her entire body before he slides on, or do you wish he'd rip your clothes off as he chases you around the bed? How comfortable are you expressing your sensuality? Will you enter the bedroom stark naked, dressed in lingerie, or maybe with a sheet draped oh so seductively, or in just a sports bra and panties? In the love scene of your dreams, is there music playing? Is it jazz, blues, rock, classical, new age, accordion, funk? Are there scented candles burning, bright lights or no lights? How do you ask your lover for what you want? Do you write a love note describing your fantasy lovemaking session? Are you the type to give directions during or before, or do you say what you want by guiding his hand or head or hips? Do you see yourself having a complete discussion of your likes and dislikes before you ever touch each other so that you are more comfortable when sex actually happens? Set your mind up like a movie camera and try seeing yourself in different sexual situations. Then remember the ones that feel most like you, that make you feel comfortable with your own style of sexual expression. Those are the ones you are going to aim for with your lover.

While you are working on those mind exercises, don't forget to practice the power of fantasy to bring yourself to orgasm with or without a man. Rock and roll in the freedom of your imagination! You may even wish to experiment with naughty scenes that you would never consider acting out in real life. Especially women who are caring for children up until the minute they are ready to hop into bed may find it hard to move their stressed thoughts and worries into sexual ecstasy mode without a little help.

Another important thing to think about is, How you are going to act if your lover doesn't give you what you ask for or doesn't like your style of sexual expression? "I had been dating for a while, and this was the second man I'd had sex with since the divorce," said Maria. "Believe me, I worked hard in that first relationship trying to get rid of all the negative thoughts, ghosts from my past, so I could begin to express just me. So we'd had a lot of foreplay before this bedroom scene, and I start guiding his head downward in the hope of a little oral sex when he said that he doesn't like it and never does it. That was fine with me; I've never been one to force someone to do what they don't want to do. When he started guiding my head downward, I said, 'Sorry, fair is fair!' I felt incredibly empowered in that moment. No, he never called again, but then I didn't like him that much anyway, and I obviously wouldn't have enjoyed a long-term sexual relationship with him." Maria's refusal to get into an unequal dynamic made her feel a sense of empowerment.

Sometimes the sexual scene you create can bring up feelings of insecurity in your date. "I had an experience once with a guy who was so uncomfortable with his own sexuality, he said my sexy behavior was making him impotent!" said Tara. "I really liked him, so I was willing to back off a little until he was comfortable. I think I ended up being sort of a sex therapist in a way. I wasn't willing to stop my sexual expression totally. In fact, it was kind of fun playing with it and learning how to tone it down and pump it up. After a few months he certainly wasn't impotent." Both Maria and Tara found ways to deal with a lover whose idea of sex was different from theirs in ways that suited their new sex esteem.

Sexual images are all around us, in both positive and negative ways. Learn to use the images that make you feel good about your sexuality, and let go of the ones that feel degrading or make you feel inadequate. "The strangest thing happened the other day," said Christine. "I was cleaning out the garage and found a box of my ex-husband's *Playboy* magazines. It always upset me when one would arrive in the mail, because I felt that he was comparing me to the airbrushed, perfect bodies he probably masturbated over. I decided to open one of the magazines to check out what he found so appealing, and I was surprised that I started to get excited. I think it was the look of desire on the girl's face, combined with the realization that men actually look at these pictures of naked women and become sexually aroused. I've never looked at a picture of a naked man and felt aroused—maybe I'm the only one who doesn't. I had this impression that those pictures would be so dirty, but they weren't. Then I found a few *Penthouse* magazines in the stack, and I looked at those too. They were much more graphic, with each picture showing girl after girl with her legs spread wide. When I looked at those I had another thought. I had been raised to believe that a woman's vagina was not the prettiest sight, and yet that is exactly what the men were paying to see. My thinking sort of shifted that day to liking my body more and feeling that maybe I could be more open during sex, since men seemed to like that kind of openness. I don't have a body like the women in the pictures, but then the men I'm attracted to don't possess a physique off the cover of *GQ* magazine either."

Foreplay Begins with the First Phone Call

Don't worry, this section isn't about phone sex, it's about how to show up with your full power as a sensual woman from the very first encounter. It's not about showing cleavage or giving a man what he wants. It's about the way you let yourself flow with feelings of desire and creativity of all kinds. It's the expression of pride and pleasure that you are a woman with skin that's sensitive to touch, breasts quickening with desire, and a vulva that engorges with delight. It's how you laugh, the way you present yourself, the gestures you make. All point to a woman who is content within her own skin and is in touch with her sexuality. If you aren't that woman yet, turn back to chapter 5 and read it again, because you are going to need to understand your sexual soul if you want to create the kind of passionate sex that allows you to express and play with your own desire and longing.

Foreplay is a sort of promise of what is to come as the sexual encounter moves forward, a measure of response from one body to another. But every interaction we have from the first meeting is a form of foreplay that sets the tone and direction that the relationship might go. It helps if the first impression you give is an accurate picture of who you intend to be, from the new starting point you have imagined and established, instead of who you might have been in the past. When you are able to set your fears aside and be honest with your thoughts, beliefs, and experiences, then it is likely that the other person will meet you on that same level and show up as themselves. If you can establish this level of honesty, it is easier to discuss your views about sex as a topic of conversation that has no bearing on whether or not you ever decide to have sex with that person.

A lot has been written about first impressions—how to use the correct words or body language to communicate your intended meaning the very first time you meet someone. These first impressions become the image of who you are in the other person's mind. True, over time these impressions may change, but it is much easier to be bold and let it all hang out in the beginning than to hold bits of yourself back and release them piece by piece when it feels safe. Let's say that you have created a new image of yourself as being outgoing and friendly, but you begin the relationship shy and reserved like your old self. If you do this, it will take a long time to create a different image in your date's mind. You may well be feeling shy and reserved in this situation, and if that is an accurate picture of who you are, then that's great because you're being yourself. But if you don't feel shy and reserved inside, yet you act that way on dates because you are afraid to act otherwise, then that isn't so good, because your date may well form a picture of the woman you are based on what he sees, which is based on a fear that you haven't yet been able to get past.

Many women find the initial meeting less intimidating if they have communicated a number of times first by phone or e-mail. "My favorite part of on-line dating is writing back and forth," said Melody. "You get to reveal intimate things about yourself before you see the person, and you can sort of decide whether or not the person's basic life views might fit with yours. I have also used these interactions to practice being honest about myself. I'm willing to say things I might not say in person. Somehow I don't fear rejection so much on-line because at that point I'm just interacting with a computer screen. I wrote back and forth with one man for a few months, and I thought we had so much in common. We had seen each other's pictures, but when we met in person, there wasn't that feeling of attraction for either of us that we'd felt behind our computer screens. Still, we have maintained a very nice on-line friendship and have been supporting each other with stories of our dating triumphs and defeats."

If you are able to be fully yourself from the beginning, it can allow the person you are beginning a relationship with to be honest in return. Have you ever noticed that most people share of themselves at the same level that the other person is sharing? If you start to talk about your pain about not being the kind of mother you wish you could be, chances are the man is going to dig into his pain and talk about something in his life that felt painful just so you are conversing on the same level. The question is whether you are the type of person who waits for someone else to take that plunge and then follow their lead, or if you have the courage to be the one who sets the tone and the direction of the discussion?

"I had been out with this guy Gary a few times, and we had talked on the phone almost every night for two weeks when I felt like it was time to talk about my sexual past," said Denise. "I was raped, robbed, and beaten when I was in college. I've had years of therapy and have really dealt with my trust issues toward men and have gotten to the place where I thoroughly enjoy sex. But that experience is still a part of who I am. My husband never wanted to talk about it. When we made love, I would ask him not to do things like put his hands anywhere near my neck. Then he would back off and say that I completely ruined the mood. When I found the courage to tell Gary what had happened, he listened, asked questions, let me talk, and showed obvious compassion as he told me a few of his sexual experiences that left a mark on him. I felt closer and more real after that conversation." Once you are well into a relationship, it is expected that you will be able to reach an intimate level in conversation, but in the beginning, when you are trying to decide how intimate you want the interaction to be, this skill becomes a great tool.

Once you have established this level of honesty, it is easier to bring up sex as a topic of conversation that is no scarier than discussing your excitement over a new career choice. When you are able to be up front with your thoughts and feelings about sex, it makes your first sexual encounter more relaxed since you already know, in general terms, what the person likes or doesn't like. It is a great subject to discuss on the phone all those nights when you don't have time for a date. Talk about what each of you liked and didn't like about your sex life within your marriages. That will give you a lot of information about a man and may help you anticipate if you would enjoy each other sexually.

"Ben and I had so many sexual discussions before we actually had sex," said Ingrid. "One night he told me how his wife would scream when she had an orgasm and how much he hated it. Well, I make a lot of noise during sex. It is a form of self-expression, and most of my lovers in the past have said it turns them on. So I decided to ask him to explain the scream. Was it a series of sounds or a high-pitched, one-time yell? I then told him that I liked to make sounds during lovemaking, so we had this discussion and he had a chance to clarify his feelings—that he did like to hear sounds of enjoyment but it was the screech at the end that he disliked. In my less confident days, I would have listened to the first part of that conversation, heard him say that he hated when women scream during orgasm, and then would have been silent as a mouse if we ever made love. What a shame that would have been, since I really enjoy the sound part and now so does he." When we are afraid of the answer, sometimes we don't ask questions about what someone means. Then we draw our own conclusions that hurt both our partners and ourselves in the long run. We create a relationship based on assumptions made from passing comments rather than from shared feelings and experiences.

Sex Can Happen the Way You Want It To

Insecurity. We all feel it. We wish our butts were smaller, our breasts firmer, our skin clearer, our legs more muscular, our eyes a different color, our hair a different texture. How do you throw all your insecurities to the wind and take hold of the present moment? The answer is simple, but the action is very difficult. You just make a decision that you are going to, and then you act like, you love every piece of yourself—and after a few times of acting this way, you may begin to believe it yourself.

What does insecurity about our bodies get us? It just makes us feel uncomfortable as we participate in an activity (sex) that we are going to do anyway. We enjoy it less because our minds are so busy deciding what the man is seeing and feeling that we can't see or feel our own desire. Chances are we'll also overlook the genuine desire written all over his face. If you've had children, the process has left its mark on your body. If you don't have children, you won't look the same at forty as at twenty. It's about time we started viewing these marks of birth and of age as joyful triumphs instead of things to be ashamed of. If one man doesn't enjoy your body, another will come along who does. Hiding in your Wonder bra or feeling insecure when you could be feeling unabashed ecstasy will only be your loss.

That said, let's get down to the act of sex itself. How can you make sex happen just the way you want it to? Are you a woman who dreams of a man who will feed you strawberries as he massages your skin with scented oil and dusts a feather up and down your body while you lie naked on satin sheets? Give me one reason why your sex life can't be incredible! You can make anything happen if you are willing to take ownership of what you want. We are all sexual creatures, so we need to acknowledge that sex is important, especially if we share it with only one person.

There are many ways to take ownership of your sex life. You could begin by making your bedroom a sensual place that reflects who you are—a woman who is interested in sex rather than the matron of the house. Think of all the years you spent married, with a bedroom that reflected your combined taste in decor. Now would be a good time to redecorate in a way that reflects the real you. The mood you set in your private spaces can help you move from your daily role as a hardworking mom into a sensual woman. Clear your room of miscellaneous clutter. Decorate with fabrics, pictures, candles, flowers, stones, or anything else that creates a sensual space. It doesn't have to be a costly transformation; you need only a few things that reflect the fact that you own this space. Music can also create a sensual mood, so tune those radio-preset buttons to stations you like, or buy a portable CD player and stack a pile of your favorite CDs on the nightstand. Scent the room with essential oils like ylang-ylang, jasmine, or other erotic aromas. Paint the walls in a color that reflects your personality and brightens your mood; paint may be the best way to change the entire feel of the room without spending a lot of money. Make sure your bed is inviting, with many pillows in case you're blessed with an adventurous lover who might enjoy various positions! When the rest of the house is covered with finger paint, the floors lined with backpacks, tennis shoes, and Barbie dolls, this room will become your sanctuary. Your bedroom will also send a clear reminder to yourself—and a message to any man in your life—that you have a sensual side that is completely separate from your organized mother role. If you will be having sex outside of your bedroom, put together a small bag of items that would help you feel ready for a romantic interlude. (Yes, being prepared communicates clearly that you want sex. You won't be able to use the excuse that he talked you into it!)

Next, learn how to clear your mind of the day's stress and move into a relaxed state, one in which it is easy for you to think about sex. Inhale slowly, saying something to yourself that helps you to let go. Turn on wild music and shake the stress out of your body for a few minutes—whatever works to bring you into a peaceful state instead of thinking about the fight your daughter just had with her friend or your son's unfinished India report.

"I feel so disappointed sometimes when I can't get in the mood for sex," said Trisha. "I think about sex all day at work. Then I get home, feed the kids, get them all packed to go to their dad's house, and by the time I begin to make a small romantic dinner for my boyfriend, I'm ready for a nap. The kids are gone only one night every two weeks, so I like to make that night a date we spend in my home. Lately I've been trying to be more ready for the evening by making a clear break when the kids leave the house. I shut the door, stretch as tall as I can, then bend forward and touch my fingers to the floor, saying, 'Let everything go. Don't think about them for twenty-four hours. They will be safe; they don't need me now.' Then I do five minutes of stretching and breathing before I start on my plans for a romantic evening. I know it sounds silly, but marking the transition in my emotional state from mom to sensual woman really helps me get excited about the evening ahead." Experiment with ways that help clear your mind of stress and static so you will be able to create and enjoy a sexual experience.

Be clear within yourself about your boundaries and expectations, and make a commitment to be true to yourself no matter what your partner asks you to do. "I don't want to be in a relationship where I can't honor myself," said Julie. "I did that once. I allowed myself to get carried away with the man I was dating because he was the most sensual person I had ever met. It felt so freeing to be able to express myself in all sorts of ways, but I allowed myself to go too far with that when I agreed to let two of his friends join us. I didn't really want to do it, but he convinced me it would be so much fun. While it was happening, I didn't feel like I was in control of what they were doing to me. They weren't listening to me because they were having such a good time. I loved him and wanted to turn him on, so I didn't scream 'stop' or anything. Instead I just sort of joked with them, telling them to stop."

Having an idea of how you want sex to happen doesn't mean you can't also be spontaneous. Setting a boundary and expectation is more about how you develop the ability to say, "I don't want to do that" or "What do you think about trying this?" or "Let's be adventurous and try that." Don't let your desire or possibilities for enjoyment depend on a man's ability to guess what might turn you on or what might hurt you. Instead, speak up when you don't like something, and create the opportunity to get what you want by being clear about your feelings and needs. Maybe you do want the man to be completely in charge so you can be taken for a ride. But that is also a choice that you make to let go and let him take you, which can also be a vulnerable, sexy, and fun way to play. The direction the sexual experience goes needs to be a conscious choice. If you are lying there and saying to yourself, "No, please don't, I don't like this, please hurry up," then you are not making sex happen the way you want it to.

Show up ready to enjoy the experience; know what turns you on, and be prepared to be equally responsible for the direction the lovemaking takes. And don't forget to lighten up the mood with humor. "The first few years after my divorce, I was so happy to have men interested in having sex with me that I didn't really think about how I wanted it to go. I would just show up and go along with whatever they were comfortable doing," said Amanda. "Then I met this man who encouraged me to take charge, to be able to express myself to create what I wanted out of our lovemaking experience. He would plan one get-together, and then I would plan the next. Once we even decided to write out our own fantasy experience and give it to each other so we could incorporate some of those elements into the night each of us was planning. I never thought it would be fun to approach sex as a planned event. We didn't plan every encounter, but it was nice to have these to look forward to. This relationship taught me how important it is to know what turns me on and to have the courage to plan for it." If you aren't sure what turns you on or how to make yourself have an orgasm, get familiar with your own body. Don't be afraid to touch and explore so that you know what to ask for.

While making love, open your senses to the experience, be present in the moment, letting go of thoughts of anything outside that room. When you move your hand down his back, actually feel the texture of his skin, and make every part of your hand connect. When you kiss, listen to the sounds your lips make. When he touches you, let your body respond completely to that touch, moving toward him and into the connection you feel. Be there for the experience you have created! "There are times when I'm making love that I feel each quiver my body makes, when time stops and all the sounds in the room get louder," said Delta. "I'm in my body, in touch with my needs, and I have this feeling of exploding into my lover with sensations. But at other times, as hard as I try, I can't get my thoughts off some problem at work."

Men I interviewed said it is easy to tell when a woman is not having a good time but not at all easy to know what to do about it. "I can feel when a woman is just lying there, not really enjoying the way I'm touching her," said Jonathan. "It's frustrating to figure out what to do. I have to act like I feel all this desire, but it is hard to feel that without a woman's desire meeting yours at least part of the way. It would be much better for her to roll on top of me, move my hand, or suggest something else we would both enjoy."

Barb said that sex in her postdivorce life is less engaging than it was in her marriage. "Sometimes I feel all these great sensations when I'm making love, but I'm afraid to lose myself in them," she said. "So instead I stay in my head, not really letting the experience touch me in any way. In my marriage I was able to be in the moment and feel that connection. I guess I'm afraid to go to that depth with a man unless I know he is going to stick around." Each of us comes to the sexual experience with our own issues, day-to-day stress, and feelings of insecurity. The goal is to set all that aside and simply focus our minds on the action of loving.

After you have made love with a new partner, take a little time to think about the experience. Decide what you liked and didn't like, and notice what you wanted to do but didn't. Pat yourself on the back for the desires you were courageous enough to make known to your lover. Use this information as you go into new relationships or as you think of ways to make sex with the same man the kind of sex you want. After her first postdivorce sexual experience Janine said, "To my surprise, not only can I have sex again, I was completely capable of enjoying something I hadn't enjoyed in a number of years. I feel a deep gratitude for the experience and its lessons. I was very grateful to learn that I could trust a man sexually and that I wasn't the frigid bitch my husband thought I was!" Every sexual encounter will teach you something about yourself. Look at dating as an opportunity to learn more about the woman you want to be in the new relationship you are trying to create.

Last, but still very important, make sure you have girlfriends you can scheme and laugh with, who you trust with your stories and fears. Nothing heals an embarrassing or humiliating sexual experience faster than a friend who will laugh with you and exclaim in total support, "He did *what?* What a butt-head!" Most of us would still enjoy a monthly slumber party with the girls to talk, to ease our fears, to laugh our heads off, and to be supported in however we feel: insecure, powerful, sexy, or depressed. However, as we sit in our individual houses, with our lives full with kids' needs and the responsibility to support a family, we often forget that in the next house is a woman who feels just like we do—a woman who might make a wonderful friend.

10

Falling in Love

Here we are. All the work, the inner searching, the outward practice, and the dating dilemmas have led us to this place. Now we look inside our hearts and decide whether or not we have the courage to fall in love again. Poets describe love as a mighty power that transforms the soul, something that brings one glory, life, and new energy. But as we all know, love also has the power to attack life's foundation and shake us senseless with pain. What a statement of transformation and growth when a woman can say, "I understand both the light and dark sides of love, and still I'm ready and willing to try again."

The moment I laid eyes on Al it was energy at first sight; desire, longing, and lust at first touch; endless days of sharing our past and countless nights of lovemaking before we uttered the words "I love you." I knew I was in love weeks before I said anything and wondered whether he felt the same way. It had taken three years, many dates, and one serious postdivorce relationship for me to come to this place of being ready for a man to share my life, my future, and my kids. I struggled to understand what had gone wrong in my marriage, to move from despair to hope, from poverty to self-sufficiency. I felt independent and for the first time in my life really had an understanding of what it meant to love myself. I was ready to open up to love, and I was strong enough to go on if my man didn't love me. But I was still too chicken to say it first.

It was August, one month after we had met on the set of the church musical. My kids were visiting their father, so we were alone. I'd just made a delicious dinner, we'd taken a long walk, and we were sitting outside on the patio when he pulled me onto his lap and said, "There's something I need to tell you." For a moment I just stared at him, wondering if he was going to tell me something awful. Then he said, "I'm in love with you."

Love is one of the glories we are all seeking. Many believe it happens all by itself, with a look or a touch. But there is no look or touch powerful enough to unlock a heart that isn't ready for love. Now is the time to let love creep back into your thoughts, for you stand changed by divorce, made whole by self-acceptance, and strong with practice and the desire to survive. You've become a mighty force! Let's take some time to look at what we learn from love, why we crave it and are willing to sacrifice for it. Then we can talk about what love means to us today so that we can begin to create a healthy new love relationship. With this basic understanding of love, we'll be getting ready to welcome love into our lives, open our hearts, accept the pain that might come despite being in love again, and dive in with hope. Last, we'll celebrate finding love, growing love, and letting love go when it isn't returned.

Why We Crave Love

Love is a great motivator. It moves us to do things we don't want to do—to make sacrifices for the sake of those we love. I work longer and harder than I want to because I love my kids and want them to live in a safe neighborhood. I stay up late, even when I'm exhausted, and talk to a girlfriend who is going through a difficult time. I cancel long-standing plans when my son is having a problem at school. I prepare dinner for my husband when I'd rather be reading a book. My heart is too attached to choose otherwise; I like the feeling of connection and the knowledge that my presence makes a difference. Many proclaim that to love and be loved in return is the greatest gift we can give or receive in life. Maybe it is the feeling that someone is there for us, likes us, and wants to be with us that has us all searching for love, the longing for that one person who will accept us unconditionally.

Many of us crave love because it feels good. For some that is enough. "I've fallen in love three times since my divorce six years ago," said Wendy. "All three times I was the one left, sadly wishing the relationship could continue. It hurt when each relationship ended, but the hurt could never outweigh all the great feelings that came with the loving. I love for many reasons; one of them is to overcome the loneliness I feel when it is just me and the kids. I like having a man to talk with at the end of the day, to share my thoughts, to discuss my problems—and, if I'm lucky, a passionate lovemaking before falling asleep. It is sad when love dies, but it is so glorious when it is alive. I learn so much about myself when I'm in a relationship. I grow, I am challenged to work on some of my bad habits, and I learn about the other person's life, problems, and bad habits. I also find a lot of humor in relationships." Wendy accepts her craving for love as a natural part of her life, and she has learned to go on to the next relationship if one doesn't work out.

In some instances the craving we have for love comes from not getting all the love we needed or wanted as children. "I feel like I've lived my whole life trying to be good enough for someone to really love me," said Audrey. "My parents were good parents; I know they loved me, but I also felt there were expectations that went along with receiving their love. When I wasn't good at something, didn't get good grades, had trouble making friends, or came home drunk from a party, like most teenagers do once in a while, I felt complete rejection. I know that my parents' generation didn't have much instruction on how to parent kids, certainly nothing like what is available to me. I'm trying to do a better job with my girls to support their talents, to listen to them, and to love them just for being themselves."

Like Audrey, many of us are looking for that ideal, nurturing relationship that we needed from our parents—for a lover to listen wholeheartedly, to support our talents, and to love us whether we are successful at things or not. We go through life constantly trying to dig up that feeling of acceptance. When we begin to fall in love, each person has this incredible ability to be nurturing and accepting in a way that even our parents didn't live up to. We hang on to each other's every word, think every story is interesting, and are willing to sacrifice whatever is asked just to be with them. The problem is that after a few months or years, even lovers become ordinary human beings, and as human beings (just like us), they lose some of the initial motivation to be the all-accepting parent figure we were looking for—the person we thought we found when we first met. In this way love can be a great teacher—showing us what we long for and nudging us into the relationships that will both stir and satisfy those longings.

In love, we learn to laugh with our whole body, to experience our environment in full color, to take on challenges with gusto, to scream in anger, and to weep with despair. "You ask me to describe what I've learned from love," said Casey. "Well, only everything that is important! Love has taught me how to work together with someone who is completely different from me, how to accept not getting what I want, and what it feels like to get exactly what I want. I've learned how to be honest, to understand my feelings and then communicate them, and how to share my most precious children." Love reveals the secrets within our hearts, putting us in touch with feelings of compassion, making us more open, vulnerable, and loving human beings.

The longing we feel to love and be loved can lead us to make great sacrifices. Some of us leave family and home to be with a man we love. Candice met a man from Australia. "We fell madly in love, and I moved to Australia with him. We got married, and two years later we had our son. I left my home, my family, my friends, and all that was familiar just to be with him."

"I'd been divorced for two years when I fell in love with Micah," said Emily. "We dated for a year before he admitted to me that he couldn't have kids. I had one child and desperately wanted more, but I loved him and we decided together that we would get married and deal later with the choice of adopting or my getting artificially inseminated. I always thought that I'd have a few more kids with the man I married, but I've accepted that this isn't an option."

Some of us have to sacrifice for love because of the prejudice that others show us. "I met Jared in a marketing class we were both taking as part of the MBA program at a local university," said Bev. "Neither of us had been in a mixed racial relationship before. I didn't think it would be any big deal to my educated and progressive family, so I took him to my cousin's wedding to introduce him to everyone. My parents were furious, first because I hadn't told them, and second because I was exposing my kids to such a difficult situation. I didn't think it was difficult, but the deeper we got into this argument, the more hurtful it became. As my relationship with Jared went on, my family made it very clear that I had to choose him or them. Well, I chose him, and it's been two years since my parents have spoken to me." Lovers have to be very brave. They risk a lot for the gift they receive.

Love Then and Now

Most of us, having been married and divorced, feel that we have a much deeper understanding of love at this point in our lives than we did the first time around. When I married at twenty-two, the attraction I felt toward my husband was the strongest feeling I had felt in my life, so I easily labeled it love. Then after having children and feeling a different kind of unconditional love for them, I began to see how many conditions my husband and I placed on love. I loved that he was good-looking, successful, athletic, financially stable, original, and unpredictable. He loved that I was pretty, capable, compassionate, creative, and good breeding stock! Would I have loved him just for being himself if he'd had no accomplishments to his name? Probably not. The same would have been true for him. All we had to go on was the depiction of love we saw in movies or what we'd felt in our teenage romances or what we saw in our parents' relationships, which wasn't much, since people of their generation kept their love lives to themselves. We didn't understand what loving someone meant, and we had no idea what love would ask of us.

Many of the women I interviewed told me they felt the same way. Most of us didn't receive lessons in love: what healthy attachment is, how easy it is to mistake lust for love, or how to show compassion without being codependent. We just fell into it—our family and friends saw the look in our eyes, and by then it was too late. Nobody talks about the natural progression that love takes as we live day to day with someone who is completely different from us.

"After my divorce, in all the soul-searching I realized that I did not know what love was," said Debbie. "Now I know. It is having someone there for you emotionally, physically, and mentally. It is knowing that you can count on this person to be there, that he loves, respects, honors, and cherishes you. It is knowing that when you have an argument, you can talk it out. It is about being grounded and calm, not screaming, pushing, and then storming out. We made some of these vows on our wedding day, we said some of these same things, but the actual living of them made no sense to me. They were part of some pledge that I hoped to honor, but I didn't learn what it meant to cherish someone until I felt cherished by the man I'm in love with now."

Maybe this new understanding of love is possible only after the experience of failure and inadequacy. Perhaps the pain we feel after divorce or other great loss opens us up to experiencing love at a much deeper and more honest, sustainable level. Divorce might have helped us redefine love in more realistic terms. "Nothing really bad had happened in my life before the divorce, nothing that made me feel that depth of despair," said Heidi. "The divorce closed the book on the fairy-tale image of love as being undying passion and tenderness. Sure, I'd learned about love during the marriage—that it was hard to feel kindness or even to like someone day after day. But I just thought the negative feelings I had for my husband were unusual to me and that I had picked the wrong person. Now that I've been out in the dating world and have fallen in love once, I realize that falling in love is the easy part. At some point, lovers have to switch from seeing each other as the other's savior and begin to accept all the faults and imperfections that make us who we are. My marriage failed partially because I never got to that point of acceptance. I wanted my husband to create within me what I thought love was supposed to feel like." Heidi now has an understanding of how to be independent and to fulfill many of her own needs, so she comes to a new relationship able to give as much as she expects to take.

Loving again requires the same kind of courage it takes for a woman to have a second baby. Before the birth of the first, you are oblivious to the physical pain you will go through to deliver that baby. When you approach giving birth a second time, you may feel excitement, anticipation, and a desire to have another child, but in the back of your mind you also know what it is going to take to give that baby life. In the same way, we go into our first marriages full of hope and trust in the power of love to get us through all difficulties. Then we experience divorce, with its loss of love, broken dreams. Over time and with much work, the heart heals and we open ourselves to a new way of thinking about love. It takes courage to create that new view and then to step forward into a new place of uncertainty, opening ourselves up to love and the renewed risk of pain.

"I'm really proud of myself," said Valerie. "I did the whole postdivorce thing—gained weight, felt sorry for myself, was depressed for months—and then I swung into full gear, pulling my career and my personal life back in order. I began to date, fell immediately in love with a man who was only interested in sex, got hurt again, and figured that maybe love was just too painful. Then a month later I decided I'd thrown myself into love before I was ready, so I backed up and decided to take things slowly. I wanted to get to know myself as a new woman instead of the woman who had been married for fifteen years. Now I can stand back and see that I wasn't in love with that man; I had fallen in love with my own potential and the possibilities I saw within myself that loving brought out." Understanding ourselves and love at this new level brings out the courage to love again.

Many of us went into our marriage believing that love and sex go together. With years and experience we now know that there is a big difference between wanting to have sex with someone, needing to feel close, being tired of feeling lonely, and opening yourself up to love. It is fine to have sex, to enjoy a man's company, and to experience intimacy without opening yourself up to love. All romantic interactions do not need to have the goal of love in mind, even though the moment love is realized seems to be the climax of the romance novels millions of women read as they sigh with hope. Most of the time these novels show two strong characters. The reader knows they are falling in love, but the lovers themselves are the last to know, and often their love needs to overcome some adversity. Not so different, although often more glamorous, than our own love affairs. There is this vulnerability we get to see when the two characters admit their feelings to each other. Rarely do they come to the point of making love, spending months together, and then deciding that love just isn't going to happen. But keep that option in mind, because even if you do have the courage to open your heart to love, it doesn't mean you are going to feel it in every relationship. That is why love is called a gift. If you are open to receiving it, love will find you. The only unknown factor is *when* it will find you.

Getting Ready to Love

Many women, when I asked them about falling in love, said, "I'm not ready yet." What does that mean exactly? On one hand, falling in love just seems to happen. A man walks into your life, and your body takes a free-fall seemingly out of your control. But is it really so unexpected? Would we fall in love if we hadn't opened up something inside of us that allowed those emotions a place? Think of other times in your life, like right after the divorce, in the depths of the worst pain. Could you have fallen in love? We all recognize that some preparation of the heart is needed for love to take root.

But how does one prepare a heart for love? Taking time to do our emotional healing after divorce is a big ingredient. But where the subject of new love is concerned, it helps to have a few positive emotional experiences to help replace the bad ones. "I met one special guy on-line," said Jean. "After my kids went to bed, I would have 'my' time, and we would type madly to each other, sharing thoughts and feelings I'd never shared with a man before. After a few months we began to talk on the phone as well, developing a friendship. Over a six-month period, I felt myself open up emotionally, and the scars that had been left from my marriage started to be replaced with these new images of what relationship could be. He started telling me that he loved me, and we hadn't even met in person. I knew I loved him too, but I was skeptical not knowing whether or not there would be any physical attraction. We arranged a meeting in a nearby city and had a lovely weekend. The intensity of the attraction was unbelievable! I cried the whole way home; both of us were distraught about being apart. After my divorce, I didn't think I could ever feel for someone again, because I felt so hurt by my ex-husband. I guess the relationship progressed at a slow enough pace that I had a chance to heal and to be ready for love." Part of getting ready for love is being willing to take it slowly, to feel your way around to see what still needs healing, and to be comfortable before committing yourself to love.

"I knew I was ready for love when feeling came back into my life in every area," said Jaclyn. "I began to laugh more, to have more energy to do fun things with my kids and friends. My problems didn't seem to rule my mind. I began to notice men and feel flirtatious energy beginning to stir. I knew I still had a lot of love in my heart to give after the divorce, but I didn't realize how much I had been craving being loved in return. It had been so long since I'd been told I was beautiful or had someone who couldn't wait to hear about my day." Like many women, Jaclyn began to feel the yearning inside her to give love another try. Life seemed to lighten up as she became more in touch with the feelings she didn't have time to feel or acknowledge following the pain of divorce.

"I knew I was ready when I began to say it to those around me," said Candice. "I had been in counseling for a few months, and one day I told my therapist it was time to date. We discussed what type of man would work best for my personality, and I said I'm very type-A and thrive with people who go '100 miles an hour with their hair on fire.' The next day I needed to visit a friend in the hospital who had just had a baby. I was green with envy as I thought she had it all—a second baby, which I also wanted so desperately, a devoted husband, the option of staying home with her children. The whole way to the hospital I kept saying, 'Why can't I just meet a nice guy? He doesn't have to be rich or good-looking, just nice.' Well, I was running late and drove too fast into the parking lot and almost hit this guy. There he was, looking very much the bum after a hard day of work! Here I am, Miss White-Collar, private-college-educated, and Gary a country bumpkin who owns his own company and drives a beat-up truck. We talked a little before I went into the hospital. When I came back out he was still sitting on the bench next to my car. He had waited for *two hours* for me! At one point he'd had to go but called a friend to wait on the bench, telling him, 'If a woman tries to get into that white car, stop her!' We've been together ever since." Ideas are more powerful than we give them credit for, as Candice demonstrated with her announcement to the world that it was her time to date. Everything just fell into place after that.

It Only Happens When We Love Ourselves First

Recently, Al and I had an interesting conversation about self-love. I suggested that in a relationship where both people are self-loving, each takes responsibility for filling their own life with positive experiences, taking care of themselves instead of expecting a loved one to do it for them. Self-love would say, "I don't need you to create peace in my life. I will do it myself, then invite you to join me." It doesn't mean living selfish, self-centered lives. Rather, it means thinking enough of yourself to set limits and expectations that don't make you dependent on the relationship for your happiness. If both people could develop this sort of self-knowledge and self-love, then it seems the neediness would disappear. Neither person would feel the burden of the other, and they both could share and enjoy what the other had to offer the relationship.

Al agreed that the concept sounded good, but he said that every great spiritual leader has taught that the highest form of love is to love another above yourself. As he kissed me goodnight that evening he said, "I'm still going to try to love you first."

I lay awake thinking about his comment, uncomfortable with its implications. That is how I had loved my ex-husband—above myself. The problem was, both of us were putting his needs first. I loved him first, and he loved him first. So I had no energy or love left for myself. Through that tough experience, I had learned that if you place your center of love within your partner instead of yourself, then you can lose yourself if the other person leaves. "I placed all my love safely within my husband," said Fiona. "Unfortunately, all that love disappeared when he left." But if the center of love is within yourself, then you are free to choose to be in the relationship with a full heart.

I believe the real challenge is to love our partner as ourselves—not more than, but not less than, either. Discernment can help us determine, one incident at a time, how we will express our self-love and our love for our partner, and how we will balance our own wants and needs with those our partner has expressed to us. Sometimes that may mean putting our own needs first, while other times we may need to work out a compromise in order to achieve a shared goal. Compromise is a valuable skill to have in one's relationship tool bag; it's the ability to give up some of our images of the relationship at those moments when our partner has a different image than we do. But the burden of compromise must always be shared. Relationship is *never* about doing just what one person wants, without any feedback from the other. In a healthy relationship, both partners will constantly be considering what are they giving up and what are they getting in return and how they balance the two in a way that reflects both their self-love and their love of the other.

How a woman learns to love herself is outlined in chapter 4. The challenge in the present chapter is to figure out how to maintain that self-love while in intimate relationship with another. It takes loving ourselves unconditionally to stay in a relationship for the long term. Some of us grew up feeling loved because we earned it; we received good grades and did what our parents expected of us. We may still only love the parts of ourselves that meet our personal standards and believe that we need to act or be a certain way to earn our partner's love. Love that has to be earned is not a healthy love; it forces us to make choices we don't want to make just to be loved. It is especially hard to love ourselves with this kind of unconditional acceptance if the person we love still operates from a place of judgment over us. So how can we love ourselves with this unconditional acceptance if we have not yet experienced it in our lives? How do we learn to stand our ground and take care of ourselves in relationship?

"It has taken me years to understand what the word *unconditional* means," said Hilary. "It means loving my body even when it doesn't look great, loving my talent even when a script I write is turned down, loving the home I've created even if I don't own it. Believe me, the word sounds nice, but it's very hard to make it real. I've been trying to love my boyfriend unconditionally too, and that is even harder. Especially when I'd like to go for a walk rather than drink beer and watch TV after dinner. I have to go for that walk anyway, with or without him, knowing that this is a way of expressing love for myself instead of turning my disappointment into judgment of him." Hilary's story is a great example of how we can balance self-love with love of other. If our partner can't support us in one moment in something we need to do for ourselves, then we do that thing alone. We hope that next time our partner will participate in ways that nurture our own wholeness, but if he doesn't, we still have to take the time to do it for ourselves.

Many women say it takes a complete shift within them to reach this level of acceptance. "One thing my therapist suggested I do to help me focus on my positive attributes instead of all the negative ones was to make a list of adjectives that describe me, both positive and negative," said Holly. "She told me to repeat the positive words with acknowledgment and joy that I have these gifts. With the negative words, she said to ask myself if there are positive things about them. For example, my ex-husband used to call me manipulative and bitchy, but those words could also mean directed and assertive, which are good qualities." This small exercise helped Holly view some of her qualities in a new light. What others see as negative may be pointers toward our inner strengths; sometimes our wounds become our greatest gifts.

Love of self can also lead us to make decisions that may cause problems in the relationship. "I've been with my boyfriend Jack for five years, and I love him with all my heart and soul," said Kay. "I have been living in Arizona for twenty years and have felt for the past five years that I don't want to live here anymore. I want to begin a new chapter of my life up in Washington. Jack doesn't want to go, but he could easily go since he has no family here and could get a similar job in Washington. We've talked about this for years without agreeing, so I've decided to make the move. We are not breaking up; I just need space to get myself together and validate my need to be someplace else. We have decided to see each other every three months and at the end of a year decide where we go from there. I'm hoping to get a business going and have him move to Washington. I'm sure he is hoping I'll come back to Arizona. We don't have children together, and we aren't married, so I guess making this decision is easier." Kay has taken a scary step, but in being true to who she is and what she wants, she may risk losing the relationship.

There are no easy answers in love. It is possible to fully love another, to listen with an open heart, to love that person unconditionally, *and* to love yourself with the same intensity and value. It just takes practice and a willingness to examine how our actions affect both ourselves and those we love.

Celebrating Your Love

When love happens, embrace it. Celebrate the incredible gift you have been given. Make a promise to yourself to take it all in, to sparkle with the glow, to let yourself have it for a while without pulling out your notebook to analyze whether or not the man is exactly who you want. Let love fill you. Set aside all your fears and doubts, and play with all the new feelings. Pull some of them inward and let them wash through your body, taking with them the past pain that is stuck in hard-to-reach places. Be childlike and dance in celebration in your front yard. Stand in front of the mirror and giggle. Wrap yourself in the warmth of love. "The week after Nathan told me he loved me, I planned a party for all my girlfriends," said Tess. "I was just so full of energy and thankfulness. All my friends, and my mother and sister, had listened for years to my agony. They consoled me in my tears, took my kids when I just couldn't cope, and stood by my side even when I was wrong. I called each of them and invited them to the party without telling them what the party was for. I took the time to write a note to each of them, thanking them for loving me through my darkest time. My kids helped me decorate with crepe paper, and then I made posters that said 'I'm in Love' and hung them with the balloons. When they arrived, I announced that it was a love party. We drank wine, listened to music, laughed, and celebrated together my transition from despair to hope." Tess wasn't afraid to enjoy her love for what it was. Whether or not it was going to last wasn't the point. She was celebrating the courage it had taken her to open her heart to love.

Too often, love walks into our lives and we dampen its impact with a list of all the things that are wrong with the relationship: "He lives in another state, doesn't want to live in the country, talks too much about himself." All these things dull the glow of love, almost as if we are afraid of the power of our own feelings. "The first time I fell in love after my divorce, I only felt happy with it for a week. After that, I started to pick the relationship apart," said Irene. "Granted, some of the things would have kept me from marrying the man, but not all love has to lead to marriage. Sometimes love just happens and is part of your life for a while as a tool to learn and heal. I regret now that I wasn't able to celebrate that love because it took me three years to fall in love again. I wish I had given it at least six months before I started trying to set up the perfect marriage. My probing into everything turned the exciting part of love into what felt like a business meeting. When I fell in love the next time, I didn't make that mistake. Instead I went along for the ride and figured out all the relationship stuff in tiny bits and pieces along the way, while we were having fun." There will always be time to work on the parts of the relationship that need it, but there will not always be another chance to enjoy the beginning stage of falling in love.

It is possible to celebrate love even if the love isn't returned as you had hoped or if you can't take the next step toward building a life together. If you entered the relationship loving yourself, honoring your desire to experience love yet knowing that you would still be a whole person if the relationship ended, then each new love experience has the potential to add to your life. "I met and fell in love with Wayne three years ago," said Leah. "We lived in different states but tried several times to make a long-distance relationship work. I flew back recently hoping to come up with some sort of plan, but we ended the relationship instead. I now know how much courage it takes to move forward. New love is very frightening. It takes a willingness to risk again. Realistically, I knew that this first relationship right after the divorce might not work. I knew there was no guarantee, but it was time to risk opening my heart."

Leah reflected that this time she had a much healthier definition of love. "I was not willing to be in a relationship again where I was the only team member. I was not willing to dangle on a string in the hope that one day I could earn more of his love. I now understand love to be an exchange that must be negotiated from the beginning. Although the relationship ended, I am happy that I had the courage to risk opening my heart again. Because of that, I trust myself more. I was able to beat back the fear. I still care very much for this man. However, I won't need months to get over this failed relationship because I walked away asking myself, what can I learn? For me, I grew in the ability to negotiate a better deal for myself and also to respect that he was trying to do the same. It didn't work this time, but maybe next time it will." As Leah found out, love doesn't always go the way we wish it would go. Still, what we gain from love can outweigh the loss we feel if it ends.

The intensity of the first love relationship after divorce defies description; all the pain, the longing to prove to yourself that you are lovable, the work you've done to know yourself better, and sexual starvation get poured into your partner. This new relationship is healing to you. Love removes all flaws and places the loved one beyond reproach. Enjoy this stage with every cell in your body, because you are going to need those memories if you want to build the kind of long-term love that makes for a solid relationship.

11

Building the Relationship

When you fall in love, things may feel crystal clear. You enter the relationship fully prepared to share yourself with this man who seems to fit every requirement you ever imagined. He actually knows how to listen—and remembers everything you tell him! The new relationship is healing to you.

Yet in the whirlwind of new love, all things are *not* clear. It takes self-control to step back and acknowledge that this man, a human being with flaws yet to be seen, is not your savior and to live each day of the relationship as it comes instead of projecting into the future (and how incredible you *will* be together). Yet if you can do that, you may get a clearer view of whether or not the relationship is a long-term, committed possibility or a short-term place to grow, heal, and learn more about yourself in relationship.

"When I fell in love with David, my world stopped, and I remember telling friends that I would do the whole divorce over just to feel for two weeks the way I felt with him," said Sylvia. "One of the women in my single-mother group shared the experience of her first love relationship after divorce and the mistakes she made moving so quickly into plans for the future. They ended up getting married a year after her divorce and then getting divorced three years later. She said they went right from this intense being in love to planning their future life without dealing with the more mundane step of building a foundation for the relationship. With her advice in mind, I decided not to worry if we had any future together and instead to give myself all the time in the world to get to know him. It's been two years, we are still together, still taking the relationship one small step at a time, and we still feel a passionate desire to be together."

The first step in building a lasting relationship is to build it slowly. Don't rush. Avoid the temptation to prove you've succeeded in getting your life back on track. Instead, learn, grow, and be willing to walk away if you realize that during the growth process your needs have changed and the relationship no longer works. The goal is to take it slowly enough so that everything you want to know about your lover, about yourself, and the way the two of you work together in relationship can be revealed layer by layer.

Choosing to love someone brings with it many relationship options. You might be hoping that this is it, the love that will lead to commitment and forever. Or maybe you're skeptical, willing to experience love but not sure whether you're ready to do the work it takes to build a relationship that will lead to marriage. You may be afraid that the relationship will fail, compounding the damage done by the loss of your marriage to you and your kids. Maybe you are struggling to balance your role as passionate lover and nurturing mother. Perhaps you're confused about how to introduce your kids, what to tell them about the relationship, or how much parenting power to give to your lover. This chapter will try to shed light on many of the confusing thoughts that occur as you move forward in a love relationship.

So Many Questions

It took a while for me to settle into the love Al and I had professed for each other. In the beginning I wondered about the little things, like how often he should come over, how involved he would be with my kids, whether or not I should allow him to stay the night. I began to look hard at his strengths as a father, how he might be as a husband, if he would remain my friend after the passion subsided. I worried most about his ability to handle the reality of my having four kids and a job. It wasn't a problem when he only came over for dinner two or three nights a week; I made a point to have all the kids' homework done, manage any of the major issues from the day, and be relaxed and ready to enjoy the relationship by the time he walked through the door. But that was a pattern I knew I couldn't sustain on a daily basis. It was also clear that we would get little to no time alone since my ex lived across the country and we didn't have any kind of regular visitation schedule. I was afraid that over time Al might resent the fact that on his weekends away from his kids, mine would be ever present. Every hard-earned moment of alone time would have to be orchestrated. Also, my kids were old enough to figure out that if we were going away for the weekend, we were sleeping together. It was easy with Al to bare my soul, to tell him everything I felt about most everything, but it was harder for me to talk about my fears about the relationship. I wanted so badly for it to work. There were times that the list of questions and decisions to be made just to be with him had me throwing my arms in the air and vowing celibacy!

The relationship needed room to grow. It was up to Al and me to create the space, to establish the honesty, and then to choose the direction we were going to take as a couple. It will be up to you to fit together all the pieces that make up the relationship you want to create in a way that works for you, your lover, and your kids. There will be many questions that only you can answer. This may feel scary at first as you turn to others, hoping that they will validate your life choices. Later you may discover that the clearest answers must come from your own heart and inner understanding of who you are and what you want. Of course, all the issues discussed in this chapter will happen within their own time frame, perhaps over many months or years. The idea is to give yourself a place to think about where you want to go with this love and to determine how it will fit into your current life.

Here are a few of the questions that crossed my mind when I was ready to open my life up to loving again.

1. When is the right time to tell the kids about a new relationship?
2. How much do you tell the kids about the person you are dating?
3. What role will the relationship have in your family life?
4. How will your boyfriend interact with your children?
5. Is there a way to build the relationship through fun and friendship?
6. How much of the couple relationship should take place with the kids?
7. What if the kids don't like your boyfriend at all, but you love him and want to stay with him or even marry him?

My first thoughts were not about establishing a solid, private relationship with a lover; instead, I was wondering how I'd introduce the concept to my kids and how everyone would get along. The answer to the questions helped me feel comfortable with the shift I was making from the solitude of my inner healing phase to having a man share my life and possibly the lives of my children. There are many things to think about and all sorts of situations to take into consideration when making decisions on issues like these.

The most important step in answering the questions is to trust your own intuition, to go with your gut feeling even if you wish the answers you receive were different. Remember the exercise we did in chapter 2 to learn to recognize our own voice? Sit with a pen and piece of paper, and ask yourself the question that is on your mind. Write down the first thing that pops into your head. This is your intuitive, gut-level response. Now, as you enter an intimate relationship with another, is the time you will appreciate all the hard work you've done in learning to listen to and trust your own voice.

Next, try to imagine the results of your answer for a few days as you go through the routines of your day. Imagine your lover eating dinner with the family or helping with homework or attending a school function. Then decide how you would feel about it. Last, be honest with yourself about how you feel when you use your imagination and slip your lover's face into family situations, like a holiday celebration or your mother's birthday party. If you are uncomfortable with anything, wait until you feel good about it.

When is the right time to tell the kids about a new relationship? "I've always liked keeping my kids informed about relationships that last past three dates," said Kacey. "I keep it light, mention where we go, like if we saw a good concert or movie, tell them a few things I like about the guy, maybe what he does for a living, but I don't introduce him to my kids. I don't think it's fair to the kids to say nothing at all. They are curious, just like I am curious about the friends they spend time with. Maybe I don't tell them about dates I go on when they aren't at home, but I try to be as honest with them as I'd like them to be with me."

Some children, depending on their age and temperament, will want to hear more or less about their parent's private life. Justin, a boy of eleven, says, "I don't really want to hear any details about my mom's dates. I want her to have a good time. I don't mind hearing where she is going or with whom, but details would just embarrass me." Paige, who is thirteen, says, "I think it is kind of fun to hear about dating. I wish my mom would give me more details. I don't know yet what it's like to go on a date. Getting that from my mom gives me information that helps me prepare for my own dating someday."

How much do you tell the kids about the person you are dating? "If I go out with someone more than a few times, I'm willing to tell my kids about my date," said Gayle. "I used to sit down with the kids and tell them all about the man. Now I tell them it's up to them to ask me what they want to know, and I'll be happy to tell them. In the beginning of this process, I wanted to be so careful to do everything right, to say the right thing at the right time. Now I know that my kids are caught up in their own lives and problems and don't really care that much how I spend my free time. I mean, they care about me, but it isn't like they are sitting at home waiting for a complete recap of the date, like I would be if it were them!"

Kelley said, "I think it is better to draw a line of privacy where my personal life is concerned. Sure, if I fall in love with someone, the relationship is getting serious, or the kids are going to meet him, then I'll tell them a little about him. I think it is better for them to have just a few basic facts and then build a friendship, just like they would if they met anyone else for the first time. I don't say a whole lot about my kids to my dates either. I know how embarrassing it can be for a kid to meet an adult who seems to know their life story." The range of responses women give here shows how each woman must answer the question in whatever way fits her personality and beliefs and those of her family.

How do you want your boyfriend to interact with your children? "Like a family friend," said Kelsey. "I don't want there to be any thought in my kids' minds that this is someone who is coming into their lives to tell them what to do. I would talk to my boyfriend about basic rules in our house, would expect that he follow those rules, and that he understood fully that kids learn by what they see. If he has kids of his own, we would most likely discuss his style of parenting, how he interacts with his kids, and in whatever ways we differ would have to come up with a compromise. Which to me might mean that we both agree to act whichever way the child's parent asked us to."

"I would hope to build the kids' relationship with him through fun experiences," said Faith. "I don't think I'd have my boyfriend over for chore time. Instead, I'd plan some sort of outing like bowling or ice skating. I'd probably do that for the first few months of interaction before I invited him to participate in family time in our home."

How much of the couple relationship should take place with the kids? "It was so uncomfortable the first time Matt was around me and the kids," said Alice. "We didn't know whether or not to hold hands. We would reach for each other, then pull away when we registered that the kids were there. I didn't know if I should sit next to him at the movies or between my two kids, where I usually sit. Matt usually paid for our dates, but I felt that since the kids were with us, I should pay. He grabbed the bill just as I did, and we kind of stared at each other, questioning. After this first family date, we both realized we needed to talk about how much of a couple we were going to be in front of the kids. We came to the conclusion that holding hands, putting arms around each other for short times, and looking into each other's eyes were all fine. We decided not to kiss each other, even a small good-bye kiss, until the kids seemed more comfortable with the situation."

"The major issue concerning couple time for me," said Clair, "is that I don't have much time for anything. I work full-time, with different hours than my boyfriend, so it works best for me if I can see my boyfriend while I'm home with my three-year-old. My son seems to have a great time when we are all together, and we get him to bed at an early enough time so we can enjoy dinner and a movie at home. I hope in the future to be able to afford a baby-sitter more often and to get our work schedule on the same page. But for now, I think this works."

And what if the kids don't like your boyfriend at all, but you love him and want to stay with him and are considering marrying him? This can be the toughest question of all. "I spent many a night crying over the first man I fell in love with," said Violet. "I loved him. He thought the kids were all right, but they hated him. He didn't have kids of his own, and I think they picked up on his attitude that they should be better behaved. He never made a comment to them, but he would say things to me, like when I would start to pick up the kids' backpacks and stuff. Or if I would get them a glass of water, he would tell me I wasn't the kids' slave. There were also a few times when my son made a negative comment about me that he jumped in and told them how wonderful I was and that my son should appreciate me. I liked that, but the kids didn't. I didn't want to break up with him based on my kids' opinion, because I was afraid they would then get power hungry and think they could decide who I loved. In the end he gracefully left the relationship to date someone who had no kids, but I was heartbroken. I'm not sure what I could have done to help the kids like him more."

Most kids like positive attention of any kind. If you want your kids to like your boyfriend, encourage him to take an interest in something the child is interested in. Maybe he could attend a sporting event with them or take them to an art museum or a skateboard shop. If he finds newspaper or magazine articles on a subject of interest to your kids, ask him to cut them out and give them to the child, or encourage him to bring up topics they're interested in. Too often adults think it is the kids who should be the welcoming ones, but it rarely works that way. The adult who is entering the family needs to do some important work so that he'll be seen as a fun, interesting, caring addition to the family, especially if marriage may be in the works.

Think about the questions you have as you move forward and begin to build the kind of relationship you really want. Don't be afraid of the answers. Instead, use them to inform yourself as you mold and shape your future.

Stay Committed to Yourself

Whatever choices you make as the relationship unfolds, one thing is important: don't forget yourself or your needs. Many women get so involved in the loving that they don't invest in themselves as much as they invest in the relationship. I'll repeat it one more time: self-love is important! Pay attention to the ways you enhance your own life so that you can keep your individual identity no matter what happens to the love. "It is really hard for me to focus on myself in any area of my life," said Sonja. "I think the definition of love that I hold in my heart has to do with sacrificing self for people you love. My boyfriend and I have gotten to the stage where one of us is going to have to move in order to be together. If I were focused on loving myself, I'd ask him to move to our town. After all, I have kids who are already in school and he doesn't. But I also know that in order for the relationship to work, there is compromise involved all the time." For Sonja to practice loving herself, she will need to give her own point of view full consideration, regarding it as just as important as her boyfriend's. Then she can make her decision not from a place of being a martyr, but instead with full knowledge of what she is choosing to do.

A good beginning discussion is how the two of you will make sure that neither one of you is making all the compromises. If the compromise always seems to be weighted in one person's favor, then do something to even things out. This makes for true partnership rather than one person sacrificing all, as women used to be asked to do. Doing whatever it takes to become a whole person might mean making choices your lover doesn't like or agree with, but in the long run working through these choices in a way that respects each person's right to the life of their choice is going to do more for the relationship than sacrifice. Stand up for yourself as you love your partner.

It is equally important to invest time in the relationship. Ask the intimate questions, find out about your childhoods, discuss your beliefs, ask what his goals are and how he views family. Time away from the kids to enjoy each other as a couple is equally important. "Within the first six months of our relationship, Kevin asked me to go on a rafting and camping trip," said Carol. "He loved camping, and we had decided early on that we wanted to share in each other's hobbies as a way to get to know each other. All I could think of when he asked me was that there would be no hair dryer and probably little camp-size mirrors, outdoor toilets, and a river shower if I was lucky. Immediately I began to negotiate a weekend in the wine country if I made it through the trip. Throughout my marriage, we always did whatever my ex-husband wanted to do, and I didn't want to get into that self-sacrificing habit again with Kevin. The trip was an absolute blast! We slept in a tent with a flap that allowed us to look up at the stars. Even though it added weight to his back-pack, Kevin brought an inflatable mattress so that my first camping experience wouldn't be so hard. He even brought candles to put on the ground while we ate our freeze-dried and boiled dinner. Being away from everyone and every-thing gave us hours to talk about our childhood memories, what scared us, just little things you don't always get to discuss in dinner conversations when you have to leave in two hours to get the baby-sitter home." Sometimes to grow in relationship, we have to take risks and do things that aren't exactly our first choice. The fun part is finding out ways to spend time together that we might never have enjoyed in the past.

Different ages and stages in life also present a challenge for lovers. You've been married before—maybe he has too—so you have different starting points. Perhaps one person has children and is through with that stage, but their lover has no children and was looking forward to parenting. Maybe one person was hoping to retire at age fifty, while the other has too many financial responsibilities to retire before age seventy. This may not be a problem if your plan is to have a short-term love affair, but if you are looking at a committed, long-term relationship, it may be important to clearly define the stage in your life you see yourself. "My daughter was two when I met Mike," said Virginia. "He was twelve years older than me. His kids were starting high school, and he wasn't sure he wanted more kids. I wanted at least one more child because I was an only child and had felt lonely all my life. As time went on, it became clear that we were not going to be able to bridge this gap no matter how much we loved each other."

"I had been in medical school for one year when I met Harry," said Jade. "From the beginning, I could feel his resentment build toward the time I had to put into my studies. I kept reminding him that I had to support my kids, that this was a dream of mine, that there would be some amount of sacrifice if we wanted the relationship to work. He left after a year, telling me that he loved me but needed to be more important in my life. Six months later he called and we started dating again. He said he used that time to process his neediness. He decided that he fell in love with me for all the traits that had landed me in medical school with the goal of doing something with my life. After a few dates with the type of woman who would set her life aside for him, he decided he wanted the kind of independence our relationship had from the beginning." Jade said she learned a huge lesson from this experience. "In the past, if I wanted a man, I would do whatever I had to in order to hold on to him. In this case, I was very clear with Harry about where I was in my life and where I planned to go. It felt great!" Both Virginia and Jade were able to step back from the love they felt in order be clear about the stage of life they were in and then honestly accept the outcome without trying to manipulate their own dreams so that the relationship might work. It is important to address these issues early on and make sure your own stage of life goals and needs are given room before moving ahead to build a long-term relationship.

Balancing Your Life

A big challenge for many women is learning how to balance the life they want to create as a girlfriend with the responsibility they feel to be a good role model and loving mother. From the first months of my relationship with Al, I struggled with this. I felt a growing passion and need to be with him, to devote my energy to the relationship, and to find time to get in touch with myself as a woman. But my kids still had the same needs and expectations and were very used to having me all to themselves. "One difficult situation for me is that my kids expect me to stay home with them *all* weekend whenever it is my weekend to have them," said Lana. "I've started dating, maybe four dates a month, but I have the kids three weekends a month. My daughter complains ruthlessly about how I don't care about her at all if I'm willing to leave her when she doesn't see me that often. I try to point out that my mother, who is usually the baby-sitter, would like a little time with them as well. I work all week too, take care of all the household responsibility, and I want some time for a social life without having to explain myself to a ten-year-old. I'm not sure what to do."

Balance is the key here. When I had the same issue with my kids, I told them that if I couldn't go out on dates, then they couldn't go to friends' houses either, and we would spend all of our time together! My kids are all over ten and value their own social time, so that made this conversation much easier to have. This explanation may be harder with younger kids, who may need more reassurance of their mother's devotion. In any case, it is necessary to set some expectations with the children about your need for a social life. Kids have friends; they will understand if you explain that just as they would rather play games with their friends, you would rather see an adult movie with an adult. This doesn't mean you don't love them with all your heart.

Georgia said, "When I told my kids I was ready to start dating, I assured them that I was not looking for a replacement father or someone to walk into our lives and take over the household jobs their father left behind. I was looking for fun and friendship, and I made that very clear. I told them that they would not be meeting any of my dates unless the relationship got to a point where I loved that person. My kids were teenagers, so I had to add a few extra rules: they were not allowed to ask me personal questions about my date, like whether or not we kissed. In exchange, I had to stop asking them similar questions, which I greatly missed!" Dating is a natural part of a woman's post-divorce life. It isn't easy to begin this process under your kids' noses, with the inevitable questions and opinions that accompany life as part of a family. If you find a way to take it lightly like Georgia did, making it seem perfectly natural that she would want to meet and to spend time with men, the process is much easier.

Balance between your mother and lover selves is needed also as you develop the physical side of your new relationship. Children are likely to want you to wear a mother uniform, not a sexy dress, a bit low cut, like the one I wore on the first fancy date with Al. So I shouldn't have been surprised when their first comment on seeing me was "You're wearing *that?* You look like a prostitute!" So much for my budding self-confidence! I went back to my closet to look for more conservative options, but this was the first dress I'd bought in over a year. No, I decided I would wear it. I wanted to feel good in it and to let Al know that I wasn't just a mom who looked okay in jeans, I could also be sexy. My children had a right to their own opinion about how I dressed, but I also had a right to express myself as a woman. I sat in my room, brooding and sad that I had to feel so conflicted about the roles I played in my life. I tried to be understanding toward these children who weren't happy that the man at the door was not their dad and who I'm sure would have been delighted if I lived manless for the rest of my life. Yet I felt confused, wondering if I was doing the right thing.

A few months later the second mother-lover conflict arose. I wanted Al to sleep at my house. There were no other options if we wanted to be together. In order for me to go to his apartment, I had to hire a baby-sitter, which I could afford only once a month. The kids rarely went away as a group or left me alone with time enough to create a romantic interlude. But I didn't want my children to get the impression that it was okay to sleep with just anyone. So Al and I decided that if he slept over, he would park his car on another street and leave before any of the kids got up. This arrangement worked wonderfully for about six months, until one morning my daughter got up early to go swimming. She caught a glimpse of Al heading for the door and screamed, "I knew you slept here!" That evening Al and I talked with all the kids about our feelings for each other. Al told them how much he loved me and that he planned to stay in my life. But that whole day I felt like a terrible mother, scared that I wasn't a good role model and sure that I had ruined my kids' view of relationship. I would much rather have had the space and opportunity to conduct our love lives away from my kids. In hindsight, I might have done some things differently, but I did the best I could at the time.

You will make mistakes, learn by trial and error, and sit confused at times as you try to balance the conflicting needs and demands on your time. But one thing is sure: if you don't carve out a space in your life for your relationship with a new partner to grow in a natural way, you will begin to resent your life, your kids, and the responsibilities you have. "My kids were pretty cool about my dating from the beginning," said Madison. "Maybe that was because their dad left me and I'd been a wreck for a few years. They were happy to see me laughing and enjoying myself again. When I fell in love, their attitude changed slightly. It was a time thing—they still wanted me to be available to them whenever they needed me and wished my life would continue revolving around them. I got fed up with their expectations and decided to have a family meeting. I talked to them about how divorce, a new family structure and having to work and manage the home were all new concepts to me. Dating was a new concept too, something I hadn't done in seventeen years. By the end of the conversation, everyone had a much clearer view of the teamwork it was going to take to get us through this stage in our lives. None of us had really chosen it, but I wasn't willing to sit back and have no fun in my life just because my kids set unrealistic expectations for me." As Madison discovered, women who give themselves some of what they need are happier and more fulfilled, which ultimately allows them to be both good mothers and exciting lovers.

Introducing the Kids to Your New Love

How lucky for your new love: you are a package deal; you come with a life full of children who will expand his opportunity to learn about love! You have to go into a new love with this attitude, because your kids aren't separate from your life and, for that matter, his kids aren't separate from his life. They belong to you. They are the ones who taught your hearts to love in the first place. Too often I talk to women who feel they have less to offer a man because they have children. They are afraid to give a man an accurate picture of their life for fear that if he had the whole picture he might run. And he might, but better to find out before, not after, you fall in love. "The most embarrassing thing happened when I began dating Kirby," said Ruth. "I told him I had one daughter. It was the first date, he had no kids, I was really attracted to him, and I wanted to give him a chance to get to know me before dropping the bomb that I had three kids. We went out for a couple of months, and I was trying to figure out a way to tell him the truth about the kids, when we went to a barbecue at one of his friends' house. My son's first-grade teacher was there with her husband. She walked right up to me and asked how my son was enjoying his summer. I thought I was going to faint, and Kirby looked at me like he'd just been told I robbed grocery stores in my spare time! He was pretty mad, but once I explained why I did it, I think he felt kind of sorry for me, especially when I told him how many men were interested in me until they heard the kid count." Ruth found out the hard way that honesty is always the best course of action when it comes to explaining the presence (and number!) of kids in your life. Try a gung-ho attitude—"I have the greatest kids, and you would be lucky to spend one moment with them"—and then see what happens.

One issue for many mothers is when to trust a man enough to share the kids with him. "I wonder if I will ever trust someone enough to share my son with him," said Rena. "He's my son, not anyone else's. I wouldn't want a lover to have any disciplinary participation, wouldn't want him to be anything but a friend. I would like to raise my son the way I was raised, with no spanking, and I would have a very difficult time if my lover had conflicting parenting ideas. I would tell him, 'This is how I'm doing it, and you have to stick with my rules or you can't be around my son.' That is one reason I'm not involved yet. I'm not ready to let someone else be close to my son." Trust is hard earned after divorce. It takes small steps. Most women agree that when a relationship with a man gets to the point of wanting to introduce their kids, they've had many parenting discussions and have figured out a way for their lover to build a friendship with the child in a nonthreatening way.

Some women find that the actual introductions go better when they play it cool, taking as much pressure off the meeting as possible. Georgia said, "When I did fall in love, I never gave my kids the impression that I cared whether they liked my new boyfriend or not. Of course, I did care, but I didn't set it up in such a way that he was coming over to meet them to get their approval. I love my kids, and I wouldn't choose to love a man who would hurt them in any way, so I trusted my own judgment." As Georgia found out, a positive attitude and a willingness to trust yourself with regard to the timing of the meeting can go a long way toward helping children get used to the presence of a new love in your life.

First Comes Love, Then Comes—What?

There are many paths to take when forming new relationships. Some women decide that they will date until their children leave home. Others choose to live with their partner, and still others choose marriage. Finding the path that works for you and your children is a matter of following your intuition and your heart. Sometimes it is difficult in our society to decide what is best for ourselves, because many people have opinions and they seem happy to offer opinions, along with their own value judgments, freely and often. Trusting your own decision-making process is a big part of becoming an independent person. Learning how to make difficult decisions as a couple helps to build the foundation of a working relationship. Unfortunately, the only way to learn these skills is to practice making decisions. With each decision, you will be learning more about yourself and each other.

I was raised a Catholic. Until my divorce, I believed that living together was a sinful and inappropriate choice if children were involved. Then, after going through my own traumatic divorce, I decided I would never get married again. When I met Al, I changed my mind, and we began talking about marriage. Both of us felt that, with six kids between the two of us, living together to see how the whole crew would get along would be a good first step. We purchased a one-bedroom, one-bath cottage and moved in. It was really more like camping than home living. My four kids shared the den, his two boys had a bunk bed in the living room, and we all used the same tiny bathroom on a rotating schedule. Four months later, we began remodeling, adding five bedrooms and two baths. Given the new situation, the close quarters, the impending construction, and a shared bathroom, one would have expected the experiment to end in disaster. But it didn't. The kids were fabulous, and in many ways we bonded through the suffering. Living together gave us a chance to see what marriage might be like. We learned how to work together as a family, how to make joint decisions, how to create the environment, the rules, and the friendships one small step at a time. It hasn't always been easy, but it's almost always been rewarding.

Then one day my daughter asked me if we were ever going to get married. I didn't really see a need for marriage. We were committed to a lifetime together and didn't need a piece of paper making that legal. My first marriage had been legally binding, but that didn't make it permanent. I was also afraid that marriage would change the way the relationship was working, that both of us might slack off in effort if the other one was "cornered." When I asked my daughter why she wanted us to get married, she said it was embarrassing to introduce Al as my boyfriend and then have to explain that we lived together. Al and I talked about it for a long time, wanting to make the right decision for all our kids. We concluded that it was time to get married. That was the next step if we wanted the kids to grow in relationship with one another and with each of us. The shift for Al and me was minimal. We knew the commitment we were making when we decided to live together, but it did mark a new starting point for our joined family.

I'm always amazed at how complicated love can be—all the thoughts that go on in each person's mind as they try to figure out what they want for their life. What if one person wants marriage and the other is terrified of it? How do you make the big decisions as a couple? "The first year of our relationship, I couldn't stop talking about getting married," said Gwen. "The relationship was everything I ever wanted. He liked my kids, my kids liked him, we loved each other. All I wanted to do was to walk down the aisle and to move into a house together. I'd spent three years before we met taking care of my husband, who had died of cancer, so I was ready to make a new start. Dwight wasn't ready that first year. The second year rolled around, and he started to be more open to the idea of getting married, but I was beginning to feel independent and wasn't sure if I wanted to get married, even though I did want to stay with him. We decided to go on an engagement encounter weekend so we could have some time to look at both of our needs and decide what we should do. I learned on the weekend that part of my problem with committing to him was that I was hurt because he had turned me down the first year, so in a way I was getting my revenge. Once I got past those feelings, we were able to discuss what was best for each of us, for the kids, and for the family. We ended up getting married three months later in a small wedding with only our family and friends." Wading through the issues surrounding how to be with each other in a way that each person is comfortable with may take some time.

When couples can find a way to communicate their feelings and needs in a way that is straightforward and honest, it makes the decision making much easier. In our relationship, Al and I try to put all the issues on the table, discuss them, and then somehow determine whose needs are more important in that situation or whether a compromise can give us some of what we both believe is important. In all decisions a couple makes, there has to be this kind of laying out of options, fair division of labor, time for each to think it through, followed by compromise if necessary.

When the decision being made is a life-changing one, like whether or not to live together or to get married, it helps to have had lots of practice communicating as a couple in making small decisions. The way you work together with small conflicts sets the pattern for how you will manage the bigger, more difficult situations that inevitably arise in life. It is important to give each person plenty of time to say everything that is on their mind before brainstorming possible choices or solutions. Then keep listening to each other until a decision can be agreed upon. A solution exists that will allow your relationship the space it needs to grow.

Building a relationship after divorce offers so many new and inspiring opportunities to do things differently. You've had time to think through past mistakes, learn about yourself, decide what you really want from a love relationship, and piece together all the good skills you already have to create the kind of intimacy you have always wanted. Try to set your fears aside and trust that you have everything you need to help the relationship to grow—or to let it go and move on to the next opportunity.

12

Blending Lives

Y ou love each other and want to spend every waking moment together. You feel full of energy and hope for the great new family that you both want to bring together, a family that will be strengthened by the love you share. You are sure that things will be different this time—you will create a new family unit that is stronger than the biological unit, which was laden with problems and stricken with divorce. Finally you have ended this painful journey and found new love, and you are prepared to take the step toward a shared life with the man you love. On the other hand, your kids aren't in love with anyone, feel incredible loss from the divorce, wish you were still living with their father, and have gotten used to having you all to themselves. That is when the moments of doubt creep in, when you aren't sure how to make it work, what a stepparent is supposed to do, or even if you want to take on the responsibility of extra children whom you knew nothing about one year ago.

It became clear to Al and me early on that our six kids didn't share the same enthusiasm the two of us had for our blended life, the dream of our wonderful home, and the lifetime of fun we were going to have together. As soon as we moved into our one-bedroom cottage, we began the plans for construction. Issues immediately surfaced. With all the kids in bunks, including in the living room, everyone had to go to bed at the same time, or someone would complain that they couldn't sleep. The computer used for homework was in the living room, so there were nights when kids typed papers with towels over their heads so the light wouldn't keep the others awake. We had a ton of yard work to do, so weekends were pretty much taken up by family projects. That may have inspired Al and me, but it also had the kids swearing at us under their breath. Then the rain came, and the whole place was nothing but mud. The kids had to wear knee-high boots just to walk to the end of the driveway, changing to school shoes as soon as they hit pavement, muddying their hands and clothes in the process. With only one bathroom, the group had to work together to create a schedule for using it.

I refused to have a television in the house, expected all the kids to do chores, wanted the Christmas tree lights hung the way our family had always done it, and had a hard time explaining to my kids why Al's kids got to open their presents the night before Christmas instead of like we did, on Christmas morning. Al was less opinionated, didn't mind if he had to adjust to new family patterns, tried his best to maintain peace while living full-time with four children who didn't belong to him, and was basically a saint through the entire process. I guess the good news was that both of us expected it to be hard. We had six kids and had moved in together four months before construction began. After sharing a house with others, my kids were so happy to be in their own home again that they rarely complained, and all the kids lived in hope of the new rooms they had been promised. The building of our home in many ways gave us a chance to create something that belonged to and defined us as a family.

We began living together four years ago, but blending our family is still the greatest challenge we face. Second marriages have a higher divorce rate than first marriages, and among that group, the highest divorce rate is among second marriages that include children. Still, every year couples take this risk though they have heard the statistics because they are sure their love will be strong enough to overcome any difficulty. The goal of this chapter is to give a realistic view of what blended family life is really like, with both its challenges and its triumphs.

Usually by the time a woman marries for the second time, she has worked through and understands her childhood fantasies of what love and marriage were supposed to feel like, but sometimes she still clings to a fantasy of the perfect family. She may believe that her new relationship is so stable and loving that it in itself will cause the kids to fall in line behind their parents with enthusiasm over the new union, and everyone will embrace the family unit with open arms and loving hearts. When this doesn't happen, great disappointment can set in, as the reality of the new relationship is eventually judged closer to average than to exceptional.

I'm not trying to paint a bleak picture or dash anyone's hopes because the journey of the blended family is also full of great rewards, but those rewards come with a bit more work than many are prepared for. It's important to take a look at the challenges that blended families face so you'll recognize them as normal and expected ingredients in the process of blending lives. Challenges bring with them opportunities to learn, to grow, and to experiment with new ways of thinking, acting, and problem solving. Many families learn, through trial and error, what works to build a strong family unit, and I'll share some of those ideas. We'll take a look at some of the questions that must be addressed if the family is to come together: What is yours, mine, or ours? How will the finances be divided? What happens if the two sets of kids have drastically different house rules? How are the family traditions blended? We'll end the chapter with stories of the triumphs you may feel when things within the blended family begin to click, when love takes root, and as individuals start to see themselves as part of a new family unit.

Fantasy Versus Reality

The biggest disappointment I have with this wonderful new relationship I've created with Al is that at times I still feel like a single mother. Somehow when I was envisioning my new life, I imagined that I would start all over again and that when I found the right person my family would once again feel complete. I planned to find a man who would become another full-fledged parent for my children. My kids would think he was awesome and appreciate all the little things he did, like nightly homework, fixing bikes, and giving guitar lessons. They might protest at first, but I was sure that over time we would all settle into a familiar groove. I wouldn't be attending back-to-school nights alone or sitting through endless children's sporting events by myself.

Just as I had expectations about the kind of love relationship I wanted to create, I had a another set of expectations that outlined the family life I longed for. The first four years of our relationship were full of unbridled passion for the family life we had together *and* unspeakable disappointment for the family life we couldn't create. Seems strange that those two descriptions could live in the same life, but they did. Whenever the disappointment would come up, I'd try to explain to Al what was so wrong, and all I could say was that it just wasn't the way I thought it would be.

We all carry a bit of fantasy into a new love relationship, a dream of what it could be. The fantasy for me was my belief that the family would just happen. Both of us were exceptional people: the kids couldn't help but see that and would love us for it. We were providing a better life and home than either of us could provide on our own. Over the years, I watched the blending happen in reality, but it took *way* more time than I thought it would. I wanted to feel love for Al's kids, to have him love my kids. I learned that the best I could do was to create shared experiences to get to know his kids. After all, you can't love someone you barely know. I expected Al to be ever patient with my kids, more patient than I was, since I made up the rule that I could scold them for bad behavior but he could only be a friend to them. All my choices focused on this ideal family that solved problems logically and thoroughly enjoyed one another. But in reality, even biological families have problems of their own, which I chose not to think about while I easily pointed out all the failings of our blended family.

One step at a time, couples move from their fantasy ideas into embracing the realities of the new family group within which they live. "My thirteen-year-old son Drew had some behavioral problems when we got married," said Grace. "Paul knew about these problems and had been so helpful with them in the past, working with me to set appropriate consequences at home. When we got married and moved into the same house, the problems that Paul had only heard about and dealt with on a limited basis began to fill every moment of our time together. Paul would complain that when we were dating he would come over and Drew was well behaved and talkative. Now it seemed that I yelled at Drew about something every night, and Paul and I had no peaceful couple time. It took us a few months to work through the reality that we were no longer a dating couple who had places of our own to retreat to as well as time away from each other. Paul was no longer visiting us. This fantasy idea that it would be like dating every night, quiet words to each other, antici-pation of hearing about each other's day, and well-planned outings, wasn't quite the reality we faced day after day. We did talk about this and came up with a plan that worked for all of us. One night Paul took a class he had wanted to take so that he had a night on his own. One night a week I took Drew out so Paul would have the house to himself. And one night Paul and I went out so we could have more couple time."

Heather said, "The fantasy I held was that we would have more time to make love once we were married. Since I have two young daughters, I had never invited Stewart to stay overnight at my house. We were both excited at the prospect of sleeping every night in the same bed. The problem was that by the time we got the girls in bed and were sure they were asleep, we were both too tired. Sure, the first few months we made love every other day, enjoying this luxury of sleeping next to each other all night and being so into our mar-ried life that we would put the girls to bed as early as we could. Over time, the girls started complaining that I wasn't playing games with them before bed, telling them stories, or rubbing their backs. They missed their bedtime rituals, so Stewart and I had to come up with a new weekly plan that would give me some nights to devote to the girls and other nights to devote to love-making. I know many couples say that lovemaking is much better when it happens naturally, but our solution was to pick two days a week that were our nights to make love. I explained to the girls that on Tuesday and Saturday nights Stewart and I needed time alone together. Tuesday became early-to-bed night, when I let them play in their rooms for an hour before putting themselves in bed. And Saturday became movie night, when I would put the movie on and then come and put them in bed two hours later. Now the reality is that we do have couple time, we do get to make love in our own shared bed; it just took a little planning." For both couples, communicating about the adjustments that needed to be made helped them move from the fantasy of blended lives into the reality without building resentment toward each other.

The next step in moving from fantasy to reality is accepting and appreciating the life you have together. It is easy to list all the good things in your life—that the kids aren't sick, that you have food on the table and friends who love you. It is much harder to really act every day in a way that embraces the life you have, even when it isn't everything you want it to be. I still struggle with this every day. It is easier for me to pick and complain about our problems than it is for me to be grateful that I have kids and a family to cause the problems. It is a shift in mind I'm still working on: how to let each day pass without reaching any major goal or measurably improving as a family. On the other hand, Al can at any moment list half a dozen things that are going great in our family, usually with a sense of humor: "Everybody is still talking to each other, we haven't had a fire in a month, nobody has crashed the car, the grass was mowed, everyone had a good report card, dinner tasted great, and I still love you."

"For me, acceptance is difficult on all levels," said Sadie. "I really want this family to work. The divorce was so hard on everyone, and I refuse to go through anything like that again. That feeling alone makes me really sensitive when anything is a little off with our blended family. When Jake's son argues with my son, or something gets broken that belongs to Jake and it looks like it was my daughter's fault, I start to get this 'us against you' feeling, and it scares me. Sometimes I do a really good job accepting the many issues that seem to block our growth as a family and try to see them as little steps on a long road toward growing a family. It is really a lot to expect, putting two groups of kids together that barely know each other and expecting everyone to get along and to be excited about it. We've found that the more realistic we can be—telling the kids that it is normal to not like the arrangement or to have conflicts with each other—the more we are all able to relax and accept this process."

Acceptance is not something you wake up with one day and have it mastered for the rest of your life. It takes daily effort to accept the good and bad things that come your way as part of your life. The sooner a family can accept the challenges of blended life, rather than blame the new family structure for any unhappiness, the faster family members will begin to respect and to care for one another. Your stepfamily will be different from your biological family—not necessarily worse, just different. So don't waste time comparing them, complaining, or feeling sorry for yourself because it takes a little work. At this point there is no going back to the biological family, so you might as well do the best you can to appreciate what you have and to create new relationships that will bring great joy to your life!

The Challenge of Blending Families

The major challenges blended families face have to do with time, money, loyalty conflicts, family identity, lack of direction, and a couple's lack of alone time. The first few years our family lived together I would feel resentful toward Al for not spending as much time on the house and garden as I did each week. I expected him to put in a few hours each weekend, and I wanted all the kids to help with general maintenance. Month after month I would arrange family meetings where I would outline each child's jobs, type them up on cards, and tell the kids that unless the weekly jobs were checked off by Saturday, they could not go to any social events or sports practices. The kids would look at one another, and then someone would say something infuriating like, "Don't worry! She'll forget about this like last month." Being a working mom made it difficult for me to act like a prison guard, making sure that teenagers did their assigned jobs. More than anything, I was looking for them to want to take responsibility and help out. Al didn't think it was such a big deal. He wanted to spend more of his free time having fun with his kids on weekends and made comments about his boys not wanting to stay with us on weekends if all they did was work. Then there was the question of how many jobs should each child be required to do. If my kids lived with us 100 percent of the time and his boys 50 percent, shouldn't they have to do 50 percent of the chores? It took weeks to get my kids to understand this division of labor as being fair.

Then there is the challenge of money, which always seems to run out, no matter how much you make! From the beginning of our relationship, Al and I had completely separate bank accounts and paid for each of our own family's costs. We divided household bills equally and didn't combine our funds in any way. In the beginning, I felt this was reasonable. Then came the months when I wasn't making enough money to pay my bills, and I began to resent him for what looked to me like an easy life. He had a salary he could count on, while my income varied month to month. Besides, he made more money and had only two kids to support. So even though we agreed to the original setup, as we lived together I began to feel like we were living like haves and have-nots. Logically I could understand why Al shouldn't have to support my kids; he had his own child support to pay, and his ex-wife was in school, so he had to pay all her expenses. But I was living each day stressed to the max having to pay for and take care of four children full-time, while his life looked measurably easier. I began to question why I got married at all.

Since that time, Al has helped in many ways to support my kids when I didn't have money coming in, but I still feel it is his money. The feeling I had in my first marriage of it being our money doesn't exist in this marriage, and sometimes that hurts me enough that I become cold and resentful toward Al. The longer we've lived together, the more we have been able to trust the marriage and to trust our future together enough to talk about blending our assets. Of course, if you live in a community property state, this question is legally addressed the moment you marry, since all assets become jointly owned unless you have a premarital agreement. However, a feeling of trust may still take time to develop. With divorce, some people lose half the assets they had worked to gain, and usually both people feel they have been screwed by the time the settlement is final. Many people find themselves reluctant to give again for fear they will lose everything if the relationship doesn't work out. The only time money doesn't seem to be an issue in blended families is if there is plenty of money to go around, which is rarely the case.

Conflicting feelings of loyalty are another difficult area. Two kids are wrestling, neither parent is in the room, each kid blames the other, and Mom and Dad run into the room and feel a need to defend their own child. Then the kids start talking, saying that the stepdad favors his kids, that he isn't fair, or that the stepmom loves only her own kids. Battle lines are drawn, and siblings stick together and treat their stepbrother badly to get him back for the pain they feel.

How do parents cope when they are obviously going to be more attached, at least in the early years, to their own children than their stepchildren? "My biggest sadness when I got married to Alice was the realization that I would spend more of my life with her kids than I would with my own," said Peter. "Since my kids were only with us two nights during the week and every other weekend, I wanted to make my kids a priority when they were with me. Alice's kids could immediately feel my shift in attention. Instead of helping her by reading bedtime stories, doing homework, or playing games with her kids, I was fully focused on reading to my own kids and playing with them. Alice would tell me how much it hurt her kids to see what a different relationship I had with my kids, that her kids could see they weren't as loved by me." It is unrealistic for anyone in the family to think that every child is going to be treated the same by both parents. Kids all come to the new blended family after experiencing the loss of divorce. Both parents are trying to give their kids all the love they can so they can heal and feel good about themselves. Both parents need to make every effort to care deeply for the needs of each child, but the kind of love and loyalty a parent feels for his or her own biological children may take years to establish toward stepchildren.

The big question creeps into everyone's mind: Who are we now as a family? Maybe the birth order has changed, and a child who was the oldest is now one of the youngest. Maybe the kids have never lived in a household where both parents work. Family traditions or religious beliefs might be drastically different. How does each individual family retain a sense of its own identity, its history, and at the same time blend with a new family that has a different past? "In the beginning, my kids would put down the way Scott's family did things," said Matilda. "They would say his kids were wimps because they were afraid to stay home alone, they ate strange food, and they couldn't put themselves in bed at night. Scott and I had to work very hard for shared family time where we could establish new memories and find out who we were as a family. The kids wanted to hold tight to how their old family was. Scott and I wanted to bring some elements from both our past family lives into the new family we were creating without feeling attached to the old. It was exciting to see it all reveal itself. When we stopped holding on to our old family roles, there was plenty of space to let the personality of each new family member grow and express itself. After a few years, my kids stopped making comments about the things Scott didn't do as well as their father, and his kids stopped making comments about how I cleaned the house." As Matilda and Scott found out, family identity is built on shared life experiences. It requires a certain willingness to let go of the old family in order to create space for the new one to emerge.

Many parents complain that they have had no training to prepare them for the most difficult job of their lives—parenting. Most of us go into this area of our lives armed with a few books, a birthing class, and memories of how we were parented in our family of origin. We learn through years of practice what works in our family, how to discipline our kids, and how to communicate effectively. But with remarriage, in walks a new family of kids as well as a new parent, and somehow the two of you are supposed to set out together in a new direction as a family unit. "I can clearly remember the look on Lauren's face when she said that we had to get someone to watch our five kids for the weekend and go away together so we could come up with a new family game plan," said Chuck. "She turned on her heels, slammed the bedroom door, said under her breath that she must have been crazy to have chosen this, and then the crying began. I understood her feelings. I also felt like I was drowning in the middle of a lake, reaching in every direction for a life preserver. It didn't help that all five of our kids were under eleven or that both of us had just finished long and grueling divorces, so our energy was naturally low. Somehow I think we both expected to maintain the same sense of order, rules, discipline, and daily rituals that we had with our own kids in our own houses. Then we just got married and threw everyone together and encouraged our kids to share rooms with their stepbrothers and -sisters so they could get to know each other."

Lauren and Chuck did schedule that weekend away. "We talked, listened, read a little about stepfamilies, and decided to start from the beginning, and take it much slower. The kids moved back into rooms with their siblings, just as it had been in their own houses. We each spent time making a list of all the things we really liked about our family traditions, which disciplinary techniques worked for our kids, family rules that the kids were used to, and all sorts of other little things we didn't know would matter until we were all living in the same house." Lauren and Chuck had the clarity of mind to turn toward each other, admit they didn't know what direction to take the family, and carve time out of their lives to meet as members of a team who were open to any and all solutions.

The years following divorce allow both men and women to develop a personal identity that is often different from their identity in the first marriage. Often each person has learned to live alone, manage a home, parent his or her children, and earn a living without the help of another adult. When the couple first comes together, some of that personal identity blends with the new partner, and some of it flows over into the new roles they expect to play within the family. In order for a couple to maintain the love relationship that brought them together, to adjust to the new roles within the family, and to accept the sacrifices asked of them by a larger family, they have to make their time together a priority. This is especially important when the blending of families isn't going as well as everyone would like.

"I remember telling Brian that we had more time together when we were dating," said Alia. "Once we were all living in the same house, we didn't make as much of an effort to see each other, to spend time doing fun things, or even to talk about subjects that didn't revolve around finances, the kids' problems, and house upkeep. We'd already shared with each other everything about our childhood. We knew each other's dreams and had spent hours in the dating phase to share our intimate desires. It seemed that all of that went out the window when we took on the role of managing the group together. When I pointed this out to Brian, he agreed wholeheartedly that some of the joy he felt in sharing a family had left him because he didn't have any time with the one he loved the most—me. Neither one of us wanted to make the kids feel like we didn't want to spend time with them." Often it takes a bit of planning to find couple time, especially in the beginning stages of blending a family. If couples make their relationship a priority, communicate lovingly, and model the belief that the family is secure, then the kids will follow suit and fewer problems will arise for all involved.

Trial and Error

Unfortunately, there are no step-by-step instructions for building a strong and happy family unit, natural or blended. The best you can do is deal with issues as they come up and be as creative as possible in your attempts to create shared family experiences. "Before we were engaged, we started to talk about how we would bring our family together," said Ben. "One of the issues for us was that our thirteen-year-old daughters had been friends but had a falling-out a year before we started dating. Neither one of them wanted to see the other or discuss the problem. So instead of starting out the dating process with an open mind, both girls were clear they would move out if we ever got married. We decided to leave the girls out of the equation and focus on outings with the rest of our kids.

"The first outing was a hike at a park that also had boats for rent, the kind that you pedal like a bicycle. Angela and I decided that she would take one of my kids with one of hers in the boat, and I would do the same. The day went really well. Later that week, Angela's son wanted to invite my son to go to a movie, so Angela called my ex-wife to ask permission, just like she would any other friend her son would invite on an outing. These sorts of casual, joint activities went on for about six months. Angela and I didn't make any big deal of our being romantically involved, didn't kiss each other or make the kids feel uncomfortable. When we got engaged, each of us talked with our own daughter and told her that the four of us were going to sit down and talk through the issues that had them so mad at each other. It all worked out. By the time the wedding came around everyone basically liked each other." Ben and Angela didn't push their kids into accepting the relationship. Instead, they acted like friends and found fun things the kids would enjoy doing together as a way of building their family history.

Al and I worked hard to help each of our kids feel part of the family unit. We began with little things, like letting each child pick out the paint and carpet color in their new rooms, and later moved on to bigger things, like taking a weeklong family vacation on a houseboat. The highlight for me was our wedding. Our children were our only attendants, and during the entire ceremony they stood in a semicircle behind us. Our vows were divided in half, with the first half directed to the children. We started with the oldest and told each one all the things we admired about them and enjoyed sharing with them and how they were a blessing to the family. Then came the part that had the audience chuckling: we wrote vows for the kids to say "I do" to: "Do you promise to respect your brothers and sisters and treat them with kindness?" We even slipped in "Do you promise to clean your room, do your chores as asked, and help maintain the home the family lives in?" All the kids looked at each other and started laughing. The minister then read some paragraphs we had written asking the kids for their support and love as we began our life together as husband and wife. Traditional vows then followed. The service ended with a blessing, where all of the kids came forward and put their hands on both of us as the minister blessed the family. It was a beautiful way to include everyone and to begin our new life together as a family. I'm sure the kids thought it a little sappy at the time, but I guarantee that they will never forget the feeling of belonging we created together starting on our wedding day.

Some families schedule mandatory family outings. "The first thing we did after our honeymoon was to get all the kids together to plan monthly activities," said Anna. "Each child was assigned one Sunday to plan something fun for all of us to do. An adult was assigned to be the child's assistant, to check costs and help with travel details. We put a monetary limit on it so that each child had to work within a budget. The first Sunday we went to a movie and dinner, the second bowling, the third on an eight-mile bike ride. With each successful Sunday, the kids got more creative with their plans. The last Sunday we went to see a magician perform." It is important to plan fun into your blended families schedule. Nobody likes to work through the tough parts without something to look forward to.

One job a family has is to support each of its members. "We have four kids between us, and each child plays two sports," said Wayne. "In the beginning, I would go to my kids' events and Jen would attend her kids' events. After a while, we decided to switch at least once a month and to take the whole family to at least one child's event each month. We made a list of the family trips to make sure that each child had the experience of having the entire family there to support them." One of the benefits of a blended family is that there are more of you to create a cheering section, to be there when someone gets their heart broken, and to stand with you through good times and bad.

The ways to successfully blend a family are born through trial and error. Ideas that work can go down in the family notebook as things the group would like to try again. If they don't work, you can throw them out with a laugh and a pat on the back for the effort it took. Create an atmosphere in which the kids know that the group is going to make mistakes, that times will not always be fun, that problems will need to be solved. Do this, and there will be less disappointment all around. Bring the kids into the process; make sure they know that the success of the family is a group effort, not just the parents' job. Make it clear that this new family does not replace the old family and all its good memories. It is merely a new and different chapter in the story of your lives.

Yours, Mine, and Ours

Combining households requires a great deal of planning to figure out what's yours, mine, and ours. Where will the family live? Does each family move from its home to a new location? Who will contribute what to the furnishings and household supplies? How will the bills be paid, and who will take care of the kids? How will the chores be divided? It isn't just the physical relocation that raises issues. Family rules and patterns come along too. Soon after Al's and my families moved in together, we discovered that Al allowed his boys to stay up very late on weekend nights, much later than I allowed my kids. The problem is that the youngest two boys are the same age, so whenever I tell my son it is bedtime on a weekend, he starts screaming at me because he knows Al's son gets to stay up later and watch movies. The problem is that my son needs his sleep or he's a grouchy, mean child in the morning. To take care of everyone's needs, we have devised a little plan that works most of the time: Al's son pretends he's going to bed until my son is asleep. But if my son wakes up and finds everyone watching a movie, he feels very hurt. It's not a perfect solution, but kids are all different, and we have to remember that!

If a blended family is to get off to a good start, the parents need to see themselves as a team that works together and decides in advance the family guidelines. "Janet and I each had our own houses about twenty miles apart," said Simon. "We talked at length about moving into my house and then about moving into hers, but in the end we decided it would put everyone on more equal ground if we all moved into a new house together. That way it wasn't like one set of kids had all of their old neighborhood friends while the other kids didn't know anyone. So we both went through the hassle of packing up our houses." It helps if decisions can be made for the good of the group, as Janet and Simon were able to do, instead of looking only at the solutions that are convenient for one individual family.

The old military strategy of divide and conquer really works when it comes to parents and children. Couples have to present a united front, having discussed things at length before presenting solutions to the kids, or the kids will find a way to pit one parent against the other as they campaign for their own causes. It is common in blended families for kids to complain heavily to their own parent about the stepparent's decisions or ways of handling things. Sometimes kids can be quite hurtful and manipulative, saying that if their parent loved them, they would side with their own child. They may pout about your loving the stepparent more than them. It is important not to get sucked into this us-against-them attitude, especially if you happen to agree with some of the things your kids are saying and are a little angry with the situation already.

One sore spot in many marriages is how money is handled. Financial disagreements consistently make the top three on the list of reasons for marital arguments. Most people in our culture want their money to go to their own kids. We feel a duty to keep our children safe, fed, and happy. It isn't unusual for financial disagreements to cloud blended families with resentment. "Clara and I really see money differently," said Kim. "I save all my extra money, and Clara spends hers. Then she is short of money at the end of the month and I have to give her some of my money. In the meantime, I've brought a bag lunch to work, passed on new clothes for myself, and have sacrificed in order to save money each month. I can see that we are starting to resent each other. She thinks I'm cheap, and I think she spends beyond her means. We also don't agree about how much money should be spent on the kids. She puts her kids in every class imaginable: her daughter is on traveling sports teams that cost more than I would spend on my kids. She doesn't mind paying for airline tickets to exotic places when her kids are asked to join a friend on a family vacation. On the other hand, Clara's girls work, buy their own clothes, and pay for most of their social lives. She thinks my kids should be working too, so that I don't have to contribute to their clothes and social activities. We are both sure that our pattern of spending is the best way to be, and we thumb our noses at each other whenever financial matters are discussed." Clara and Kim have a bit of work to do if they are going to respect each other's financial positions.

Housework is another area that causes distress. In many households both adults have to work, so it only seems fair that household work be divided equally. Yet old stereotypes still exist that place a woman in the kitchen and a man in front of the TV enjoying the news or a sporting event. My mother told me long ago that if I wanted a man to help in the house, I would have to give him a list and have the expectation that he would do an equal amount of work instead of feeling like he was being kind to help me with my job. "One of the hardest things I had to do was to make a list of every household job I was doing and then to demand that my husband take on his fair share of the housework," said Janice. "It took me a few months and a friend's gentle nudging before I understood that I was still following the old pattern that had me taking care of my husband and all the kids, while his life was easier and definitely more enjoyable. He was hurt by the conversation, especially when it came down to carrying his own dirty clothes to the laundry room and my demand that he be responsible for dinner at least three nights a week. I realized during this conversation that it wasn't that he was unwilling to help, he just didn't know how much I was doing or how resentful I felt about doing it all when I worked just as many hours as he did."

But keep in mind that people are different when it comes to cleanliness and organization. Some people are just naturally messier and others naturally neater. My son Troy is a very neat person, always organizing his toys and putting his clothes away the minute I leave them on his bed. Other kids in the house are more carefree; dirty dishes, unwashed laundry, scattered books, and unmade beds are acceptable to them. When it comes to blending families, it is helpful to keep in mind that one person's "neat" is another person's "obsessive," just as one person's idea of a clean room is not clean enough for another. As with everything else, be prepared to compromise on your picture of what the ideal house will look like.

A fun way to blend families is through sharing old family traditions and creating new ones. Whenever our family would sing "Happy Birthday," it would be accompanied by a pounding on the table while the person blew out their candles. I remember the look on my stepsons' faces the first time my kids started banging; they didn't know what to make of it. Now it's a highlight of everyone's birthday, and we all get to watch the looks on our guests' faces when all eight of us start pounding.

"Our first Christmas together was a treasure for all of us," said Maggie. "Larry and I had spent quite a bit of time discussing holiday traditions in our families of origin. Those were the traditions we decided to add to the ones our children already enjoyed. Each of us had a wonderful time sharing our childhood with each other's children, telling them about our favorite tradition and how much it meant to our family. In my family we would walk down the street and sing Christmas carols to all our neighbors. So last year we bundled up all the kids on Christmas Eve. I printed up song sheets, and we went to sing to our neighbors. It was great fun! Larry has a tradition of picking names for presents within the family. That way each person can buy one big present for their special person. They were also supposed to leave loving notes, pieces of candy, and other secret presents for their person in the days leading up to

Christmas. Part of the game was trying to figure out who had picked your name. We decided to add that tradition to our blended family tradition, and the kids loved the idea." There are many ways to build new traditions. Ask each member of the family to come up with something the family has never done for each holiday, and try a few of the ideas out. If the family decides they like it, all you need to do is repeat it year after year and it then becomes part of the family history and a memory that lasts forever.

Moments of Triumph

A family is a group of people who share daily routines, support individual efforts, disagree with each other, cry with pride, laugh at embarrassing moments, and stand together through whatever wonderful or tragic moments life has to offer. In our families we learn about intimacy, how to communicate with each other, how to express our feelings, and how to get what we want (or at least some of what we want). The experiences we have within family in many ways determine who we are, how we feel about ourselves, and the direction we take in life. Family life is our first and primary experience with other people.

Stepfamilies are the second try in establishing a safe and loving unit. Each person enters the stepfamily having lost their first family, the one they trusted, the place where they shared experiences and memories and where the definition of what family meant had already been worked out. The greatest triumph is that people are willing to come together to create a new family unit in the hope that new memories will be added, kids can be supported, and adults can have another chance at an intimate relationship. Opportunities abound in stepfamilies! This time parents are older, have more experience with parenting, and are more conscious of the mistakes they made the first time around. We all have a better understanding of what it takes to make a family work.

The changes required to thrive in a blended family can also give children a head start in learning how to be flexible and in developing confidence. "My parents were divorced when I was ten," said Marci. "There were three kids in my family and two in my stepfather's family. It took work on my parents' part, planning special Sunday outings so we could all get to know each other, making sure that we ate dinner together, little things. When I went away to college and moved into a sorority house where I had to share a room with four other girls, I was way ahead of the game. One of the girls complained every morning she couldn't sleep because people would come home at all different hours, turn on the light, and wake her up. Another girl couldn't adjust to having to share a bathroom with so many girls. Another cried every night because it was the first time she had been away from her family. I sat back and felt thankful that I had already lived through many of these difficult experiences, like learning how to live in a house with many people and how to share rooms and bathrooms with strangers. I'd already worked through the loneliness of being away from one parent or the other. I was responsible and confident in my ability to deal with whatever difficulty came my way, and I owe that to the experience of living in a stepfamily." Kids in blended families also have the added benefit of being loved by more people as the scope of extended family expands to new grandparents, aunts, uncles, cousins, and friends.

The couple has a chance to use all they have learned about themselves to form a new and different example of what a loving relationship looks like. "I was thirteen when my mom remarried," said Tim. "I was angry, mean, and hated my stepfather for a good three years. It wasn't until I was sixteen and started dating that I started to appreciate how my stepdad treated my mom. He showed her so much respect and expected us to show her the same respect. He loved her. I could see that in the way he listened to her, looked at her, and was there for her whenever she was down. I remember how I felt when she was married to my father. It was like I had to step in and rescue her from his insults and be the shoulder she cried on. When I really looked back, I could see what a confident, exceptional woman she was and how my stepdad's love for her brought strength to the whole family. Ten years later when I got engaged, I asked my stepfather to be my best man. It was my way of telling him thanks for teaching me how to love a woman." You can never underestimate the power of a good example to influence a child's life path.

Al and I had been married a year when we took our first family vacation. We rented a houseboat on Lake Shasta in northern California. One of my moments of triumph as a stepparent was watching my twelve-year-old son, Rhett, begin to treat Al's fifteen-year-old son, Adam, as a big brother. They were hanging out together, making wild and spiky hairstyles with gel, and having fun. I watched Adam teach Rhett to wakeboard and was grateful that Rhett has a big brother as talented and kind as Adam. As the years pass and the relationships within the family grow, the feeling of pain and loss is replaced with the knowledge that new friendships have formed, fun memories made, and the goal of creating a shared life full of people who care has been accomplished. It all begins when you have the courage to love again, but it becomes much more real and lasting when you, your new partner, and your kids grow in love, trust, and compassion for one another.

13

New Skills

I learned from my divorce that relationships are both beautiful and breakable. No matter how strong, love is not indestructible—in my life it was very fragile. Once trust and intimacy are threatened, the love connection can turn bitter. This happens because, as time goes by, couples are not as careful with each other as they should be. We don't measure our words or weigh our actions. We may feel we have the right to say whatever we think, no matter how insulting, and call it honesty. With my ex-husband, I got into the cycle of seeing only his negative attributes. I became defensive and unable to express the depth of my feelings or to listen deeply to his feelings. It took years of therapy to learn the skills I could have used to make the relationship work, but by that time we were both so damaged by our past interactions and power struggles that there wasn't enough love left to rebuild the relationship. Simply put, the skills I had going into my marriage were inadequate. I'd spent years in school getting a degree in psychology, but I hadn't spent more than twenty hours in relationship training.

Much of this book has talked about knowing what you want from the relationship you are trying to create. We all agree that part of the relationship puzzle is knowing what you want to achieve, but the other and maybe more difficult part is learning and then incorporating the relationship skills you will need to make your vision a reality. The first year after my divorce, I was comfortable with my old patterns of interaction and believed for a time that the communication and marriage issues that led to divorce were solely my ex-husband's problem. When I started dating, I began to see that there were relationship skills that I lacked: ways of communicating my feelings, expressing my anger, and discussing important issues that helped my partner to feel loved and supported rather than attacked. Hundreds of books are available that discuss the creation of solid, respectful, supportive, and loving relationships, and I will not duplicate them here. What I will do is offer you five skills, or practices, that will give your relationship a better chance of succeeding as a healthy and equal partnership:

> Establish a trusting friendship with a man.
> Understand and use the chemistry of love.
> Learn new communication skills.
> Use conflict resolution and anger management to solve problems.
> Maintain your independence while developing an equal and fair
>   partnership.

As you begin to understand each skill, take time to practice it in the dating process. Obviously a casual date will not call for conflict resolution (or if it does, you probably have the wrong guy!), but a serious relationship definitely will. The idea is to practice these skills to the point where they become second nature to you. Then when a situation arises in which you are hurt or angry, you will automatically fall back on these behaviors instead of repeating old relationship patterns that didn't work.

Establish a Trusting Friendship

It takes a lifetime to learn about friendship. Most of us begin this process as children. I have a great series of books for children written by Joy Berry. I chuckle when I read the titles: *Breaking Promises; Fighting; Being Careless; Being Selfish; Being Messy; Being Mean; Lying; Throwing Tantrums; Being Bossy; Being Rude; Cheating; Being Lazy; Being a Bad Sport; Complaining;* and *Teasing.* The books depict children who engage in these bad behaviors, while readers are asked questions like "When you are with someone who keeps complaining, how do you feel?" Children have a chance to put themselves in the situation being described, to consider their own behavior in that situation, and to decide if they want people to like them or not. We need a set of these books written for adult lovers who would also like to be friends, because every one of the undesirable behaviors listed above has a tendency to occur in love relationships after the initial "wow."

Friendship isn't nearly as exciting as the feeling you get when a man walks into the room and takes your breath away. After all, how many of us come home from a party after talking with a man for two hours and stay up all night trying to imagine his face after deciding what a good friend he might be? It seems our society puts much more energy into sexual attraction, leaving most of us disappointed with even the best relationship when the fire of passion simmers to a low-burning flame. And yet, as women, what is it that sustains us through the good and bad times of our lives? Our friendships.

The probability of a romance lasting past the relationship's first year may well be determined by the quality of friendship cultivated by the couple from the beginning. The ingredients of friendship may not be consciously cultivated or written down. But they will be there, underlying the way you talk to each other, in your attitudes about telling the truth, and in the way you make joint decisions.

If we could list the ingredients of friendship that can make a love relationship worth staying in, even during the times when things aren't so good, what would they be? "If I could have just one thing, it would be trust," said Leah. "My ex-husband started off as a good friend, and I trusted him with my life—until he cheated on me. I had this feeling that he was with someone else just by the way he wasn't really with me, but whenever I asked him about it, he said that he loved me. Now that I'm dating, I keep thinking that my boyfriend is lying to me. I read my own distrust into everything he says. When he can't be with me, I think he must be looking for someone else. I don't know how to trust him."

Trust is the basis of all friendship. We can begin to build trust in our new relationships through baby steps and clear messages. "I told my boyfriend, Jeff, the story about how my mom used to betray my trust by telling everything I confided in her to my aunt, who would then let it slip when she saw me that she knew some really personal thing about me and was concerned," said Marcy. "I clearly told Jeff that I needed him to keep everything I ever said to him to himself. I didn't want his family to know in advance that my dad was an alcoholic or that I had lesbian sex in college. If he was unable to keep our conversations private, then I told him I wouldn't be able to trust him."

Even if trust does become broken, it can provide an opportunity for rebuilding through the openness with which you communicate about the problem. "When we first started going out," said Louise, "I told my boyfriend that I could deal with any piece of truth better than I could deal with a lie. I would really rather that my boyfriend say to my face that he had fallen in love with someone else than to find out later. Even something as simple as telling me he has plans, while what he really wants is a night to himself, would really bug me. This might sound stupid, but it worked for us. I told him to raise his right hand and repeat after me, 'I promise to tell the whole truth and nothing but the truth in this relationship.' Then we also both agreed on the twenty-four-hour rule: if we were dishonest to the relationship or each other in any way, we had twenty-four hours to confess what we had done. The other person would then have the right to make a similar choice if they wanted to, or they could forgive and let it go.

"Three years into the relationship, I cheated on him. Things hadn't been going very well, and there was this guy at work. I told him about it within our one-day rule, even though it was the hardest thing I had ever done, especially since I was the one who was so big on trust from the beginning. He decided that he should be able to sleep with someone else one time, just as I had done. Even though it hurt me, it felt a hundred times better than when my husband cheated on me. Something about the feeling of being open about our mistakes and allowing the other to determine the consequences seemed to heal both of us. We are still together, and neither one of us has had another fling since then."

Another ingredient in friendship is shared interests. Most of us have something in common with our best friends: we like old movies, belong to a book club together, go on weekly hikes, or like to travel. Lovers also need areas of shared interest for a friendship to flourish. "When I was married, I thought we had so much in common because we both loved to ski," said Gina. "The first few years that we skied together, we would go down the same runs, ride the chair lift together, and take hot chocolate breaks at the same time. Then over time he decided that the runs I wanted to go on were too easy for him. He wanted to do the more difficult ones, so we ended up skiing by ourselves. That was the one area of our relationship where we both had a passion, and when that went, it seemed we didn't have much to talk about."

Friendship is a deeply layered mystery that grows over time with shared experiences, laughter, hard times, and vulnerable moments. Lovers need to look past the outward appearances that may have drawn them like a magnet to the other person. We should pay closer attention to the way the other person cultivates his present friendships. Ask your man what kind of activities, hobbies, and discussions he enjoys. Tell him to describe his best friend's childhood. Watch the expression on his face to see signs of genuine attachment, enjoyment, and interest in the friends he has established. Ask to meet your lover's friends. If you notice a pattern of underdeveloped friendships, be aware that there may be work ahead if you wish to experience the kind of friendship you are accustomed to.

"The best thing we did for our friendship was to establish what we call friend talk time," said Celeste. "We don't discuss financial issues or problems with the kids or divorce issues, but instead just talk like friends talk—you know, small talk, with an excited energy, just to catch up and know what is going on in the life of someone you care about."

Jane reported that respect is an important ingredient for friendship. "To me, respect for the other person's ideas, life goals, and choices would be at the top of my list," said Jane. "If you respect someone, then you want to listen, and you don't feel this need to control what they choose to do with their life."

"The most important thing to me at this point in my life is that I'm accepted as part of a package that includes my kids," said Beth. "I am a great friend, and I'll try the best I can to be there for someone, but my kids have to come first. Sometimes it is hard for men to love me. They want to be with me, but they have to work around my family schedule. Well, that is hard for me too, and there are days I wish I had more freedom to be spontaneous. So I guess it is really important that my lover understand and accept that I'm not just a girlfriend; I'm a mother with kids."

Each couple will establish friendship guidelines that work for them based on what they value most in a relationship, what they need to focus on to feel secure with each other, and how willing they are to express their true self. They don't necessarily need to pass "laws" that keep the relationship in a box, but rather they can agree on guidelines that give their relationship a priority in each other's life. Everyone can learn to be a better friend, to listen more attentively, to show interest, to be compassionate, and to have fun. Expecting, defining, and practicing these friendship skills from the beginning will direct the couple toward understanding what it really means to share and enjoy a life together.

Understand and Use the Chemistry of Love

One thing seems true for all relationships: any complaints that may eventually develop didn't exist during the first six months of the romance! The beginning of love is the stage where your body is alive with feelings of love for this perfect, lovable being who has floated down from heaven and into your life. Have you ever wondered how it is that this same human being can become the scum of the earth a decade later, even if he hasn't really changed at all?

We know that at this stage of love, when we are totally flooded with emotion on meeting someone we're attracted to, we have no control over whether or not our bodies will feel turned on—it just happens. Some women have tried to conjure up those feelings, especially when they've found a man who has all the qualities they are intellectually looking for, but in the end you either feel it or you don't. Since the chemistry at the beginning can be so fleeting, why do we persist in considering it so important? If we accept the notion that a few years into the relationship the desire will lessen and the negative traits will become blatantly visible, why do we trust our body's response at all? Why don't we just find a man who fits our criteria, one who is intellectually stimulating, okay in bed, would make a dynamite stepfather, and thinks we are beautiful?

It seems to me that the chemistry we feel in the beginning is intended to be the hope we all hold on to, the feelings that we remember, that gets us through hard times in the relationship. If couples can somehow remember that chemistry and work to keep it alive, they will have that promise and excitement to fall back on as they work through any difficulties that arise. The challenge is this: to keep the chemistry alive, a couple must pay attention to other areas of the relationship, like communicating with each other and resolving conflicts with kindness, or the chemistry slowly leaves and is replaced with critical words and eventually contempt.

Each of us has failed to keep love healthy and alive at least once in our lives. We've been through the cycle of infatuation, followed a few years down the road with the pointing out of a partner's negative qualities. We either break off the relationship or learn to accept and love each other faults and all. Conscious effort is needed to keep all aspects of the relationship working toward the common goal of staying together in order for any relationship to survive. Nobody works without a reward, and when you are talking about love, that reward is the attraction or chemistry we feel toward our partner. If we can begin the relationship understanding the importance of keeping that chemistry alive and protected from immature, cruel, or hurtful behavior, then there is a good chance that the relationship will last.

So how do you nurture the desire you have for each other? You need to consciously create patterns in the relationship that allow each person to feel attracted to and appreciative of the other. Then when trouble arrives, you both won't turn to criticism and complaints.

Step one in nurturing desire for each other is to make an effort to remain attractive. Don't assume that since someone loves you, you can dress sloppily or forget about your appearance. "In my first marriage, I let myself fall apart over time," said Myrna. "I had the kids and couldn't find much time to exercise, and eventually stopped wearing makeup altogether. My husband never said anything about it. He didn't ask me to lose weight or wear something other than sweatpants. He didn't say he missed my wearing makeup, although he did shower me with compliments whenever I wore it. When he left me and the angry discussions began, the top insult on his list was that I didn't care about myself, that I hadn't made an effort to be attractive. He pointed out that he still worked out, hadn't gained weight, and made an effort to dress nicely. I thought, 'Sure, you go to work, put on a suit, go to the gym on the way home, and then get served dinner—nothing happens to mess up your life.' But after he left I lost thirty pounds, and I look great now." Stay in shape, whether or not you have a man. Wear clothing that reminds you that you are attractive and sexy and that appeals to your man as well. It's part of staying in tune with our sexual selves—to pay attention to what makes us feel sensual and helps to keep our partner's desire alive. Notice when he says you look sexy in something, and then wear it regularly. Don't cut your hair to your ears the day after he tells you how much he loves it long. Stay on your toes, and don't take his undying attraction for you for granted. Make it clear from the beginning that you expect him to make the same effort to be attractive to you.

Step two is to practice remembering how you felt in the beginning. "When I started dating Morris I put every love note he sent to me in a box," said Jennifer. "I also made copies of the love letters I sent to him. Whenever I get frustrated about the relationship, I open that box and read some of the letters. It is amazing how much I was willing to reveal about myself in the beginning of the relationship when trust was high and hope sprung eternal. The words remind me of what I saw in him to begin with, and I usually feel a little spark of love whenever I open that box." People don't change that much over time. Good qualities don't just get up and walk away unless the person has some sort of substance abuse or psychological problem. In the beginning of a relationship, when you see so many promising characteristics, make a list of everything you love about the man. When times get tough, read the list and remember why you fell in love to begin with.

Step three is to make an effort every day to compliment your partner on all levels, not just on his appearance. Let him know you appreciate it when he makes a good meal, is playful with the kids, fixes the dryer, or gives you a great massage. Make a habit to do it every day, even when you are feeling depressed, unhappy, or disillusioned with the relationship. "In the beginning it felt a little fake to give my boyfriend a compliment every day," said Helen. "I remembered from my parents' marriage how nice they were to each other, what kind things they always said. In my marriage we didn't have many nice things to say, but I decided after the divorce that any new relationship I had would need to contain an element of genuine appreciation. I found that over time, the compliments I gave my boyfriend became more genuine as I changed the negative pattern I'd fallen into during the marriage. He complimented me all the time too, and that felt great." It is difficult to feel happy or fulfilled in a relationship when all you hear are negative comments or criticisms. Make sure to notice and to compliment the good things your partner does.

Step four is to find some activity you can do together, an interest that you both enjoy. It is much easier to appreciate and feel attracted to your partner when you have a chance to see him regularly outside the family home. It also gives you a chance to have fun together. "Matt and I met at a beginner's tennis class through our town recreation league," said Karen. "We were attracted to each other from the first lesson. He approached me and asked if we could set a weekly practice time. Well, he set that practice time conveniently close to dinner on the days I didn't have my kids. Practice turned into a date. We have been married now for three years, and we still play tennis once a week. It is a great way to stay in shape, stay connected, and remember the relationship we have that doesn't involve my kids or his kids." All relationships thrive when partners make such shared experience time a priority.

Step five is to establish good friendships with couples you both enjoy. If you begin to feel disenchanted with your partner, call on your friends and ask them to remind you why you are with this man in the first place. Members of your own family can do this as well. Talk to your family about your desire to stay in the relationship. Tell them that when you are feeling critical, you would like them to remind you of all the good things you love about your partner. Friends and family can offer balance, perspective, and a sense of history that couples often overlook when times get tough.

Learn New Communication Skills

I'd been involved in my first postdivorce relationship for about six months when my boyfriend said, "Hold on for a minute, you have to stop responding to me like I'm your ex-husband! You are so defensive—I'm not even sure where this is coming from." He had wanted to see a movie that I didn't want to see at all, but I hadn't told him ahead of time that I didn't care to see it. Instead I said, "You know I hate violent movies, why would you even suggest it!" Then I felt myself withdraw from him, deciding that he didn't care about me. It took me a few minutes to center myself and realize he was right. My emotional response came directly from my interactions with my ex; they had nothing to do with the present moment or with him. I decided that day that I needed to learn new communication skills if I wanted to navigate this new relationship successfully.

Communication is talking, listening, understanding, responding, and problem solving. So many things affect what we hear: the words we choose, the way we say them, and the body language that communicates how we feel even when no words are said. Communication styles are passed down in families. Some people talk quietly, while others yell, discuss, or argue. Many of us spend most of our time talking, stating our opinions, and expecting others to be interested in hearing what we have to say. Yet most relationship research points to listening as the key to good communication. Learning to really listen to someone can transform how we understand, respond, and problem-solve. Most important, listening is a skill that can be taught, practiced, and easily incorporated into all of our relationships, including those with family and friends.

Active listening is the first skill to learn. In its simplest form it means listening to what someone says and then repeating what you heard back to them to make sure you understood the meaning. It sounds simple, but often what you heard was not what they meant, so the feedback you provide in active listening is very important. Here is a sample "active listening" conversation:

Jill: It really bugs me the way you do the dishes but leave all the counters dirty so that even when it isn't my turn I still have to participate in cleaning up the kitchen.

Active listener: You don't like it when I do the dishes and don't clean the counters.

Jill: Yes, it makes me feel like I'm the primary housekeeper and the only one who cares whether or not the house is a mess.

Active listener: So you feel like I don't care whether or not the house is a mess or not.

Jill: Well, maybe you care, but you are willing to sit back and not do anything because you know I will clean it up.

Active listener: You think I sit back and let you do more of the household work.

Jill: Yes, and I've been thinking maybe it would be better if we sat down and went through what needs to be cleaned each week and divide it up between us.

Notice how the active listener didn't defend himself, he didn't tell Jill how she should feel, and he didn't get angry and tell her to stop bossing him around. Instead he simply listened, and the conversation worked its way into discussing some of the feelings Jill had about dividing household work.

Often problems or irritations begin with one behavior, but after a while they develop a history and take on a life of their own. Taking the time to hear someone out until they've expressed everything they have to say about the situation gives both people time to consider and understand what is being said. It is easy to practice active listening with your partner. Just write four problems that have nothing to do with your relationship on a piece of paper, and take turns playing each role.

It is easy to practice active listening with your partner in a nonthreatening way by picking a few problems to discuss that don't really have anything to do with the relationship. That way neither one of you will have to focus on the issue at hand; instead you can practice the format of active listening. Here are three problems to get you started.

- Somebody leaves their wet towel on the floor of the bathroom every time they take a shower.
- Each week you buy special food at the health food store that you don't want to share, but your partner keeps eating it.
- Your partner is constantly having costly car problems, the expense of which you split, and you are convinced these problems occur because he/she skips routine auto service.

Another kind of active listening happens when there is no problem to discuss, just information to be shared. This listening exercise is practiced by many of the engagement or marriage workshops offered around the country. It can also be used by parents and children with great success. The concept is simple. All you need is a clock to keep track of talk time. Decide how much time each person will get to talk; ten minutes each is a good starting point. The rules are simple: no interrupting, giving advice, or saying anything at all. Look the person who is speaking in the eye, nod your head, show you hear them with your eyes and your body language, and listen intently to every word they say. When the time runs out, it is your turn to talk. You can choose a topic that both of you will speak about, like childhood memories, what is going on at work, future dreams. Alternatively, each of you can use your ten minutes to talk about anything you want to say. This is about hearing fully what the other person wants to say. It isn't about having your say, correcting the person, or giving advice or opinions to move the person off what they believe. During these talk times the listener has the opportunity to hear with their whole heart instead of thinking of what they are going to say while the other person talks. If the listener has a hard time remembering everything that is said or feels they just can't stand not saying anything, they may take a few notes, but they should still maintain eye contact as much as possible.

Another way to listen is to pay attention to behavior. A person lying on a couch with red eyes obviously has had a bad day. Nonverbal clues can allow you to piece things together and then approach the person in a way that incorporates your newfound observations. Many women have told me that it hurts them when they have to constantly ask their partner for help or under-standing. They believe that if the man loved them he would do things with-out asking. The men I talk to say that they don't read minds. Nobody is interested in developing the codependent behavior of trying to figure out what someone wants or needs and then doing it for him or her, but all of us could pay closer attention to the nonverbal communication we receive all the time. "I decided to see myself as a detective solving a crime, just to make this boring stuff more fun," said Tim. "When I came to pick Tracy up I saw construction materials, glitter, glue, and pieces of boxes on the kitchen table, the water was boiling on the stove, the kids were watching TV, and the shower was on. I waited for the shower to stop. Then I went in and reported my observations in a humorous way, suggesting that maybe it would be better if I helped with the project on the table while she finished dinner for the kids. I suggested that I could get a movie to watch and a pizza for us to share as soon as the kids were in bed. I could see how much she appreciated the fact that I was listening to her just by observing what was going on. She ended up saying that she was going nuts with the kids and really needed to get out of the house, so we did go out, but I know this exchange deepened our understanding of each other." By noticing Tracy's situation and by being willing to alter what he wanted to fit the problem he saw, Tim showed that he understood Tracy's circumstances.

The most important thing is to practice your listening skills all the time. Learn them so well they become automatic during hard times, arguments, or when you feel you need to defend yourself. Listening helps all forms of communication improve. The person talking feels more open to expressing their feelings when they know they will be listened to. The person listening has a better chance of understanding the problem and of empathizing with the feelings being expressed. Both people experience a greater connection to each other when they are fully present in the exchange of information. Over time, the ability to listen builds trust in the relationship, deepens the friendship, and allows the couple to share more of life's experiences.

Use Conflict Resolution and Anger Management

One thing is guaranteed to show up in all love relationships: anger. It takes self-control and a commitment to the relationship to handle anger and conflict in a positive way. Anger is a clear warning sign that a conflict is brewing. Sometimes we are angry because we are afraid: "How could you spend that much money on a car when we have a house payment we can barely afford!" Often we are angry because we don't get our way: "Don't you dare come over now; it is too late! I told you I wanted you to come over by 8 P.M.!" Wherever the anger comes from, it seems to quicken the pulse, fill our minds with hateful thoughts, and urge our body forward into a defensive stance.

Unless a fight is the desired outcome, the first step in anger management is to calm yourself down. You can do this in several ways. The first is to remove yourself from the situation until you can talk without being on fire. Take a twenty-minute time-out from each other, think about what you want to say, and decide how you want to approach the topic in a nonaggressive way. During this time-out, *do not* rehearse hurtful comments or points you plan to bring up when you resume talking, like how much you want out of the relationship or what a shit he is. Rewrite the angry script that is swimming around in your head by thinking more positive and realistic thoughts instead: "The relationship is good; we are just having a small disagreement."

Another option is to use self-talk to remind yourself that you intend to manage your anger responsibly. My husband says the same thing out loud whenever we get into an argument: "I don't want to be saying these things to you because I love you and our connection is more important than the point I'm trying to make." Sometimes turning away from the person and taking ten deep breaths helps or going into your room and screaming into a pillow until all the angry energy seems to drain from you. Above all, remember that whatever you communicate while angry will most likely hurt the other person, who may then hurt you back. So at some point you will have to ask forgiveness and do the best you can to repair the damage. Better to skip the angry step altogether and move right into conflict resolution.

Much has been written about resolving conflicts in the past twenty years. Kids are taught healthy ways to settle disputes at school, and businesses and sometimes even governments are shifting toward looking for more peaceful solutions when people or groups don't agree. One simple form of conflict resolution is to set thirty minutes aside for a conflict meeting. That may seem like a lot of time, but it is much less time than healing from an angry fight will take. Whoever has the problem needs to ask for the meeting. The person who is upset by the problem talks about the situation—what upsets them and why. Once the problem is understood, the conflict is described briefly in writing on a piece of paper. When the conflict has been described, a brainstorming session follows in which every possible solution is recorded, no matter how silly the solutions seem at the time. Remember, brainstorming is about listing alternatives, not judging them. Once every possible solution has been voiced, the couple goes through each suggestion and circles all the solutions that both agree might work. Out of the possible solutions, they pick one and agree to try it for one week. At the end of the week they hold a follow-up meeting to discuss how the solution is working. If there still seems to be a conflict, the couple picks another solution from the list they brainstormed the week before and gives that a try for a week.

This process goes on until they find a solution that relieves the conflict. Here is an example.

Conflict: Every weekend man goes golfing instead of spending time with woman. She's not satisfied seeing him only two nights a week.

Solutions: Man could golf one day during the week, skip one weekend golf day twice a month, or compete in fewer golf tournaments so he'd have more weekends free. Both could take a day off work so they could have a weekday together instead of only two evenings, or they could see each other one more weeknight. Woman could accept man's need to play golf, find something she likes to do on weekends while he is golfing, or go golfing with man so they could spend more time together.

The important thing about this process is that the two people are showing enough respect for each other to try to find a solution that works for both of them. Throughout the process it is crucial that they speak to each other in a nondefensive way. The goal is to find a solution, not to make the person with the problem feel like it is all their fault for demanding so much. It is also possible that the couple cannot find a solution to the problem, which is when some sort of counseling might be needed.

Maintain Your Independence While Developing an Equal Partnership

The journey through divorce has offered us as women a unique opportunity to learn about ourselves, to gain new skills, and to experience independence in the running of our homes and lives. No doubt we have begun to savor this feeling of wholeness and accomplishment, even if those accomplishments feel at times like barely getting by. Still, we've traveled a journey alone through possibly the most difficult time of our lives, and most of us don't want to give up the independence that we have worked so hard to achieve. We have a new view of what we are willing to put up with in order to make a love relationship work. We may have grown up enough not to need our partner's approval for the choices we make—all in all we have grown stronger and confident in our selves, our capabilities, and our self-worth. On top of that we may be a little skeptical about men, haven't quite decided whether or not to risk trusting again, don't want anyone walking into our lives and telling us what to do, and have settled into the new pattern of our lives without a partner. Maybe we are a little lonely, stressed, or overwhelmed, but we've learned how to juggle things and adjust to the pressure of handling all of our new roles, including house handywoman.

Then into this scene walks a man, possibly the man you're in love with, and the balance you worked so hard to create is tipped again. Remember, the man in question is also walking in with his own view of what a man's role, responsibility, and rights are in a relationship. Maybe he had a wife who let him make all the decisions, never worked, and gave no financial input. Perhaps the women in his life, from his mother down to his last girlfriend, were high-powered career women, and you have just landed the first job of your life. In any case, as you become a couple you will need to pay attention to and determine the balance of power between you. This balance may shift as the relationship deepens or marriage is considered, but in any case the question has to be asked, "How do you keep what you've gained and at the same time establish a fair and fulfilling partnership?" This is a question only you and your partner can answer, based on what you have learned about yourselves. However, it is an important question to consider in depth before getting too involved, because the answer will allow you to set the relationship up from the beginning in a way that emphasizes the partnership you wish to build. Adjusting the balance of power down the road is much harder than being up-front with expectations from the start.

In postdivorce relationships, women often call for sharing household labor more equally, for greater financial independence, and for placing equal value on both partner's life goals than happened in their marriages. "When I started dating Bart, I worked part-time and he worked full-time," said Ellen, "but it seemed at the end of the day I was still working and he was relaxing in front of the TV. Since I have kids and Bart didn't have any, we spent many evenings eating dinner at my house. I would cook, we would all eat, and then we'd spend time together. After he left I'd clean up the kitchen. Even though I thought it would be fairer for him to do the dishes and clean up after dinner, I never mentioned it. Part of the problem was that I wanted to impress him with my ability to manage both job and family. We ended up getting married a year later, and division of household labor was a huge issue for us. He expected things to go as they had gone before we were married, with me taking care of everything, but I expected him to do half of everything since we were living together. One argument hurt me almost enough to leave. He said that I should be doing three-fourths of everything because I had three people to his one. That hardly seemed like a marriage to me, but part of the problem was that I wasn't clear from the beginning what I really wanted because I didn't want to lose him over what seemed at the time to be a small issue." Had Ellen been clear from the beginning that she expected Brad to participate in household upkeep, Brad would have had the chance to decide if he could meet Ellen's expectations.

"The greatest accomplishment I feel I've made over the past five years is financial independence," said Brooke. "Sure, I had to lower the family's standard of living, move from a house to a townhouse, go from part-time classroom aid to full-time teacher, and attend night school to get my credential, but I did it. When I fell in love with Stewart, I was very clear that I didn't want to increase my standard of living beyond what I could support on my own. The process of divorce, trying to get on my feet while I was grieving the loss of someone I loved, was almost more than I could manage. I know the statistics on divorce. If I do get married again, I don't want to have to go through the whole downsizing thing again, dividing accounts, deciding who owns what. Stewart also has a child, so this is a big issue for us that we haven't quite worked through. If we do marry, it's not clear where we will live, because my townhouse isn't big enough for all of us, but his house is. I'm thinking about renting my townhouse out and then paying Stewart rent, but I haven't talked to a financial advisor yet to see if that would be to my benefit. The old me would have listened to my heart and made a decision based on love. I love the power I have with money of my own, a place of my own, and the right to make every financial decision without consulting anyone. It helps that Stewart understands how I feel and wants to support me in maintaining my financial independence. Neither of us knows what direction this will go when we get married, but being aware of the issue is creating a greater bond between us instead of making it a huge conflict." Brooke and Stewart are trying to respect each person's goals and come to a fair and equal partnership with regard to financial resources.

"The saddest part of my marriage was feeling that in so many ways my life was unimportant compared to my husband's life and goals," said Margaret. "His job was more important than my job of raising the kids. His hobbies were more important than any class I might want to take because he of course worked so hard and needed a break more than I did. His friends were more important for us to spend time with because they represented connections and the possibility of financial gain. It seemed I was along for the ride as keeper of the children and sperm receptacle. I'm not ready to date yet, but when I do, I'm looking for a man who can see me as a human being with her own dreams and desires in life instead of someone to help him accomplish his dreams." Margaret wonders how she will recognize this quality in a man. "Maybe it will be in his actions toward me, if he takes an interest and places value on the things that I'm excited about." Too many of us set our lives aside for a man, and we're not about to do it again!

Many of us felt, in our marriages, like our wings were clipped. Divorce gave us the opportunity to shed those old, clipped feathers and sprout some new ones in their places. Learning relationship skills is like growing new, strong feathers on our wings. Each new skill you practice, each time you open your mind to listen, and each time you courageously step forward to define what you want from the relationship, you are giving yourself the means to fly. Pretty soon you will take off and soar, rising above your old relationship patterns to a new level of understanding. With this understanding comes the freedom to be the woman you want to be. You will have gained the ability to love a man in an independent and self-realized way.

14

The Journey Together

Having the courage to love again began with loving your inner self and worked its way outward toward loving someone else. Over time, as the relationship grew into something you would consider committing your life to, you asked many questions, sifted through many doubts, fears, and expectations, and made future plans. Perhaps now you live together in the life you have created one step at a time. The kids are settled in their rooms, finances are being worked out, you've had a few family meetings, and you've marked the beginning of your new life. Some days are wonderful, and others make you feel you have lost your mind. On those down days, you may wonder how you can make the relationship last.

An important answer is to again make the inner journey a priority—the inner journey of the relationship. For just as you as an individual found the courage to love again through loving and forgiving yourself, removing old patterns, and taking responsibility for your daily life, so you as a couple will follow a similar journey. The inner journey of a relationship is the intimacy you create—how you communicate, love each other, and become familiar with each other's thoughts, feelings, and dreams. Do not let this inner journey get pushed aside by the outer tasks of organizing family, managing finances, and making a living. Start this new relationship with the understanding that this inner journey is a priority, and you will give yourselves as a couple the same solid foundation that you gave yourself through following the process outlined in this book.

Paying attention to your relationship's inner journey may not mean spending huge amounts of time alone together. No single block of time can replace daily lust-filled glances, hugs that catch you from behind when you're busy being frustrated, catching up on the happenings of daily lives over the chatter of kids' voices at the dinner table, or a call in the middle of the workday just to say hi. Don't get me wrong—I grab at any piece of alone time that Al and I can get, but it goes much deeper than that. At the core, I believe making our relationship a priority begins with the joint awareness that our relationship is precious and fragile, so it needs to be tended daily, watered, nurtured, and appreciated.

This chapter will get you thinking about how you and your lover can become better partners, ones who have chosen to take a journey together. Neither one of you has to hand yourself over to the other or forget the dreams you have for your own individual life. But there are things you can do that might get your relationship going in the right direction. In this chapter we'll think about who you are together as a couple—the strengths you offer each other, the ways you can support your love. Next, we'll take some time to picture the life you want together—right now, but also when the kids have all left home and when you are retired. Your shared dreams can give you something positive to focus on during difficult times. Then we'll take a close look at the spirit of the relationship, the commitments you have made to each other to be kind, loving, and supportive, and how you express those words with loving actions in your daily life. We'll end with an affirmation of your own inner journey, the work you have done to be able to begin this love relationship as a strong, independent, self-knowing woman.

Who Are You Together?

When we are truly loved, something changes in our lives; we have more faith in the future. When love comforts our heart we take more chances, aren't as afraid of failure, say what we feel, and go for what we want. We all seek love, the kind of love that allows us to be truly ourselves, to be open, laughing, and alive in each day, knowing that even in the worst moments we can find comfort in our lover's arms. That kind of love requires daily attention, the conscious loving actions that define who you are together as a couple. Being open and vulnerable to love the second time around can be a challenge. The innocent view of love and marriage has shifted into skepticism in some cases, and outright fear in others. This feeling of being secure in the new love on the one hand and the pain and remembrance of past experience on the other makes it especially important that each person make the relationship a priority in their lives.

Most of us fall in love with the many strengths we recognize in our lover. I remember watching Al play the piano with a group of kids months before we met. I admired his playfulness, his patience, and the way he cared for the kids. When we met, I pulled that observation from my memory and began to record other things: he was easy to talk with, honest with his feelings, very predictable, intelligent, creative in a different way than I was, enjoyed writing, looked athletic, and was very outgoing. I'm sure that he was also making mental notes of my strengths as we dove past the initial attraction and got to know each other. Many of the strengths I saw in him were qualities I didn't possess: I love music but quit playing a musical instrument years ago, I'm not so predictable, and I'm shy around people I don't know. The strengths in him that I was drawn to are the qualities, talents, and abilities that I like to be around; they are characteristics that make me feel good when I experience them.

In the beginning, the strengths we find in our partner are like Christmas lights delighting us with each new flash of color. We feel wonder at our good fortune in finding someone so right for us. It is that sense of awe and appreciation for each other's strengths that we need to find a way to preserve. When we get used to the person, we may start to take his strengths for granted. I used to sit and listen every time Al played the piano, but now it can be just an everyday occurrence. Sometimes it takes visitors to remind me how lucky I am to have a musician in the house. Al shows our children that same playful interest I noticed that first day when he helps the kids with homework, passes a football, or shows them how to change the oil in a car. But now that we share daily life, I sometimes don't notice these same behaviors with the same attention and admiration. So an important aspect of appreciating who you are together as a couple is the ability to remember the strengths you fell in love with, to compliment each other on these qualities, and to find a way to enjoy them.

Many couples say that they were drawn to a partner when they recognized a strength that they wanted or needed to develop within themselves. "In a way I fell in love with Kevin because I needed his stability in my life. I liked the way he made time to have fun, and I was hoping that the relationship would push me to improve myself," said Jo Ellen. "One night he asked me what I needed from him. I hadn't thought of it in that way before, that we need and perhaps expect things from our lovers that are not as straightforward as we might think. It is easy for me to see when I need money or a ride somewhere or time alone together. But it's harder to define what it is in my partner that makes me a stronger person. It was a revealing conversation that led to a discussion of how we can take on some of the other person's strengths and use them to better the relationship and ourselves. For example, we talked about how Kevin's dedication to fun has rubbed off on me and the kids, in our willingness to put our serious stuff aside and to play more often." One of the beauties of a love relationship is that two people have the opportunity to share their strengths and in many cases help each other overcome weaknesses.

When we were single, the goal was to find love. Now that you have it, how do you keep it alive and well? How do you set the fear aside that you might "blow it" again? The simplest way to nurture love is to appreciate fully that someone loves you. Let this soak through your system: there is a person in your life who thinks about you daily, who wants to touch you, to hear your thoughts, and to share your future. That person is willing to put up with the not-so-good things—the issues, the baggage, and the fear—because he loves you. Pretty amazing, and definitely worth whatever it takes to keep those feelings strong. "Sometimes when life gets going and I don't have a moment to breathe, all I do is rattle off the complaints I have about our relationship: the way the family is going, how much I have to work, or the kids' ungrateful attitude," said Samantha. "I get caught up in picking away at my life without realizing sometimes that I'm picking at our love, chipping away at it with my insults and my frustrations. A co-worker pointed this out to me. She said that I seemed to be negative and never grateful about my partner. She hurt my feelings, but she made a good point. Now whenever I begin to feel negative, I say the same sentence at least three times: 'I am loved by my family, and I love them; that is enough.'" As Samantha found out, gratitude can be a simple daily exercise. It has great power to change the way our life looks.

Another way to nurture love is to care for it as you would a treasured possession. Just think of the amount of time you spend washing clothes, cleaning the house, keeping the garden looking neat, or grooming yourself. Love needs a little attention, some focused time spent sprucing it up. What do you do for your love? "Nothing replaces time spent alone with Jessie," said Meredith. "Time doing something that isn't housework or kid work but just relaxing into each other, talking, sharing our dreams, having fun. That kind of time reminds both of us why we fell in love to begin with. It gives us a chance to fill each other in on all the ways we are growing and changing. We get to feel interested in each other again as adults who have thoughts unrelated to the home we have or the kids we share. This time is the most important time for me, because it allows our love a place to live between us. Making time for sex is also important, but that is more a physical sharing of our love—our personal stress-reduction plan! But the time we set aside as a couple we call our play time, as we often have to explain to our kids that we need an adult recess too." When both partners acknowledge the importance of setting time aside to be with each other, love receives a sacred space in which to shine and grow.

Finding this time means that the couple has to make the relationship a priority in their lives. It may mean that before any other activity is placed on the schedule each month, the couple claims their own time. What it can't be is an afterthought that takes place only when you have nothing better to do.

This time alone together is especially important when the relationship isn't going so well and you'd rather get away from your partner than spend time with him. "Both Terry and I have stressful lives," said Nancy. "Sometimes it seems that the harder work gets, the more I want to be alone in the tiny amount of free time I have. When I'm stressed, the kids have issues, or my life seems a little out of control, I want to pull away from everyone. During those times, I don't like Terry very much, and I guess I don't like myself much either. He picks up those vibes and backs away too, and then we have two people pulling away from each other instead of reaching out to each other. We described this habit to a marriage counselor at our first meeting, and she asked each of us to take a few minutes to think about how we would describe the other to a good friend. Each of us had a turn to talk about the other, and we said so many great things we ended up laughing, and, even in that little room, we were relieved to be with each other. The counselor told us to devote two hours a week to a date of some sort and come back in a month. We didn't even need to call for the next appointment because both of us got the point."

Living in a blended family can bring a great deal of stress into family life. It may take extra effort for a couple to be alone together, and in that alone time too often the moment is swallowed discussing and solving the problems of the day. Making the relationship a priority means that you put your friendship and couple connection in front of everything else instead of allowing it to become something that happens after all the family issues are dealt with. Who you become as a couple is up to you. Who you are together will be an expression of how much priority you place on the relationship and how you value and nurture your love.

Picture the Life You Want Together

Once you are past the practical problems of getting two families together, how do you blend your hopes and dreams in a balanced way, without favoring one person's goals? How does the picture of the life you created in chapter 1 fit in with the picture your partner has created of the life he wants for himself and the life he envisions together with you? Now is the time to pay attention to the big picture—the hopes and dreams you have for just the two of you, the things you want to do with the rest of your lives, like retire in the south of Italy when the last child graduates from college. After all, you can't sacrifice everything for the life of the family. You have to claim some of the joy and the family resources for yourselves as a couple! Be a little selfish once in a while. Stop feeling you have to constantly make up for the past pain your family has gone through and embrace the life the two of you want. Sure, you have to take your children's needs into consideration, but the kids won't be living with you forever, so start building a foundation that includes shared dreams that reach well into the future.

Too often in second marriages, couples spend so much energy dealing with the issues of the present that they are thinking ahead only one or two years down the road. They lack a big picture of what the two of them are trying to create and work toward. Short-term thinking makes giving up easier when present-day problems get difficult. A clear and jointly created vision of the big picture of your life together fosters moments of understanding, "Oh, I see where we are headed, why we are budgeting now, or why we are dealing with this child's problems in this way." The big picture gives clarity and shared direction for both you and your partner.

It is best to share life dreams early on in the relationship, preferably before marriage, to get a general idea of how well your lives might fit together over the course of years. This kind of sharing is generally an exciting part of the dating process because it is the first view of our lover's possibilities. Once you have made the commitment to stay together, the sharing of dreams takes on a different flavor as each person tries to gauge how much the picture of what they wanted their life to look like will need to be adjusted to make room for the other person's picture. The first step in creating a picture of your life together, which includes both of your dreams, is to know what you want and to be able to share your dreams honestly. You may want to divide your dreams into stages of your life, since there is no way to achieve everything at once. Stage 1 might be from this moment until the kids are in high school or college. Stage 2 may begin when the kids leave home, and Stage 3 starts when the two of you retire. If your lives are at different stages, such as one of you having preschoolers and the other college grads, you may have to come up with a creative variation of the above.

The second step in sharing the picture of what you want your life to look like is to listen to each other with an open heart and mind. Don't pull back, throw up walls, or start in with how impossible such-and-such would be. Just listen and try to feel your lover's enthusiasm. "When Chad and I started talking about Stage 1 of our life picture, it was mostly about getting our blended family settled, adjusting to the marriage, and making a good start at becoming a stepfamily," said Stephanie. "I don't think either one of us had a picture of our lives past getting married again and paying our monthly bills. It was fun to think in terms of dreaming of a life together, but when we started to share our longer-term dreams, I could tell we were both getting a little defensive. Chad talked about having a studio-office in the house so he could do some of his architectural work from home. I was thinking that I didn't really want him home after school or over the summer when the kids would be running around with friends, making lots of noise. I thought his dream would change the flavor of our home. Then I shared that I wanted to go back to art school part-time so that down the road I might be able to switch careers, and he immediately brought up how much money it might cost." Describing your dreams to each other is not a competition for resources or an exercise in making one partner feel like she or he must sacrifice all to make the dream a reality. It is simply about letting each person express their desires. Chad and Stephanie would have been better off just listening, not making any judgments or asking for explanations, since at this beginning stage they are simply trying to discover what their partner wants out of life.

The third step is to talk about how your dreams might work together, to discuss which ones are the most important ones and how serious you are about pursuing certain goals. You may also want to look at which of your dreams could easily fit into your current life without changing too many things, costing a ton of money, or putting too much strain on the family unit. "Charlie and I decided to start a 'Picture Our Life' notebook," said Celine. We had the most fun with the stage when all the kids would be leaving home. It was nice to think of our relationship as making it through the tough years while raising three teenagers and then to picture what it would be like to be just the two of us. There seemed to be so much more room for personal growth when we would reach that stage. We talked about taking classes in something we've never had time to learn, like photography. I thought about the gourmet meals I could cook that would have to please only the two of us. We dreamed of weekends spent without worrying how late the kids would get home or being asked to chaperone a day at the beach. Charlie talked about moving to a house near a river. We'd both felt a little stuck in our current location because of custody arrangements, so the thought that we could move in the future to a location of our choice brightened both of our days." When couples take the time to seriously consider the life each person wants, there is a much better chance of moving forward in a direction that satisfies some of each partner's dreams. This joint vision helps keep the marriage strong and vibrant.

The fourth step is to pick a few short-term goals as a couple, goals that might help you move toward the life you have pictured together. "One of my dreams was to fix our home up the way I'd always wanted it," said Connie. "When I told Sam this, he asked me to make a list of everything I would want to do to accomplish that. I had a blast going from room to room with my notebook, writing down every little thing I wanted to change or fix. We then bought a three-year planning book and wrote each project onto the calendar. In the past whenever I had brought up house projects, Sam would get frustrated because it seemed everything was falling apart at once and I wanted to fix everything right away. When we started talking about the picture of our lives, it became clear that one of Sam's dreams was to live in our current house until the kids left for college. That goal allowed both of us to move forward with plans to fix things up." Sam and Connie were able to successfully combine this part of the picture of their lives. Even though he was content with the house, he was able to honor Connie's dream as they put together a home improvement plan that fit their joint picture.

Spirit and Relationship

At some point along this journey together, a couple will begin to share the values that govern their moral choices and actions, whatever you may choose to call it: God, spirit, the universal consciousness, the inner conviction to do right, to be kind, or to treat your partner as you would like to be treated. Those beliefs and thoughts form what I call the spirit of the relationship. Spirit is the bonding agent, the invisible stuff that holds you together, that allows you to trust each other, that floats between you in loving gazes and even in angry outbursts. It is not easily defined, except to say that when that spirit is missing, partners can do each other great harm. That is why some form of spirit is brought into wedding ceremonies, to give couples a foundation for making a set of agreements together. During the ceremony, in the presence of others, the couple states their promises, their values, and their beliefs.

We had only known each other two weeks when Al and I had our first spiritual discussion. It was actually our first date, lunch at a local brewery, and one of his first questions was what I studied in college. I told him that I majored in psychology and religion. Most people slide by that and go on to the next question, but Al told me he had recently taken a university class on that topic and that he had organized the adult religious education program at his church several years before. We spent the rest of the date talking about how our own religious experiences had influenced our lives. I told him why I loved to listen to the Catholic mass in Latin and how it seemed somehow more spiritual to me than English because it pulled me out of my ordinary life and into something that felt mystical. He told me how he liked to meditate by sitting still and enjoying nature. We talked about how my family used to say at least ten prayers before we would get down to eating dinner, and he remembered the German church he attended as a child growing up in Philadelphia.

Many experiences shape who we are, and many of them are spiritual experiences. It is impossible to fully know someone until that person's spiritual beliefs have been shared.

What are the spiritual ties, the moral or ethical guidelines you both live with? It is important to share what you believe and to find a way to incorporate each of your beliefs into the relationship. "Chris and I agreed to not have sex with other people," said Bella, "and to practice honesty at any cost. Recently Chris went to a bachelor party where two prostitutes stripped and were available for blow jobs. I found out about it from my sister, whose boyfriend told her how funny it was to watch the groom try to get out of it. I asked Chris if he had participated, and he said he hadn't. Well, he had. It took a few weeks for it to come out, but I told him I knew he had done it. We fought about it, and I asked him to leave the house for a week so I could think. In the end I forgave him, but it took a while before I could trust that he was being honest. That whole situation caused us to examine the promises we were willing to make to each other. I needed to find out from Chris what he believed was right and wrong." Love will not survive without the ability to trust that your partner will make decisions based on the code of ethics the two of you have established in the relationship.

Sometimes couples find it difficult to commit to a lifelong relationship with someone who has a different set of religious beliefs. It takes creative compromise to blend each person's beliefs into the fabric of a family. "My husband, Brad, is a Buddhist, and I am a Christian," said Julie. "Neither one of us was overly involved with our religion when we met, so it didn't seem like a big deal. The problem seemed to arise when the kids were brought into the picture. My daughter came home from church and said she had asked the pastor about Buddhism, and he told her that the only way to heaven was through Jesus. It created a real division for a while, with the kids putting each other down in small yet noticeable ways. At that point Brad and I decided to share with each other the religious beliefs each of us had, the things we liked about our religion, and the parts of our beliefs we felt were important to share with our kids. We found out in that discussion that our basic worldview—of love for other people, treating others with kindness, not lying or cheating—was very similar. We worked hard to understand a little about each other's religion so that we could find a way to combine our beliefs in everyday ways, like prayer before dinner, respect for each other, our pets, and nature, or doing community service as a family." A couple doesn't have to believe in exactly the same thing, but neither can they keep their beliefs separate without any blending of philosophy. When Julie and Brad noticed the negative effect their policy was having on their new family, they became willing to search for the common ground and then make an effort to share that ground with each other and with their children.

None of us is a saint. We hurt each other, and we know the best place to twist the knife if we want to cause pain. Where does inner control come from, the little voice that tells us not to speak the words we are thinking before they reach the tongue, before we damage our fragile, beautiful, and infinitely difficult-to-repair love relationship? It comes from our conscience, our past experiences, and our personal belief system. "Once I make a statement about what I believe, it keeps me on track," said Bonnie. "When we go to church, the kids hear a biblical reading about treating your parents with respect, about parents loving their children, or how it is a sin to lie, to steal, to cheat, or to hurt others. It gives the family a higher guide to follow. I seem to be the one who sets so many rules in our house, and it is nice once in a while to be able to depend on a religious belief structure that supports these rules and expectations. Because I didn't just make up these rules—I learned many of them from my parents, and from my church. The hard part about sharing what you believe with your partner or kids is that you then have to live the life you talk about or you will be seen as a hypocrite. I can't make up some lie to get off the phone without one of my kids saying, 'Mommy, that was a lie. You're not leaving the house right now.' It gives the whole family a set of similar rules to follow, which is a bonding experience in itself." Many families participate in a religious community that defines the moral standards of their lives. But it is also possible to meet as a family and set up your own guidelines on this topic without the help of regular churchgoing.

Relationships need space to grow on many levels. Couples may share intellectual interests, enjoy reading a similar book and discussing it, or taking an interesting class together. Sex usually takes care of their physical needs, along with daily hugs, kisses, and massages. But the spiritual side of a relationship is often left out. Yet the spiritual life can become a couple's greatest strength. It reaches into the core of who a person is and allows the couple to delve that much deeper into a significant part of their shared life. The spiritual topics, like what happens when we die or how God or spirit works in the world or even a debate about abortion, open a couple to greater intimacy as they share what beliefs they hold and why. When opening your relationship up to this deeper level of sharing, be sure that the discussion respects each person's right to his or her own beliefs. The relationship doesn't require that both of you feel the same way or that you agree on every issue, only that you listen with an open heart and love your partner enough to accept them for who they are instead of trying to force them to believe the way you do.

The health of a relationship ultimately rests on the integrity of each person, the beliefs the two people have about commitment and love, and their willingness to live through difficult years as they search for a way to help the relationship through the hard times. You may wonder how you and your partner will be able to keep the promises you've made to each other when you couldn't keep them the first time around. You have a better chance to succeed because you have learned from the loss of a major relationship. You have now gained a deeper knowledge of who you are. You have better skills to bring to this new relationship, and you've taken the time to develop what it takes to make a relationship work.

Ultimately, beliefs show in your actions. What kind of people will you be on a daily basis? I've often thought the best way to pick a husband would to be to put him through a suffering test. Make him run five miles, then when dripping wet and tired have him explain algebra to my daughter, then listen for thirty minutes to the problems of my day; wake him up in the middle of the night to shoo raccoons away from the trash, and then have him get up and prepare a breakfast for eight with a smile on his face. If he could come to me, after living with a schedule like that for a week, with a list of the family issues that *might* need work or compromise—willing to hash it out, throw out ideas, work within the limits to find a workable solution   then I would have found my man. I'm laughing as I write this because Al has taken on this and much more for many years, and he still comes to me with a peaceful attitude, sure that we can brainstorm a solution to any problem. Miracles do happen!

Remember Your Inner Journey

We've come to the end of the book. Before we leave the comfort of one another's stories, triumphs, mistakes, and dreams, there is something I must ask of you. I want each of you to promise that you will remember who you are. Remember the time and effort you spent on your own inward journey. Retain your independence; be ever conscious of the goals and dreams you set in the first half of this book. Don't be lulled into the security of undying love that all new relationships offer. Plant your creativity and future hopes firmly within yourself. Bring to the relationship everything you can without surrendering your individuality. Work to build the equality that allows you to remain a whole person in a balanced relationship with your partner. Believe that you deserve it all, and be willing to do the work it will take to get it. And the most important thing I want you to remember is to turn to the women around you for help if you get lost. I wish you all the best on this wonderful journey!

Acknowledgments

M y deepest thanks go to all the women who were willing to share the details of their lives with me. It isn't easy telling a stranger your most intimate, thoughts, fears, and past experiences. You gave of yourselves without recognition with the expressed hope that other divorced women might learn from your experience. And to all the women on my single mother mailing list. You inspire me with your stories, the way you support each other, and the way you have supported me. You have voluntarily given advice to others, planned workshops for single mothers in your community, all while working to rebuild your own lives. You have helped me to understand the power of community.

Immeasurable thanks to my amazing editor, Liz Perle, for her insight, direction, and support. Your ability to sum up in one sentence exactly what I needed to change to make a page or chapter work still astounds me. Also at HarperSanFrancisco, I want to thank my gifted marketing and publicity team, Margery Buchanan, Calla Devlin, Liz Winer, and Jim Warner. And to my agent, Al Zuckerman, and to Writer's House for continued belief in my abilities.

I consider myself incredibly fortunate to have talented individuals working with me. I couldn't do it without them. To my assistant, Allison Beltz, for her happy heart and willingness to be my second set of hands no matter what I ask her to do. To Cindy Friedman for designing my new Web site, and to Julia Briggs for her inspiring paintings that give personality and life to each Web page. You went above and beyond to help make an online community for moms a possibility. And to my amazing marketing team, Mike Koenigs and Vivian Glyck, for helping me to create a new vision for my writing, speaking, and media future.

I consider my greatest blessings my family and friends who with a supportive word, a phone call, a box of goodies, or a look remind me that I am loved—you know who you are. To my parents, Nancy and Dave Maley, for putting their lives back together each and every time they experienced disappointment in their lives. Without this example I might have given up on myself or waited around for somebody else to fix my life after divorce. To Julia York for all the time spent talking, hiking, and scheming with me--I do think we have the answers to everything.

My last and greatest thanks go to the people who fill my home and my heart. To my husband, Al, who had the courage to call and ask me for a date after I told him that I had four kids! This book would not have been possible without your willingness to create with me a new model of relationship. You have redefined love, partnership, intimacy, and sex for me! To our six children, Wesley, Brooke, Adam, Rhett, Eric, and Troy, for giving me so much to write about! Your unique and wonderful lives have given me the chance to laugh, think, love, admire, clap, scream, and embrace each day knowing that something exciting is going to happen. I am blessed by all of you.

Visit the author at
www.CompleteMom.com

Sheila Ellison's
COMPLETE M♥M.COM

Be sure to check out the Single Mother section of the site!

- Find a support group for single mothers in your area
- Receive free legal information
- Find out about Sheila's workshops:
    Becoming Whole Again After Divorce
    Loving Again After Divorce
- Receive immediate emergency advice from CompleteMom's support team
- Chat with other moms on the extensive message boards
- Get tips on nurturing yourself, guiding your children through the divorce process, and rebuilding your life
- Contact Sheila

For more information on books by Sheila Ellison go to

www.CompleteMom.com

365 Days of Creative Play

For Children 2 Years and Up
By Sheila Ellison and Judith Gray

Fun . . . it's what parents and kids are looking for! *365 Days of Creative Play* is a unique collection of indoor and outdoor activities that encourage your child's imagination while providing a family experience that will create lasting memories. If you need ideas—here is your guidebook!

365 Days of Baby Love

From Birth to Age 2
By Sheila Ellison and Susan Ferdinandi

Each day with your baby brings new moments of caring, teaching, holding, and growing through baby's first experiences. Filled with magical ways to create and enhance those special everyday moments, *365 Days of Baby Love* will help you celebrate each once-in-a-lifetime opportunity you and your baby share.

365 Ways to Raise Great Kids

By Sheila Ellison and Barbara Ann Barnett, Ph.D

Inspiring and insightful, *365 Ways to Raise Great Kids* will help you accomplish what all parents want: to raise bright, caring, honest, happy, respectful, and creative children.

365 Afterschool Activities

TV-Free Fun for Kids Ages 7-12
By Sheila Ellison and Judith Gray

A year-round carnival of afterschool fun! From making a monster mask to going on a bike photo safari, *365 Afterschool Activities* will let kids' imaginations soar with terrifically fun things to do during those valuable afterschool hours and beyond!

365 Foods Kids Love to Eat

Fun, Nutritious, and Kid-Tested
By Sheila Ellison and Judith Gray

Here is the cookbook parents have been waiting for, filled with carefully chosen, great-tasting, good-for-you, kitchen-tested recipes that appeal to the whole family, especially the kids!